The Arnold and Caroline Rose Monograph Series
of the American Sociological Association

Opening and closing

D1474811

Other books in the series

J. Milton Yinger, Kiyoshi Ikeda, Frank Laycock, and Stephen J. Cutler: *Middle Start: An Experiment in the Educational Enrichment of Young Adolescents*

James A. Geschwender: *Class, Race, and Worker Insurgency: The League of Revolutionary Black Workers*

Paul Ritterband: *Education, Employment, and Migration: Israel in Comparative Perspective*

John Low-Beer: *Protest and Participation: The New Working Class in Italy*

Rita James Simon: *Continuity and Change: A Study of Two Ethnic Communities in Israel*

Marshall B. Clinard: *Cities with Little Crime: The Case of Switzerland*

Volumes previously published by the American Sociological Association

Michael Schwartz and Sheldon Stryker: *Deviance, Selves and Others*

Robert M. Hauser: *Socioeconomic Background and Educational Performance*

Morris Rosenberg and Roberta G. Simmons: *Black and White Self-Esteem: The Urban School Child*

Chad Gordon: *Looking Ahead: Self-Conceptions: Race and Family as Determinants of Adolescent Orientation to Achievement*

Anthony M. Orum: *Black Students in Protest: A Study of the Origins of the Black Student Movement*

Ruth M. Gasson, Archibald O. Haller, and William H. Sewell: *Attitudes and Facilitation in the Attainment of Status*

Sheila R. Klatzky: *Patterns of Contact with Relatives*

Herman Turk: *Interorganizational Activation in Urban Communities: Deductions from the Concept of System*

John DeLamater: *The Study of Political Commitment*

Alan C. Kerckhoff: *Ambition and Attainment: A Study of Four Samples of American Boys*

Scott McNall: *The Greek Peasant*

Lowell L. Hargens: *Patterns of Scientific Research: A Comparative Analysis of Research in Three Scientific Fields*

Charles Hirschman: *Ethnic Stratification in Peninsular Malaysia*

Opening and closing

Strategies of information adaptation in society

Orrin E. Klapp
Professor of Sociology
The University of Western Ontario
London, Ontario

Cambridge University Press

Cambridge
London   New York   Melbourne

Published by the Syndics of the Cambridge University Press
The Pitt Building, Trumpington Street, Cambridge CB2 1RP
Bentley House, 200 Euston Road, London NW1 2DB
32 East 57th Street, New York, NY 10022, USA
296 Beaconsfield Parade, Middle Park, Melbourne 3206, Australia

First published 1978

Printed in the United States of America
Typeset by Telecki Publishing Services, Yonkers, NY
Printed and bound by the Murray Printing Company, Westford, Mass.

Library of Congress Cataloging in Publication Data
Klapp, Orrin Edgar, 1915—
Opening and closing.
(The Arnold and Caroline Rose monograph series
of the American Sociological Association)
Bibliography: p.
Includes index.
1. Communication — Social aspects.
2. Communication — Psychological aspects.
3. Stress (Psychology) 4. Information theory.
I. Title. II. Series: The Arnold and Caroline Rose
monograph series in sociology.
HM258.K55   301.14   77-87382
ISBN 0 521 21923 X hard covers
ISBN 0 521 29311 1 paperback

To Evelyn,
Merrie, and
Curtis

Contents

Preface

This book views society according to a theory of opening and closing. In the last fifty years it has become plain that the concept of progress is biased in favor of opening. This book asserts that closing is as needed as opening, for creativity as well as for keeping what we have. Because of bias in the concept of progress, modern society has wandered into a crisis of social noise and failure of resonance.

The book interprets a variety of phenomena according to the theory that individuals and societies normally open *and* close to information and communication. For example, closing responses are reflected by nostalgia, meaninglessness, concern about pollution, suspicion of conspiracies, wanting to close boundaries or emphasize ethnic roots, or seeking a guru. On the other hand, opening is illustrated by modernism, expansionism, adventurism, ecumenism, joining, romantic rebellion, and faddism — enthusiasm to communicate, try things, open doors, let oneself go. Opening is scanning for desired information, whereas closing is a natural response to too much adverse information broadly conceived as social noise, including information overload and entropic communication.

Nor is closing merely against such things. It is also *for* something, such as synergy as a payoff of cohesion, as in cults, and good redundancy. Such redundancy is not useless, but is playback of valued parts of one's past. It feels good because it is the basis of resonance, meaning, and identity. Nostalgia indicates need for good redundancy.

All this leads to a theory that opening and closing, by optimizing information, constitute a strategy of living systems against entropy. Four categories of information — good variety, good redundancy, bad variety (noise), and bad redundancy (banality) — are conceived of as sectors of a sort of field in which the game of life is played. Stresses such as information overload and loss of trust come from straying too far and too often into losing sectors. Boredom is a penalty of bad closing. Strategy requires sensitive alternation of opening and closing according to advantages perceived. Therefore, openness or closedness is not a fixed structural feature of a system but a changing life strategy of organisms and groups. Communication fluctuates, in amount and content, in shifting popular moods, cycles, and in what I call surges and spasms.

It is a challenge to modernization to more clearly distinguish good from bad opening. Rising GNP is of little help with problems of social noise or bad closing. Modernization, using appropriate indicators, should heed redundancy needs and the costs of social noise. Study of communication balance within the human scale should help show a better way to progress.

I wish to thank the following scholars who have kindly read part or all of the manuscript: Lawrence J. Fogel, Richard L. Henshell, Raymond Immerwahr, John H. Kunkel, Benjamin D. Singer, Anselm L. Strauss, Charles R. Webb, and the Editorial Board of the Arnold and Caroline Rose Monograph Series of the American Sociological Association.

O. E. K.

March, 1978
San Diego, California

1. Social noise

There has been a crisis of noise in modern society, of which the assault on our eardrums is but a small part. In the broadest sense, noise is the chaos from which we try to construct meaning, the continual challenge of existence. The sense of meaninglessness so prevalent today comes in part from the fact that modern society is generating more noise than it can handle. This book is concerned with how and why.

When the philosopher Schopenhauer wrote his famous essay on noise (which recommended that a driver who cracked his whip on the street should have to dismount and receive five good blows with a stick), he could hardly have realized he was contributing to what is now humorous literature. To him, noise was a threat to the life of the mind, to civilization itself. He could hardly envisage a civilization in which people would be surrounded not just by good minds but by gadgets that bark at them with strange tones and appeals, from whom and where, Lord knows. The noise we endure today is so vast compared with that of a German town in 1850 that the philosopher's complaint seems quaintly petulant. Almost anyone living in a modern city suffers more noise in a day than a tribal native or peasant does in a week or perhaps even a year. Scientists who search for the secret of long life in the Caucasus and the Andes should perhaps examine the noise a person absorbs, as well as the standard villains: saturated fats, alcohol, tobacco, and smog.

The estimate of the U.S. Environmental Protection Agency is that over half the American people live in areas where the noise level (over 55 decibels) is a hazard to health.

The commonplace nuisances of noise and sheer volume of sonic impact that our nervous systems sustain are but the tip of an iceberg, which is revealed if we take noise as a tag — synecdoche if you please — for the entire mass of extraneous, irrelevant, and useless stimuli from our environment that the mind must negotiate to find what it seeks. In broadest terms, noise is opposed to *signal*, which is everything we wish to receive or send to others by way of communication; and noise blurs

1

feedback. Then noise becomes a generic name for all that impairs communication and confuses meaning in our troubled world. Then noise is no small opponent but seems like an indefatigable enemy agent working to sabotage meaning and resonance. To see all this, however, a broader conception and classification of sorts of social noise are needed.

A broader conception of noise

From a communication point of view, the world is a sea of signals in which we swim, looking for information useful to us. All sensory inputs make up this sea — the noise of traffic, sounds of a forest at night, waves on the beach, glances of strangers at one another, words in a book, the talk of friends. In modern biological theory every living thing is made of information, from heredity (DNA) or environment — a bacterium, for example, has been estimated to contain one thousand bits (Quastler, 1964:4). Information comes most reliably through channels, as when a man sits by a telephone or a trout waits at the top of the pool below a riffle because it is the most informative part of the stream for food opportunities. Society is a name for our richest and most reliable information channels. As John Dewey (1916:5) said: "Society not only continues to exist *by* transmission, *by* communication, but it may fairly be said to exist *in* transmission, *in* communication."

If all social channels and signals were perfect, they would bear all and only the information we needed, as with auditoriums designed so that we should hear only music. But social channels give us much that we do not want or at times when we cannot use it, a rather poor mix of information with noise. When the mix is poor enough, a problem of social noise exists.

By definition, noise is anything coming in a channel that interferes with signals we are trying to send or receive. Its essence is interference, not the level of sound. For example, ordinary conversation may be noise to someone phoning nearby. Noise is always relative to strength of signal. Diffuse city lights can reduce the efficiency of a giant telescope. Noise impairs all functions that rest on communication of a signal or perception of what is real.

To broaden our conception, various sorts of social noise should be distinguished. Plain noise is nonsense with a loud voice: the blast of a jet takeoff, the bang of trash containers early in the morning. Much of the story of the impact of acoustical noise on our environment has already been told.[1]

Decibels are not a very good measure, however, for auditory noise need not be loud. We all know that small sounds can be as irritating as loud ones: buzzing, whining, scratching of nails on a blackboard, rustling of candy wrappers in a theater. Certain symbolism, such as insult, can multiply the impact of small sounds many times. In other words, acoustical volume is but one dimension even of auditory noise, and by no means the most important.

There is more to noise than meets the ear. Anyone with half an eye can see that visual pollution — litter, junk, slag heaps, gravel pits, strip-mining scars, garish advertising, graffiti, and defacements of public objects — is as prominent as auditory noise in many places. If we become habituated to ugliness and bad taste, and accept visual pollution more readily than auditory or air pollution, this has little to do with how harmful they can be.

Noise can enter any part of the sensory spectrum. For example, odors can be a nuisance and spoil enjoyment of food, perfumes fool the nose, and deodorants block the sense of smell. In the realm of touch, a callus lessens sensitivity, an uncomfortable chair might be said to be noise to the spine.

Nonsensory channels of information are also subject to noise — for example, computer "garbage," typographical errors, jammed radio broadcasts, fluctuations of current in a wire carrying signals, radio static, electronic distortion, television "snow." Even endocrine imbalance might be said to make noise from wrong amounts of chemical messengers in the blood.

From this it should be plain that all noise is not recorded by decibel readings on street corners and assembly lines. One must catch stridencies for which there are no meters, as well as soundless and invisible kinds of noise that may be registered only in symptoms such as boredom or ill will.

Four sorts of noise deserve especially to be called social. They are at least as important as those already mentioned. The first is semantic, coming from ambiguity, confusion, carelessness, or duplicity in using meaningful signs, as when a person uses a word with the wrong connotation, or "cries wolf." Deliberate misuse of symbols in advertising and propaganda is a huge source of semantic noise.

Stylistic noise comes from incompatible values, fashions, and identities. We live in an era of clashing life-styles, in which more communication has made people more aware of differences. People thrust upon one another, and life for many has become inimical. One hardly needs to mention the style rebellion of the 1960s, which generated hippie, long hair, unisex, Gay Lib, and swinging styles. Rock gave major challenge to conventional music. Ethnic groups also emphasized differences. Such signals become noise when they threaten and confuse, rather than sharpen, the sense of identity of an individual or a group. Basically, stylistic noise is a matter of compatibility: People who like the same sounds can be loud together; those who have the same tastes can do as they please together. A pluralistic society with open boundaries, however, runs into painful problems. When media publicize all types of personalities, they generate what I call modeling noise, felt by some to have demoralizing impact.

The third sort of social noise consists of perfectly good information that is irrelevant, redundant, or in sheer overload. Then it may interfere with, more than it helps, decisions, consensus, and meanings. For example, redundancy, however useful it may be, say, in repeating points of a lecture, becomes noise when it tells us what we do not care to hear again while, at the same time, filling a channel that might otherwise tell us what we would like. The criterion of noise here is not the inherent value of information but its relevance to our needs. Any signals in the wrong amount, time, place, or company can become noise. Even material goods can act as noise when their clutter prevents our finding what we want. Noise is communicational clutter; clutter is tangible noise.

A fourth sort of noise may be called contagious. Negative feelings such as ill will, hysteria, suspicion, discontent, despair, lawlessness, and unrest[2] can spread unnoticed at first (much as smog and lead contaminated the air before people became alarmed by them). People may feel a need to preserve themselves from influences spreading by example or word-of-mouth, or creeping across borders or into homes via TV. Amplified by rumor, reverberated by feedback from more and more persons, contagious noise increases entropy of all parties. When there is too much, the environment becomes inimical: Things seem to be hindering more than helping; people have trouble finding what they seek, hearing what is said, saying what they mean, liking what they hear, attuning to strangers, relating to neighbors, trusting media, leaders, and institutions.

This book treats such noise under the heading of entropic communication.

Noise is here defined relative to receivers' needs, not senders' intentions. (To those seeking beauty, ugliness is noise; to those seeking harmony, discord is noise; to those who want neatness, clutter is noise; to those trying to make sense, irrelevance is noise; to those concerned about their souls, sin is noise.)[3]

All noise — sensory, nonsensory, semantic, stylistic, informational, and contagious — makes up a burden, which modern society bears. It stands in the way of information we require to fulfill our lives as humans, and in the way of perhaps esthetic form, education, meaning, wisdom, or the secret a guru might whisper in a seeker's ear. Once society is viewed in terms of communication, noise becomes a measure of what defeats us.

How, when, why, and to whom is noise a problem?

The epochal breakthroughs by Shannon and Weaver (1949), which identified noise in communication with entropy[4] opposed to information in signals; by Wiener (1948), which determined that feedback is the essential lifelike process; and by molecular biologists, which revealed that information encoded in DNA is the basis of life, forever removed noise from its trivial status as an acoustical nuisance and gave it a central place in social analysis, both as indicator and problem. In that view, entropy is the foe of life at all levels from the cell to the communicated order of human society. Life's ability to encode information, use feedback, and organize itself temporarily defeats entropy by improbable patterns, in spite of the total increase of entropy in the universe. This tendency is represented by the Second Law of Thermodynamics, which says that confusion or shuffledness is more probable than order, and that, even if there is a decrease in entropy in some part of the universe, it is always more than compensated for by a larger increase somewhere else, this increase being, as Sir Arthur Eddington put it, time's arrow. According to this view, noise is communicational entropy. Its tendency to increase defeats signals and causes communication and information to degrade. So Wiener (1950:134) says that beauty occurs "as a local and temporary fight against the Niagara of increasing entropy." In that sense, noise is everybody's problem all the time.

In theory, progress is supposed to defeat entropy, if only temporarily, by orderly and elegant institutions. To see how far from true this is, one need only look about at urban sprawl, traffic jams, economic crises, unemployment, civil disorder, rising crime, personal disorganization, environmental pollution, the demoralizing content of the media, and so on. Progress is *not* defeating entropy in any conclusive way — even in developing countries, where population explosion and civil disorder offset rapid economic gains. Business decisions, if anything, are aggravating entropy with little concern for social costs of development (Schumpeter's "creative destructionism"). In the catalog of modern woes, noise remains a tangible and convenient indicator of entropy in progress, of how far the battle is from won.

It is an awkward fact of progress that noise is man-made. Except for events such as thunderstorms, nature is quiet. Modern noise is a product of industry, commerce, technology, mass communication, and the movement of strangers crowding one another. The fact seems to be that nothing in biological evolution has adapted us to noise levels encountered in the last fifty years.

Of course, societies, institutions, individuals, and occasions vary in their tolerance for noise. A healthy racket of work, the hubbub of a sports event, loud-spoken argument, and strange customs and styles can be stimulating. Some noise we count on, such as the warning sound of an approaching vehicle. A movie without a certain amount of audience noise is less entertaining. We have all heard of city-raised people who could not sleep in the country because it was so quiet. Total insulation, as shown by sensory deprivation experiments, is boring and unnerving. People who are ill or old suffer from noise that others regard as moderate, just as esthetes are sensitive to ugliness that others do not notice. One person's titillation is another's pornography.

Regardless of such individual and situational variations in tolerance, noise becomes socially critical when it reaches levels at which large numbers of people feel irritation and stress, threat from enemies or violation of their own identity and style by "barbarians," alienation from their world, or general meaninglessness[5] and confusion.

Crowding multiplies whatever effects noise may have, whether the pleasures of festivity or antagonism to incompatible styles. Psychologist Freedman (1975) sums up psychological evidence that crowding is not inherently bad but depends on conditions, such as whether one likes the other people. Doubtless this would be acceded to by anyone who has tried bundling.

However, noise becomes critical between generations and within the family or any group in which members are expected to have similar tastes and values. This was what made the style rebellion of the "generation gap" of the 1960s — slovenliness versus middle-class neatness, hard rock versus softer, sweeter music — so hard to bear: that they had to be endured in what one had supposed was the haven of one's home. Such crises emphasized the damage that noise can do to communication, feedback, resonance, and ultimately to the meaning of relationship, where communication and resonance are needed.

Other causes of crisis from social noise come, I think, from the fact that social status exposes some people more than others to communication, and also to an upbringing that makes them sensitive to noise. If one asks what sort of people are especially likely to be concerned about the problem of social noise as described in this book, the answer would be those who have a status in which they are exposed to communication, have developed high expectations, and at the same time don't care much for their roles. Indeed, this throws light on what might be called the alienation of the overprivileged: the puzzling discontent of many people who have enjoyed affluence. The answer could be that they experience more social noise; that is, once a few jackhammers (symbolizing physical hardship) are eliminated, stress of noise plays no favorites among the economic classes. If anything, it strikes the well off harder.[6] The first reason is exposure to communication. Not only are they likely to have leadership, which exposes them to communication, but they have more costly communication equipment, from wall-to-wall audiovisual and computerized retrieval systems to radiotelephone contact from yachts and airplanes, to bring noise to them. Not only are they better equipped but they are also more exposed by education, travel, purchasable expertise, and cosmopolitan interests and friendships. If they experience more communication, then they are more exposed to whatever comes through communication, not only the pleasure of good news, but also the stress of bad news, overload of information, boring involvement and entertainment, relative deprivation, status anxiety, envy and other bad vibes, disillusionment and loss of faith, all of which seem to reach the rich quite as much as the poor. Note that I am not arguing that the well off are on the whole worse off than the poor, only that alienating communication can strike the well off in spite of their favorable position. It was rather like that with the plagues — and we are speaking of contagious communication. I am saying that the affluent do not have it all their way, but are exposed to real causes of discontent from the communication to which they are exposed.

Second, well-off people are more sensitive to whatever noise reaches them. Their upbringing and tastes make them expect more and sensitize them to disharmonies that the poor ignore. This was conspicuous in the "sentimentality" of reformers during the Victorian and muckraking eras (Filler, 1961; Hofstadter, 1955). Romantics such as Byron, Shelley, and Hoffman came from the ranks of the well off. The historian Raymond Immerwahr (1974) finds the origin of romanticism in a middle class that could buy and read romances and began to judge life by that standard. Along with social Darwinians who view hardships of the poor with comfort, there are keenly sensitive rich people who trouble themselves far more about the world than they need to, even to the extent of radical action (contributing in no small numbers to the student rebellions of the 1960s). Such sensitivity might be symbolized by the fable of the princess who could not sleep while there was a pea beneath her ten mattresses. Deprivations are no less for being relative or vicarious.

A third reason for sensitivity to noise among upwardly aspiring people is low commitment to roles. Sociologists have amply explained why modern success-striving man gives up roots, looks forward to leaving the place he has, feels relative deprivation from comparing himself with others, so often finds himself in a job, career, place, family setting, or kind of service to which he is not durably committed. The happy professional in a career of his choice may pay no more attention to noise than does a mountain climber to struggle, cold, and gravel in his shoes. But it is another matter when commitment to roles is low. Then, so to speak, one finds ants in the picnic food. Perhaps one is in a job for which he has little heart because he has been educated for better things[7] and brought up to expect that his work will fulfill him. Such a man will feel noise and boredom keenly. Suppose he works at the customer adjustment counter of a department store. All day he listens to complaints, soothes irate customers, attends to trivia, screens claims of people trying to put something over on him. Unless he is especially fitted for the role, loves engagement, and prides himself on his ability to handle people, he is likely to feel bored, with a sense of grievance that might be expressed in a question such as: "Why should I put up with all this when I don't care much about the job anyway?" He is in a dilemma involving a conflict between *stress* leading easily to distress (Selye, 1974) and *boredom* from monotony or an overload of irrelevant information not serving his personal significance. Such a double-bind of stress or boredom from work and communication, I say, is felt especially by people whose role commitment is low, because their inner steering signal (redundancy of personal identity within that role, as I shall call it in Chapter 6) is too weak to withstand the noise encountered. Stress and boredom make a sort of Scylla and Charybdis between which a modern Ulysses sails, with second thoughts such as "I didn't want to go on this trip."

In short, there seem to be good reasons why social noise is likely to strike well-off people harder, as they are highly exposed to communication, high in sensitivities and expectations, and low in commitment to roles. This may throw light on the romanticism of rebels of the 1960s who rejected affluence, advocated return to the simple life, and resurrected Thoreau as a patron of the environment.

Today, complaints about the modern environment and culture are wider in scope, including demands for less visual pollution, more truth in advertising, and some sort of communications policy to reduce pollution from media. They, too, seem romantic. But, however impractical and far from fulfillment such proposals may now seem, does not the romantic have an important role as social indicator, rather like that of the canary carried into a coal mine to detect fumes before humans can smell them? He faints in delicate anguish, and people are saved.

The romanticism of yesterday is often the reality of today. I believe that, as the crisis of social noise is more fully seen, it will change our understanding of progress. For example, it will explain how clutter in the environment, giving rise to noise in communication, in turn giving rise to confusion in the mind, is somehow a threat to the human spirit. A things-heaped, noise-filled, information-overloaded environment makes the receptive mind like a poorly organized photomontage. This has much to do with closing responses, such as alienation, joining cults, ethnic ingrouping, and hurrying into restrictively zoned suburbs. The overall perception here is that a high noise condition contributes to the meaning gap of modern society. An overload of noise is ultimately a crisis of meaning.

Second, the crisis of social noise challenges the modernistic assumption that opening is always good, that boundaries are better crossed and walls down, that every bit of information is welcome, that changes are better accepted than rejected.

Third, it challenges the homogenization (melting pot) ideal — as opposed to cultural pluralism — so long a part of American immigration (but not religious) policy. Even if one could reduce stylistic noise by assimilation, by eliminating differences, the question would remain: Who would want it? More today are coming to favor a pluralism that protects, revives, and enriches differences of culture, style, and identity — personal and collective. They are beginning to realize the threat of social noise and banalization to life-style preservation, to recognize that one cannot easily remake a collective style once lost, and, more slowly, that life-styles require collective support and boundaries — a point that it is the sociologist's job to emphasize. This leads to the (now seemingly impractical) proposal for a mosaic of life-styles and also for concern for human scale and communication network balance, which will be explained in Chapter 8.

Indeed, during the 1970s, movements such as environmentalism, "limits to growth," recycling, planning, nostalgia, and concern for human scale ("small is beautiful") heralded general awareness that the era of unrestricted, uncritical growth had come to an end. From then on, large developments would require impact statements, monitoring, program evaluations, and so forth, in which (hopefully) indicators of social noise would have a part.

Such movements showed what I would call closing to entropy, a natural and primitive response of living systems to excessive disorder, experienced within receptors and channels as noise, as part of a strategy to gain information. When social noise gets too high, it is felt to be a losing transaction and becomes a trigger for closing rather than a challenge and opportunity of new experience and cross-fertilization. Closing is tightening boundaries and withdrawing interest in external information and communication until better opportunity for transaction — that is, good opening — can be found. In a crisis of noise, the information environment deteriorates to the point at which resonance is lost and more and more persons and groups close for their own good.[8]

Closing is not merely against noise, but for advantages of information such as resonance and redundancy. Fortunately, offsetting noise, there is a comforting sort of signal — a homing beam if you please — that I call good redundancy. It is comforting to have repeated what we already know in a way that reassures and restores us. Indeed, in the cross winds of modernity, not to have redundancy is like trying to dock a sailboat without a buoy to tie to. Good redundancy is more than the rearview mirror of which McLuhan wrote: It is an essential part of what we must look forward to. In this perspective, I see a balancing between opening as scanning encouraged by favorable information, and closing as a turning off and toward redundancy when the environment offers too poor a bargain of information versus entropy.

Both opening and closing occur within what is commonly called progress. But progress can be a poor bargain — for the well off too. It is just as important to preserve redundancy as to innovate in the game, and balance, of life. Therefore the path of progress cannot be a straight line, but has surprises and sharp turns.

We shall not understand the predicament of our society — its mounting problems at the apex of which is meaninglessness — unless we recognize how entwined communication has been with noise: that transfer of more information from person to person can be disappointing when it comes in forms, amounts, or ways people cannot use, especially when it destroys resonance and overwhelms redundancy, the tie-line. How this happens I hope will become plainer in following chapters, the next of which gives an overview of the theory.

2. Opening and closing in open societies

The artist who says, "I don't look at shows when I'm working," states a view held by many: that too much exposure to the work of others will stifle one's creativity. They retire to remote places to do their work. Writers show a similar need for seclusion for the sake of creativity. Similarly, every Ph.D. thesis writer knows the predicament of collecting more data than he can use, with the chance of being swamped by facts or forging them into conclusions that relate to no theory, so adding to clutter for somebody else.

Such things challenge the conventional belief that openness is always better than closedness, that the more information the better — perhaps that one cannot get too much of a good thing. Since Aristotle, it has been accepted that "the mind desires to know," and since the eighteenth century, liberal theorists have held that an open mind is better than a closed one (Rokeach, 1960); likewise for society (Popper, 1952). By scientists, especially, closure to information — even to views like those of Doctor Velikovsky — is censured. Some sociologists see generous limits to how open, changeable, and temporary society can become (Bennis and Slater, 1968).

What is challenging the conventional view that openness is always tolerable and better than closedness? First, there are substantial considerations about information overload (Miller, 1960, 1971; Deutsch, 1961; Meier, 1962; Toffler, 1970; Klapp, 1972). Systems theory has re-emphasized homeostasis in all living systems, as a balance between intake and outgo. There is new appreciation of the positive value of redundancy, not as merely something to be cut out as quickly as possible. Optimization is of prime concern in systems theory. Psychologists are exploring the thesis that too much knowledge smothers creativity. On the same score, a neglected educational wisdom whispers, "Assimilate to create, don't just swallow to regurgitate."

From this point of view, too much input is a threat because creativity is essentially an outflow from within,[1] not an inflow from without.

It is an inner change in configuration, not a recombination of pieces poured in from outside (as in a hand dealt in cards or a rather mechanical notion of cultural cross-fertilization). Creativity is a surge of vitality reshaping the world outside, discovering what is needed to complete a pattern — and because of this is a *closure* to what is not needed for the jigsaw puzzle, too many pieces of which might hide forever the finding of the fit. Once a pattern is perceived, 90 percent of information becomes irrelevant.

Also challenging the ideal of openness in the nineteen-seventies are what might be called spasms of closing among ethnic, religious, and other groups. Archie Bunkerism has been on the rise, and its enormous popularity is by no means due merely to its message of the bigot *put down*. It is an era of nativistic revivalism and separatism asserting the spirit of unmeltable ethnics (Novak, 1971), provoking antiforeignism and backlashes of one kind or another, such as the furor over school busing (Rubin, 1972), "seething intolerance" among longhairs, Chicanos, and Anglos for each others' styles in Taos, New Mexico (Melville, 1972:140–3), or efforts to restrict Hutterites in Alberta, Canada. Other signs of closing are nostalgia for the good old days, reemphasis of nationalism, immigration restriction, and the "police dog and padlock" syndrome in large cities.

Along with such closing spasms, however, are paradoxical movements to *transcend* restrictions felt in the supposed freedom of information and goods and progress of modern society, such as romantic rebellion, dropping-out, and forms of cultic and occultic seeking such as witchcraft, astrology, flying saucers, extrasensory perception, biofeedback, and mysticism of many kinds often based on religions from the East (Klapp, 1969; Braden, 1970; Roszak, 1972). Such seekers claim something is missing from an overly technological, bureaucratic, matter-of-fact, secularized, sensate, denotative, positivistic, banal, or one-dimensional culture — a restriction of some kind in the very abundance of modern society separating people from wonder, mystery, meaning, and cosmic consciousness. Progress, not an Inquisition, has produced this box.

In the two sorts of collective response mentioned, we have illustrations of spasms of closing, on the one hand, and surges or tides of opening, outpouring enthusiasm, and seeking, on the other. Surges are overflows of social energy, characterized by catharsis and synergy, as in the hero worship of Lindbergh after his flight, or the election of a popular president. The enthusiasm of a surge might be in terms of gratitude, welcome, rejoicing, market optimism, gambling fever, gold rush, or spiritual fervor. During such movements, there is a greater willingness to try fads, open doors, let oneself go.

Spasms of closing, on the other hand, are more negative in feelings like anxiety, alienation, and hostility. They may contain with them both the backflow of the spent wave, due to fatigue and other limiting factors; and defensiveness against threat, invasion, or dissonance, perhaps from another group's opening. Closing might reflect a sense of entropy widespread in society, as medieval people locked themselves up to escape the plagues. Closing ranks with one's own kind seeks not only defense but reinforcement and intensification of "good vibes" (needed redundancy) within. The more positive side of closing is illustrated by the following statement by a member of an American Zen community:

I feel there's great harmony here . . . we tried to find and emphasize that harmony rather than the discord. And then we try to help people outside the building to experience this harmony. . . . Here I am trying to learn a life style, a way of living that turns life into a constant creative thing. I want to open myself to growth, instead of living in a way where I'm always having to protect myself and fight things off and be afraid. I really like the people here. They're trying to be careful about themselves and each other and their lives. There's a feeling of order and preserving, taking good care of things, not being destructive and careless and wasteful. (*Wind Bell*, Publication of Zen Center, San Francisco, Fall-Winter 1970–1:4)

Such things illustrate how the cult opposes entropy by enclosing its members in a fellowship providing both needed redundancy and creative synergy in terms of meaning, faith, or rebirth (Klapp, 1969).

A natural rhythm

In larger terms, we may see opening and closing as not just a feature of human collectivities but as part of a natural tide or rhythm throughout the living world. The sea anemone in a tide pool outstretches and retracts its green tentacles. The turtle and snail withdraw into shells when openness gets to be too much. Hibernation is a seasonal closure. The Old Testament says: "to everything there is a season . . . a time to get and a time to lose; a time to keep and a time to cast away . . . a time to keep silence, and a time to speak" (Ecclesiastes 3:1–7). The sabbath is a traditional closure to worldliness once a week. The pupil dilates when light is dim and contracts when it is bright. Youth is a time of risk whereas old age is one of saving and stocktaking. The child crawls, reaches, tastes, then curls up to rest. From such things, we see that what we call aliveness — resilience, adaptability — is noٽ continual intake, nor any constant policy, but sensitive alternation of openness and closure. The mind listens alertly, then turns off to signals. The natural pattern is alternation, and the more alive a system is, the more alertly it opens and closes. In such a view, closing is not, as some suppose, merely a setback to growth and progress, but evidence that the mechanisms of life are working, that the society has resiliency. More alarming than swings to closure would be a lack of public response. A perpetually open society would suffer the fate of a perpetually open clam.

In this light opening and closing may be looked on as a strategy to gain information while defeating entropy. At the organismic level closing is governed by needs for homeostasis, growth, and adaptation. At the psychological level, it responds to conditions such as arousal and satiation (Berlyne, 1960), consonance–dissonance (Festinger, 1957), and structural features of belief systems (Rokeach, 1960). At the social level, opening and closing is a transaction through communication, with factors such as noise, information pollution, or signals of threat to a group playing a large part. When things are going well, there is no gain of entropy; should signs warn the reverse, the gate slams, if but momentarily.

At the social symbolic level, I suppose that a focal point of opening and closing is a feeling about "we" or collective identity, embodied perhaps in style, "soul," heroes, or other group symbols. The more closely knit a group is, the more sensitive it is about its honor, the more resistant to criticism, and the more defensive against enemies and traitors. A major concern, triggering the closure noted, is threat to collective consonance from noise generated by outsiders, and attrition of collective identity — too little belongingness, as in alienation and anomie. The assumption here is that normal identity requires both self-identification and collective identification; losing either, beyond a point, may provoke closing to extremes as represented by schizophrenia or closing ranks in a small separatist group.

Collective identity is built and maintained by sufficient flow of "we-relevant" information in appropriate nets and channels. Historical inputs, such as conflicts and the deeds of heroes, nourish collective memory and pride. Ritual recalls and intensifies such images and feelings of togetherness. Interpersonal interaction supports — or denies — them by verbal and nonverbal, conscious and unwitting signals in daily life. Intrusion of outsiders and their noise into a group might challenge and strengthen collective identity; or in other circumstances, perhaps high mobility, dissolve it. Some hypotheses are offered elsewhere (Klapp, 1972, Chapter 1). For a well-developed collective identity, members of a group should perform functions of the *gatekeeper* (reading the incoming signals, screening and interpreting them for group benefit); *elaborator,* retouching and embellishing the image of "we" (poets, artists, biographers); *custodian* of collective memory (arbiter, archivist, storyteller); *decider;* and *actor* (effector, agent) for the group, in public drama as hero (Klapp, 1964a). Anything interrupting such flow weakens collective identity.

When a lot of people feel too much entropy as a crisis to collective identity, they close to protect the net, exclude noise, intensify signals affirming common values, and perhaps define more clearly an enemy. But sometimes there may be no particular enemy triggering closing, only a generalized sense of malaise, of entropic signals coming from one can hardly say where. Entropic communication is a huge subject, including such things as mass contagions, semantic corruption, insincerity and manipulation of information, betrayal of trust, inconsistency of rules and expectations (including the "double bind" of schizophrenia), and "information pollution" from the media.

So when one interprets closing spasms such as the furor over school busing or the rights of kith and kin versus immigrants, one sees them as more than merely "prejudice," in the light of the communication context and societal rhythms of opening and closing that even open societies display. As I see it, all living systems balance variety and redundancy in this way.

What are conventionally called "open" societies close in different ways from "closed" societies, and at different points on a range, one end of which might be an authoritarian system allergic to small increases of information, and the other an ideal liberal society with a progress ideology emphasizing the modern and devaluing the old — hence vulnerable to crisis from information overload and loss of redundancy. The closing of such a society would occur largely through ingrouping (intensified pluralism if you please), in such things as increased college fraternity enrollment or "snob zoning" in suburbs. But one would not expect it to swing to authoritarianism except under extreme conditions of entropy. An open society oscillates within a range different from that of the closed one, on a continuum stretching theoretically from high solidarity (cohesiveness, morale, esprit de corps, and so forth) at one end to total alienation at the other.

If all societies are naturally subject to opening and closing, some revision in current assumptions about progress and the "free market of information" may be necessary. Is it possible to get too much of a good thing? No living system takes an unlimited input of anything. Does information have a special exemption? Or is it, too, subject to overloads and entropic effects comparable with overproduction in economic markets and polluting side-effects of "growth"? If closing is as necessary as opening to any human system, then perhaps redundancy is insufficiently appreciated in modern society. At any rate, closing needs to be seen in a more sympathetic light than just the bad end of a continuum of which open is the good end. And perhaps Archie Bunker represents more than the ignorance end of a scale of which the opposite is knowledge.

I do not, however, wish to erect a straw man here. Most system theorists recognize that unlimited increase of anything good is not better. But it can hardly be denied that in the literature there is some bias in favor of openness over closedness, whereas the present argument puts them on a par. Opening to *any* feedback is usually regarded as more adaptive than closing to poor (e.g., noisy, irrelevant, misleading, anxiety-provoking) feedback. For example, Hampden-Turner (1970:79) finds competent, creative people to be openers, whereas closers tend to be anomic and to cling to the formal system: "Man's anomic failure to exist renders his perception narrow and impoverished, his identity 'locked in' and stagnant . . . [he] avoids trying to bridge the . . . distances to others."

The information game of opening and closing

This book suggests an amendment to the open social system model. A flabbily open system is no more viable than a rigidly closed one. Only under some conditions is the "free market of ideas" of J. S. Mill closely descriptive of pluralistic society. A more accurate picture, it seems to me, is continual oscillation between relative openness and closedness — resilient adjustment to intakes of information/entropy. When such oscillations are properly analyzed, we may have better understanding not only of how open systems work, but of such things as ethnic revivalism, cultic movements, mass contagions, fads, and fashion cycles.

But a mechanical picture of oscillation is not intended. Three qualifications are needed regarding its synchronicity, selectivity, and game-like character. First, though cyclicity is implied by the hypothesis of opening and closing, synchronicity is not always to be expected.[2] Cycles of subsystems may be out of step. It may be that opening of one collectivity, for example the liberalism of the countercultural movement in the sixties, provokes repressive backlashes in another. Nevertheless, one may expect that some eras would display overall fluctuations in the amount of communication across boundaries, though such patterns remain to be observed by composition of various indicators (of such things as message flow, mass media content,[3] fashion pace, neologisms, tourism, cultural exchange, joining intercultural organizations, legislative issues such as immigration or invasion of privacy, active prejudice and ethnocentrism, experiences of door-to-door salesmen, and even the conferring of exotic names on children).

Second, opening and closing are not just a matter of sheer amount of information flow. The notion of a gate swinging ajar or slamming is not meant to imply indiscriminateness in what is admitted or kept out. It is assumed that perception and communication are always selective; that information is selected according to interests, norms, codes, psycholinguistic grids, stereotypes, gestalts — templates of one sort or another. By analogy, a sport-fisherman extends his range and variety of lures not to get more of all kinds of fish but to win better trophies — his standards are as high as ever. In other words, no amount of opening or closing eliminates the gestalt figure/ground dichotomy, unless it were certain psychedelic and ecstatic states (Huxley, 1954; Lewis, 1971; Greely, 1974). Openness then might be characterized as readiness, as it were, to look around a gestalt while widening the range of scanning, as artists try to do (Ehrenzweig, 1970). But culture is a powerful determinant of what is of interest, so the social system even at its most open is choosing some kinds of information at the expense of others. It might, for example, have a bias toward military opportunities while neglecting those of peace, or profit while ignoring environmental impact, or (as critics like Roszak, Matson, and Heidegger have said) overload with "objective" facts while neglecting intuitive awareness. Even faddism, as a form of collective search, though scanning and dropping varieties quickly, is discriminating according to standards of taste as "nice," one may presume, for rock as well as for classical music, though its judgments are not so long lasting. Selectiveness of perception and communication also implies that opening and closing apply not to the entire horizon of information but to range of scanning within some *sector.* A business might diversify investments without being venturesome in labor relations, a modernizing country might welcome technological innovation while strongly resisting "immoral" Western influences. Again, it was apparent in North America and Europe during the early seventies that there was a nostalgic yearning for redundancy (closing to the pace of change and variety), while in another sector cultic and occultic movements were opening to transcendental experiences. Such oscillations, with occasional swings from one sector to another, seem to me to be part of a trial-and-error strategy by which societies seek to remedy imbalances and optimize their information.

As to the correct moves, we get a clue from classifying words in the English language referring to opening and closing in terms of "good" or "bad." *Bad opening* is implied by words such as folly, crime, lawlessness, waste, error, amok, indiscriminate, dissipated, vulgar, tasteless, tactless, promiscuous, depraved, licentious, libertine, easy mark, gullible, suggestible, corruptible, dishonest, two-faced, disloyal, treacherous, susceptible, permissive, fast, loose, easy, blabber, tattletale, bigmouth, pollution, information overload, mongrelization (interbreeding), hemorrhage. Such words imply transgression of needed boundaries. On the other hand, *good opening* is implied by words such as expressive, open-minded, tolerant, broad-minded, receptive, omnivorous, liberal, libertarian, indulgent, outspoken, charitable, sympathetic, understanding, cosmopolitan, curious, persuasible, inquisitive, inquiring, adventurous, experimental, permissive, seeking, searching, free, independent, forthright, informative, news-bearer, well informed, cross-fertilization, circulation. These words express gains of information flow. *Bad closing* is referred to by words such as repression, inhibition, bigotry, censorship, puritan, intolerant, straightlaced, chaperone, prig, prude, arrogant, insular, provincial, hidebound, narrowminded, dogmatic, fanatic, sectarian, secretive, timid, tight, pinchy, cut off, isolated, ignorant, sterile, uncreative, stereotyped, shallow, monotonous, inbreeding (degenerative), embolus, anorexia. These show loss from overstressing boundaries. *Good closing* is referred to by words emphasizing norms, restraint, and discrimination, such as loyalty, self-control, prudence, conservation, conscience, morality, connoisseur, judge, expert, epicure, critic, discriminating, selective, guardian, gatekeeper, discreet, cautious, incor-

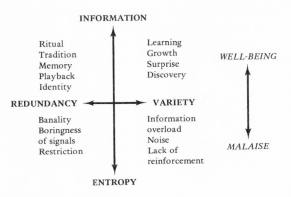

Figure 1. Sectors of the game of life

ruptible, pure, clean, antiseptic, saintly, united, settled, rooted, firm, sturdy, sound, brave, accurate, solution, answer, discovery, design, well bred, selective breeding, coagulation. From such lists, it is plain that no case can be made for *all* closing or opening. Studying the situations to which such words apply may help us to distinguish success and failure of various strategies. There are inherent risks either way: Scanning for news, discovery, or growth runs the risk of excessive noise and other costs of bad opening; closing for redundancy, memory, reinforcement, or cohesion risks narrowness, ignorance, and stifling banality.

 So we may think of opening and closing as part of a shifting strategy to get the most of the best information and the least of the worst noise, depending on a tradeoff in the signal-to-noise ratio. When the environment becomes adverse, from noise or information overload, more closing is needed. A society or person who tried to take in everything would be like a clam who tried to siphon all the sludge at the bottom of a bay. In strict accounting, every bit of information and noise, beauty and ugliness, enters the human reckoning. Oscillation between opening and closing is the normal way to play the game. Good moves take one into advantageous sectors. Mistakes — opening or closing at the wrong time or to the wrong things — may land one in deeper trouble. Such alternatives are indicated in Figure 1, which depicts the "playing field" of the game of life. Oscillations can there be conceived of as moves on the playing field to gain variety or redundancy as needed in the particular state of the system. In general, bad closing calls for moves toward good opening (the upper right-hand sector), and bad opening toward good closing (the upper left). Bad opening consists of being overwhelmed by sheer noise or signals of amounts and kinds that a system cannot use for its own growth, as when cultures become "victims of progress" (Bodley, 1974), or cities so open that they become crime jungles because communities cannot define "defensible space" (Newman, 1972). On larger scale, Sorokin's (1941, 1950) crisis of altruism in sensate culture may be another example. In such circumstances, more opening is hardly the prescription; rather, closing through ingrouping, traditionalism, nostalgia, ritualism, and so on, as I have described, aims to increase good redundancy with its contribution to resonance and identity (as in the warm feeling of an anniversary celebration). On the other hand, bad closing (as in banality) calls for scanning to find a better "mix" of information — hopefully a fortunate encounter with the right clues for discovery according to one's needs. In society, scanning might take forms such as wit, clowning, artistic creativity, experimentation, romantic rebellion, existentialism, mystical transcendence, or frenetic fashion change.

Tipping points occur when enough people perceive a *communication imbalance* that can be remedied by scanning or closing, as the case may be. My theory, stated in following chapters is that various sorts of communication imbalance make deciders aware that a sector of the environment is giving a disadvantageous noise/signal ratio. Such imbalances need to be empirically determined for various kinds and states of systems, by channel and symbolic content-analysis. In addition to sheer information overload or deprivation, for example, one may find imbalances in the relative amount of oral communication (face-to-face dialogue and gossip) to impersonal media output; nonverbal to verbal information; pattern and meaning to disconnected bits; negative messages (ill will, anxiety, and so on) to good will and reassurance; or banality to redundancy that is warm and reinforcing.

One imbalance having much to do with whether people experience information as overload, as I will suggest, is the proportion of *exogenous* to *indigenous* signals. Indigenous signals are familiar, high in redundancy, local in reference, communicated from people one knows; so they are immediately understood without definition and trusted; whereas exogenous signals (strange in origin, referring to things with which one has had little direct experience, coming from people one does not know) require continual definition, calculation, and testing if one is to know what to make of them, so they carry a greater decoding burden while contributing less to any particular identity — until the world may seem flooded with information one cannot own, a jigsaw puzzle that does not come together. In such cases, the overload is not in sheer amount of communication but in too high a proportion of exogenous signals. Another imbalance having to do with whether information is experienced as overload is the failure of a modern society to supply enough information relevant to identity, personal and collective, to avoid attrition and crisis to the sense of who one is (Erikson, 1963; Klapp, 1969). There are also important questions about human versus economical scale, taken up in Chapter 8. When such parameters of communication balance are defined, we shall better understand when closing and opening are good and when not.

I try in this book to put the claims of closing on a par with those of opening, seeing them as part of the same life strategy. Opening to variety — for learning, progress, evolution, and control (Ashby, 1956) — has been emphasized in modern society to the point of bias. When the need for redundancy — helping cohesion, resonance, reinforcement, tradition, memory, identity, and continuity of purpose — is equally recognized, then oscillation of opening and closing is expected as normal and necessary for living systems.[4]

What does this mean for our modern society? I begin by looking at how the information environment deteriorates into social noise — informational, semantic, contagious, and stylistic — thus impairing communication and resonance and making it harder to find meaning. Then I consider how society responds by closing and opening aimed at communication balance for a better quality of life.

Let us see how much more there is to noise than meets the ear.

3. The feast of the media

Hungered for in countries where books are scarce and films a novelty, information has a different value in a country plastered with billboards, where paperbacks are thrown away on trains, students complain of study loads, and television is regarded by some as a nuisance, if not a menace. Here the supply of information enters the range of overload for many people.

This is a surprising ending for a story that began with information hunger.

Information hunger

As they rattled off down the road in the cold, clear morning, the boys, round-eyed with excitement, studied every house and barn with such prolonged interest that their heads revolved on their necks like those of young owls . . . Rock River had only one street of stores, blacksmith shops and taverns, but it was an imposing place to Lincoln . . . When Lincoln spoke he whispered, as if in church, pointing with stubby finger, "See there!" each time some new wonder broke on his sight . . . The buying of boots was the crowning of joy of the day . . . Then there were books to be bought, also, a geography, a "Ray's Arithmetic," and a slate . . . At last, with all their treasures under the seat, where they could look at them or feel of them, with their slates clutched in their hands, the boys jolted toward home in silence . . . Lincoln was pensive and silent all the evening, for he was busily digesting the mass of sights, sounds, and sensations which the day's outing had thrust upon him. (Hamlin Garland, *Boy's Life on the Prairie*, 1899:17–18)

This glimpse of boys' life on the prairie during the 1870s is meant to illustrate how it was in North America before our transition to a media system, how thrilling were the simple sights and sounds of a small town to a boy who had no notion of movies, television, or, for that matter, newspapers.[1] His world was quite as interesting to him, it seems, as ours is to us, though not so loaded with sensations.

Such a natural interest in the sights and sounds of one's own world soon loses ground to the more alluring experiences offered by the media of opportunities and adventures beyond. So an agricultural expert who has lived in African and Indian villages tells of the "true contentment" he found in self-sufficient traditional societies, which is lost when people enter the worldwide system of trade, jobs for wages, and mass communication.

Unless there is a famine (and in twelve years in Africa I never saw one), everybody gets enough to eat, and people who do not hanker after the flesh-pots of the white man live a very good life indeed.

Teach these people to read, though, and you immediately get a completely different situation. The children grow up no longer content with village self-sufficiency. They must have books, and books cannot be produced in the village (although I have seen paper being made in an Indian village in a mill; the chief constituent was a cow walking round in a circle providing the power), they wish to see the other parts of the world that they now become aware exist, they long for the sophisticated clothes, the machines, the gadgets and the other things that can only be produced by a city-based civilization. The Indians have two useful words: pukha and kutcha. Pukha means with a civilized finish on it. Kutcha means rough — made in the village without outside help. The man who has learnt to read, and been to town, comes back and wants a pukha house — one that makes use of glass and cement and mill-sawn timber and other materials that cannot be produced in the village: his old kutcha house is no longer good enough for him. He also wants white sugar instead of gorr, which is the unrefined sugar of his own sugar-cane, tea instead of buttermilk, white flour instead of his own wholemeal. He — and eventually his whole village with him — are forced into a money economy. (Seymour, 1976:8)

Giving up contentment seems a small price for participation in the larger world. Not until much later do people wonder how large a price it was and whether contentment is gone forever. But when information is novel and the adventures are promises for a better future, it hardly seems to matter. The wave is welcomed.

The advancing wave

All over the world, wave upon wave of media, beginning usually with transistor radios, transforms the experience of people in less-developed countries from direct to vicarious or mediated. Layers of experience by battery-run radios, tape and record-players, telephones, films, and even television, usually precede newpapers and books. Travelers in remote regions tell of surprise at hearing music of a transistor radio coming from an ox-cart, or tramping from a jungle trail into a clearing to find loin-clothed natives squatting to watch a film packed in by USIA; or, as was the experience of one sociologist (Glassman, 1974), finding in the back-country of Puerto Rico barefoot villagers standing before a large-screen color television set absorbed in "typical everyday fare" of warmed-over American commercial TV (with a dubbed Spanish sound track, of course). Media hunger is strong in developing countries not yet saturated. For example, after import controls imposed by the Allende government had been relaxed in 1974, movie fans rushed to see new Western-made films such as *The Godfather, Death in Venice, Cabaret,* and *Le Mans,* trying to catch up on what they had missed, while placards urged, "Hurry up, we are three years behind." According to a UNESCO survey, by 1975 about 364 million television sets were in use throughout the world.

Rather late compared with audio-visual media, dependent as it is on literacy, comes a hunger for books, coupled with a strong wish for children to be educated to share in the careers and benefits of modernity. A UNESCO report of 1973 noted that, since the world's reading population had more than doubled in twenty years, there was in Asia, Latin America, and parts of Africa a book hunger amounting to starvation, while the other half of the world was saturated by the printed word. Because of such eagerness for input from media, people in transitional countries grasp almost whatever is offered. Lucien Pye says they are unselective because the media are novel and can still provoke curiosity:

In many Asian and African countries there is only one local radio station or at best two stations that compete for attention; and the volume of newspapers and magazines is so limited that competent readers are usually constantly hungry . . . Under these conditions of relative sparsity of media it appears that people do not develop the same attitudes of selectivity, and therefore . . . the media can in fact play a far more potent role in political education than in the saturated societies. (Pye, 1963:126)

Their avidity is the opposite of the alienation felt by many today toward the wonders of "the tube."

General impacts of the media wave on developing countries became plain. As Daniel Lerner (1958) showed in his classic study of the Middle East, media aided modernization in a cycle which began with urbanization, as people moved from scattered hinterlands to centers where markets, jobs, and media might be experienced. Then literacy became the pivotal agent increasing media participation, generating new desires, and providing means of satisfying them in a modern system; as media participation increased, people lived more by what they heard of in the press, radio, and TV, so increasing their empathy and psychic mobility. Finally came public participation, as people played a larger part as voters, buyers, bank depositors, political party members, and so on. Although it is rather a chicken-egg problem to sort out which of these phases is the prime mover (Schramm, 1964:50), there is little doubt that media open up countries, increase mobility, generate new needs, speed political change, and vastly aid markets for manufactured goods — to a degree in Latin America that Wells (1972) called "picture tube imperialism": consumerism leading to dependence on imported goods at the expense of indigenous productive capacity. In a broader sense, media bring about growth of a public domain of information, as distinguished from local tradition and esoteric teaching, which belongs to nobody in particular and, if not publicly known, is at least accessible to everyone.

But a price has to be paid for such benefits of the media wave.

Fading indigenous signals

As media bring their exogenous signals into developing countries, other signals become harder to hear. Lerner's study (1958), while showing the benefits of the mobile, modern life-style, also captured the drama of a struggle: that media in modernization were somehow pitted against networks of oral communication, and that in this struggle direct communication and relationships based on it were the losers. For example, in the unforgettable picture of the chief of the Turkish village of Balgat, who, having bought a radio to please and instruct his sons, tried to control the picture people were getting from it by a ceremonial:

Each evening a select group of Balgati foregathered in the Chief's guest room as he turned on the newscast from Ankara. They heard the newscast through in silence, and at its conclusion, the Chief turned the radio off and made his commentary. "We all listen very carefully," he told Tosun, "and I talk about it afterwards." Tosun, suspecting in this procedure a variant of the Chief's containment tactics, wanted to know whether there was any disagreement over his explanations. "No, no arguments," replied the Chief, "as I tell you I only talk and our opinions are the same more or less." (Lerner, 1958:26–7)

The old Chief was a custodian of traditional wisdom, a gatekeeper for news, and was trying to maintain his opinion leadership by interpreting messages to shape the views of those who were used to listening to him. But he did not know what a loser he was: Already the grocer, who had been to the city and had had opportunities to listen in the coffee houses of Ankara, was undercutting him with views at variance. The chief was a traditional, trying to hold to old views and his position as opinion leader; the grocer was a leader for those who were no longer listening solely to the old voices ("We are stuck in this hole; we have to know what is going on outside our village"). Whereas the younger generation rushed to be modernized, traditionals had "constricted" views, objecting to exposure to radio and cinema, for fear that accepted standards were being undermined ("It spoils our youth . . . Movies show films with naked girls . . . with gambling . . . They teach them how to kiss girls." [p. 193]). Traditionals preferred gossip, local affairs, indigenous music and culture; whereas transitionals, and especially moderns, were empathic, cosmopolitan, and oriented toward radio, news, and film as the source of their opinions and values. But it wasn't just a matter of old ways and culture versus the new. How fundamental this change was in the *kinds of relationships* by which people got information was shown by Lerner, who contrasted the oral and the media communication systems. There are four main dimensions of change: (1) in channel, from personal (face-to-face give and take) to broadcast (mediated, one-way) transmission; (2) audience, from primary group to heterogeneous mass of strangers; (3) communication content, from prescriptive (rules, norms) to descriptive (news, facts); and (4) source, from hierarchical (status in one's own system) to professional (skill and job as communicator — for example, a newscaster or television actor). Because the professional communicator lacks the authority that goes with status, his messages, if they are to be persuasive, must be descriptive and factual rather than prescriptive, that is, having the character of moral injunction or command. But the main point is the kinds of relationships one has with sources of information in these contrasting systems: the oral spreading messages by mouth-to-ear among people in natural primary groups of kinship, work, worship, and play; the media spreading messages through impersonal channels such as print, film, and radio, to large mass audiences coming from all walks of life, having little in common, unknown to each other and to more or less anonymous communicators. The oral system is richly dialogical whereas media are monological — full of information yet unresponsive (Matson and Montagu, 1967). Such a transition, if it went far enough (that is, if people got most of their information from media), would be no less than what sociologists have described as the mass society.

Indeed one does see a kind of rootlessness in modernism as a set of attitudes that come from a life in which there is high media participation, stress on individual achievement, and low integration with relatives and other status groups. According to Kahl (1968), the marks of a "modern" man, perhaps anywhere in the world, are: (1) activism rather than fatalism, including planning the future and using technology to shape the world; (2) role stratification of life chances, that is, seeing a system open in which status can be achieved; (3) low community stratification; (4) occupational primacy, or determination and driving ambition to succeed; (5) low integration with relatives; (6) individualism, that is, independence of close ties and pushing one's own career; (7) low distrust of outsiders (contrasted with ingroup mistrust of strangers); (8) high participation in mass media (versus gossip and the oral system); (9) preference for urban life; and (10) accepting work with big companies and bureaucracies (versus the primary group). So we see something of the state of mind and style of life of the psychically mobile participant in the media system.

Of course, transition to a modern communication system does not mean wiping out the oral system. The gatekeeper and informal opinion leader are not driven away by the professional communicators of the mass media. Rather, the media system is laid over the oral system, which has become looser in the process. The analogy might be used of water (representing mass-media messages) flowing so rapidly through a lawn that it loosens the roots of the grass and separates clumps from one another. Such a view of how a media system coexists on top of an oral system of informal opinion leaders is given by Pye (1963:24–9), who said that mass media do not always weaken the oral system. The real test of modernization is the extent to which there is effective feedback between the mass media systems and the informal, face-to-face systems. Very often transitional systems (for example Greece or Turkey) have a "bifurcated and fragmented" relationship between the media and oral levels, an urban-centered media system that penetrates only erratically into a separate village-based system, which is autonomous in the sense that it does not interact with the urban system. Further, the villages are actually isolated subsystems, which have less communication with each other than they separately have with the urban centers; this linking might be likened to "the spokes of a wheel all connecting to a hub but without any outer rim." The adjustment problem of a transitional society, therefore, is to bring the informal rural systems into relationship with each other and to the mass-media system rather than just pouring investment into the modern sector, which might create even greater imbalance.

The point is that modernization with prominence of the media system does not easily defeat indigenous communication networks, and if it did so, it would be at great cost. What we get from such pictures of modernization is not unequivocal welcome but the fact that indigenous systems were resisting — by what now might be called homeostasis — the oncoming wave of information. In modern society such resistance to media by oral networks is often called two-step or multi-step: that is, certain messages from the media are picked up by opinion leaders, who pass them on by personal influence to their following or circle of acquaintances, thus working as buffers, filters, and reinforcers (as Katz and Lazarsfeld, 1955, showed for women's fashions). If not so picked up, media messages are weak or slow to get people to do things. Innovators are not followed at first; only somewhat later, after opinion leaders adopt an idea or technique and influence flows through interaction, does diffusion move without haste through stages of innovators, early adopters, early majority, late majority, and laggards (Rogers, 1962; Rogers and Svenning, 1969; Rogers and Shoemaker, 1971). That is, steps of diffusion because of selection by indigenous nets might be seen to either help media messages get accepted or retard them — depending on the scale of comparison, say, for example, the speed of news diffusion versus how long it takes for a rumor to become legend, or for people to be persuaded to change habits such as smoking. For our purpose (explaining information overload) the important point is that indigenous systems resist and retard absorption of media messages, maintaining their boundaries by gatekeepers and selective assimilation of what is useful to *them* from all messages offered. Media hunger is not the natural state of an indigenous communication network. In the early stage of exposure to media messages, a traditional society may not get it at all because it simply isn't relevant to their frame of reference, as Allan Holmberg (1968) reported in his contact with Indians of the Andes of Peru: Shown a public health film, villagers were unable to see any connection between it and their life, grasp the meaning of photographs, or recognize a flea when it was magnified — only patient talk and demonstration could finally get the message through. Such information was exogenous both in that its content was unrelated to their culture and in that it came to them by a channel they were not used to; it therefore could not pass their mental boundaries. The same phenomena is shown in a study by Eisenstadt (1952) of immigrants to Israel coming from Yemen, Yugoslavia, North Africa, and Central and Eastern Europe: Where people are enmeshed in group relationships, they are hard to reach except through their gatekeepers; if exposed to mass media, they do not respond readily but prefer to have messages given personally to them by their leaders. This is illustrated by the effort to assimilate some 250 families into the modern State of Israel. A program of oral and written instruction was provided in three spheres: economic, to instruct them as to working opportunities, and housing and relief facilities; cultural and educational, to induce them to send their children to schools, study the Hebrew language, participate in lectures, folk dances, festivals, and so on; and political, to instruct them about civic rights and duties. However, it was found that the way in which information was transmitted had a great deal to do with whether it was accepted. Three types of transmission were tried: (1) direct, impersonal appeals to the whole group in meetings, or through newspapers, proclamations, and the like; (2) personal appeal to a specific individual or small group by an official; and (3) transmission of messages to them through their communal leaders. As might be expected, the formal, impersonal contacts were least effective; the best way of reaching them was through their opinion leaders, and they fully accepted nothing unless it came to them in this way. Data showed that after six months of communication effort, only 10 percent had been affected by formal, impersonal methods of instruction and 25 percent by direct personal appeals from an official; whereas 65 percent had changed their behavior when information came to them through their leaders. As the immigrants said: "In all these things we know that we have to rely on our teachers and rabbis as they understand these things much better than we do; and if they would have thought it right, they would have told us themselves"; or "We have joined in these social activities mainly because 'leaders we trust' have talked about it with us and have persuaded us that it is good and worthwhile. In all these matters we rely very much on them and we would heed them much more than any stranger." Moreover, even the leader's messages had to come to them in a certain way: If formal and impersonal, it was likely to fail; communication was effective only when it was direct and personal, in which authority was intermingled with primary relations and identifications. As one immigrant put it, 'We do not want only to hear orders from far-away people, even if they are very wise and know everything.

Our rabbis know that the best way is to gather all of us in the synagogue and to tell us about it and to explain it to us. Otherwise, we do not listen." However, over a period of time, such exclusive reliance on opinion leaders was lost; the immigrants began to receive more information directly from the absorbing social system, to go to the movies, and to participate more in the mass media. Among the reasons given for turning away from traditional opinion leaders were disillusionment with the elites' ability to interpret the new social system and its values, and even the feeling that clinging to the old elites blocked achievement of full status within the new society. As one said, "Lately I began to feel that whenever I meet the old leader, whenever they try to explain things to us, to organize us, I live in our imaginary world, a world of yesterday. I feel they really do not belong here. They are trying to keep us in our old life. But I feel that we really belong to the new life here, and that they are real obstructions on our way here." (Eisenstadt, 1952:42–58).

Such resistance to messages outside the familiar network should not be classed as mere ignorance, rigidity, or pigheadedness. Schramm (1964) finds prudence, if not wisdom, in the reluctance of a Southeast Asian patriarch to accept the new ideas about jobs and money that his sons brought home from school. The patriarch is not rigid but realistic in knowing that he operates on a very narrow margin, close to famine, so how can he afford to gamble? He knows a sure and safe way to farm, learned from teachers he trusts, and tested by a lifetime of experience. Moreover, he must work within the village system, so cannot change alone. So when change pushes into the village and community development workers try to make agriculture more productive, his attitude is resistant — not stupidity, but a realization of the value of a way of life threatened by information that has not yet proven itself. Exogenous information comes to such networks as noise — hard to understand or cope with, and possibly dangerous.

Another real source of aversion to exogenous information is the increase in the "want-get" ratio, as media foster growth of expectations — psychic mobility, the capacity to dream — faster than the development of means and institutions by which to satisfy them. This brings about a generation of youth alienated from parents whose old ways cannot meet the expectations, and also dangerous political instability (Davies, 1969; Feierabend et al., 1969). Ten years after his first, rather optimistic, formulation of the effect of mass media on developing countries, Lerner commented with some foreboding:

The naive idea that it is good for a nation with a very high standard of living to communicate its own image to a nation with a very low standard of living . . . is a very dangerous assumption. I think on the contrary, that we are doing such psychological harm in the underdeveloped world that our children's children will pay some of the price for this. We have conveyed a picture of a better life, of the availability to all of the good things in life, and thereby helped to accelerate the desires (and demands) of peoples for these things . . .

What we have done is to create a set of wants which cannot be satisfied within the lifetime of the people now living . . . disruption of the want-get-ratio — for people are taught by the mass media primarily to want . . . preparing a "revolution of rising frustrations." When people learn, as they must, that they cannot hope to get what they have been taught to want, there will follow a global acceleration of frustration with its attendant reaction-formations of aggression and regression. (Lerner in A. Hoffman, 1968:134–5)

Such things — resistance of indigenous networks to outside information and explosion of frustrations when information is accepted — show that stereotypical ideas about progress do not quite describe what happens when messages from the media replace the homeostatic signals of indigenous networks.

As I said, the indigenous system resists such things by homeostatic responses. The "bifurcated" state is really an effort to preserve balance by separating indigenous from media systems by a filtering boundary. To visualize in a North American setting what a bifurcated situation is like, where an indigenous system is acting as a buffer, we may turn back to a small town of the 1930s described by a sociological classic (Blumenthal, 1932). "Mineville," a Western town of 1,800 inhabitants, shows people absorbed in their own affairs and buzzing with talk and gossip, to which media are a secondary input. In this hotbed of gossip the main hobby was to talk about somebody else. Since everyone knew everyone else, there was plenty to talk about. Most of the people took part in this talk, though if asked about it, they would outwardly condemn gossiping. Whether or not one was a "bad" gossip depended on one's relationship with the teller. The chief gossipers were "social historians" who could remember everything about everybody. In two hours a story would completely circulate around the community, though most would know it in a half-hour.

Telephones helped: Over half the residents had them, and the women were able to gossip on the phone while the men were at work, then at night summarize for their husbands, who in turn had their share to contribute. Intimate tidbits of personal information were usually fed into gossip through betrayed confidences. Blumenthal analyzed the reasons for the inability to keep a secret. Because all the townspeople were so closely related by kinship and friendship, there was no one in whom anyone could confide who did not have some other relationship equally confidential. So the spread of information was due not so much to irresponsible information purveyors ("bad" gossips) as to normal disclosures of intimacy. Many people simply forgot they had received the information in trust. Moreover, if the relationship was broken, as in a quarrel, the situation was ripe for a wholesale breaking of confidence. Some disclosures came from accidental slips, in the effort to tell an interesting story, to win a point in an argument, or to seem important in other people's eyes. Not only did people tell what there was to know, but they also knew each other so well that they could deduce the channels through which the news traveled and thereby evaluate its reliability.

The chief gossip centers were the school (children were important agents of gossip) and "Sid's Tailor Shop," which was for Mineville's men what the modern beauty shop is for today's women. It was a center for discussion of everything by way of news and the best place to sense shifts in public opinion. The tailor was like a newspaper editor in that he would hear both sides of a story quicker than most others, and try to arrive at an assessment of the truth of the situation. He took pride in his informal status. Thus, if one wanted to find out quickly what was going on, one went to Sid's Tailor Shop to talk to those who liked to "hang around and talk."

Here we see a community fascinated by gossip yet afraid of it — ruled by Dame Grundy (as we epitomize that sharp-eyed little old lady who looks out from behind the lace curtains). Gossip was not only the main channel of information, but also made every person's tongue a whip to discipline his neighbor (Blumenthal, 1932).

This means that gossip was the main means of informal social control, and also an oral, public, opinion-forming agency, its power to work as a sanction lying in the fact that, along with what parties knew about each other, moral judgment was passed along the chain from *A* to *B* to *C*, taking shape as social opinion (consensus) and leading to various activities of control (whereas a stranger's values would be of no significance). This ability of gossip to formulate moral judgment is what makes it so important to the community. However, we must not conceive it as simply cruel (as it might be to strangers) but protective and even forgiving. For example, in Mineville, police found certain difficulties in law enforcement: They could not easily arrest their own neighbors and buddies; an offender was not merely an individual but a member of the Jones family, whose reputation helped him. There was a general concern of people for each other and a sense of responsibility to those they had known all their lives. There was a unique credit system, in which, knowing everyone, merchants extended credit to everyone. The community took care of its own, and outside agencies such as the Red Cross were not called on. Gossip played a part in this by telling who was in need. So we see how an indigenous network serves its members.

The main point here, however, is how exogenous information is handled: All filtered through the oral network. For example, the Tikopia, according to Firth (1956), have no word that distinguishes news as we understand it (as a verified, known source) from hearsay or what people are saying, though they do take an interest in whether accounts are true or false and suspend judgment when in doubt. They have a great interest in news, both from the outside world (such as the arrival of a ship) and from the local area (the fishing, an illness or death, what the chief in the next village is doing), and get it by word of mouth daily.

Folk are continually traveling up and down the beach and along the inland paths, and exchange of news is part of regular social intercourse, as it tends to be in any rural area. Between districts there is less contact. Formal visiting is not very frequent . . . when it occurs, as for a dance festival or some other large-scale ceremony, or when a vessel arrives from overseas, the visitors are apt to remain separate from the local residents, to hang about together under the trees or to sit together in a house. But even then there is plenty of exchange of information between the parties. . . . An arrival from one side of the island at a ceremony on the other is usually asked first for news. (Firth, 1956:123)

News is also passed from one island to another by ceremonial whooping and firing of guns. Similarly, drum signals are used to extend the oral system.

Oral communication networks may work very widely, spreading news almost as well as mass media. Rural villages of India, for example (Dube, 1967), showed an amazing ability to discover by word of mouth what was happening far away. In 1962, when Communist China attacked a remote part of the Himalayan border, a national survey of 198 villages randomly chosen from different states, some far away from the event, showed that 83 percent of the villagers had heard of the attack shortly after it occurred. Only a small proportion of the communication could be attributed directly to radio and newspapers; by far, the majority had gotten their information from face-to-face oral communication through traditional channels. "The proverbial isolation of the Indian villages is a myth. The economic, social, and religious networks that join together a number of villages are accompanied by their own channels of communication" (Dube, 1967).

What an oral system does is quickly carry what is relevant to people, leaving the rest. Seeing the system's vitality and usefulness when it is thriving helps us to see what may be lost if media pour in too heavy a load. As a news service, the indigenous network acts as a buffer to signals coming in from the media. What it does is homeostatic: shrinking outside events to scale and shaping them to meaning by word-of-mouth interaction, surrounding and supporting the individual by identity-giving feedback and norms.

Though it does not diffuse news with such mechanical efficiency, we should appreciate the many advantages of the oral over the media system. Chief among these is the high rate of personal feedback in day-to-day transactions, giving expression as well as support and control to identity.

A balanced oral system allows maximum interplay of person on person throughout a day, week, or season — continuous dialogical exchange at many levels, a time for joking, love, solemn ceremony, convivial eating, physical contest, body contact, debate, drama, rhythm, even orgy — all the modes of interaction that together can make a full person. (Which is not to say that oral systems cannot make people dour, stilted, puritanical, paranoid, and so on, as anthropologists can well attest.) But the potential range of interaction makes great self-expression possible. Nonverbal cues and interactions by tone, manner, gestures, etiquette, and kinesics (Hall, 1959; La Barre, 1967; Birdwhistell, 1970), together with the whole range of ritual (Klapp, 1969), are important parts of the oral system — it is never a matter of words only. Even where the rule "Silence is golden" is applied, there is a great deal of personal expression and recognition; just because a person is noticed, people are responsive to him, he matters in the status system. This is one reason why gossip is of high value: Everything a person does matters, a thousand eyes and ears take account of his performance in a festival, his presence or absence from a gathering, his success in enterprises, his attitude and demeanor from day to day. He may complain about intrusions into his privacy as if he were a city person, but not about lack of concern.

All this hinges on the fact that communication in oral systems, as

Lerner said, is based on status. First, talk puts a premium on the ability to tell and remember, and so gives status. The story teller is not just an old grandmother serving as babysitter in disadvantageous competition with television, but a person with a respected function for the whole group, listened to as seriously by adults as by children. There is stress on oral performance; status goes to those who are wise, that is, those who remember and speak well. The social historian is not just a gossip (as in Mineville), but has the duty to remember protocol and tales of importance to the group, whether legend or history. As has been said of the Tikopia:

The Tikopia are great narrators. They delight not only in hearing news as items of information; they also delight in giving and hearing a presentation of news in elaborate aesthetic form, with dramatic emphasis. They dwell on incidents, the narrator taking time to explain in particular his own emotions and thoughts as an event takes place. (Firth, 1956:127)

Not only is the talker important, but status governs all communication in oral systems: that is, people want to know *who* said it and what right he had to speak; the source is just as important as the content of the information. A person speaks at appropriate times, and in different ways, depending on the status of the other; to some he speaks not at all (as in brother-sister avoidance). Not knowing the proper style in which to communicate may nullify the message. For example, the Japanese are very sensitive to status and have different modes of address for male to male, male to female, youth to age, and other communication situations. One American Nisei, who studied Japanese before returning to the country of his fathers, was embarrassed by puzzling reactions to what he knew to be excellent pronunciation, until he discovered that he had been taught a *feminine* style of speaking. Where status governs in communication, there is a high ratio of prescription (for example, advice, moral judgment, command) to merely descriptive information, because people who speak the most have the right to say how things should be done. Because they are used to this, people living in oral systems prize wisdom, proverbs, omens, moral tales, and so on, and do not prefer the "objectivity" of factual information. Where status governs who speaks when and to whom, though there is high appreciation, there may not be a democratic equality in expression of opinion, yet the status of he who speaks may include the obligation to speak for those who are silent. Thus F. and M. Keesing (1956:91—129) described opinion expression among Samoans. Few are ready to express personal opinions outside the proper communication channel on any issue of concern to the group; even leaders are not willing to give opinions or "spot" decisions in fields of their responsibility. The reason is that to know what a decision means, you must know all the "voices" involved. The leader does not know what his opinion stands for until he has been through an oral communication process:

A titleholder is essentially a responsible group representative. His "voice" is correspondingly a group voice. He must therefore correctly consult back to his adherent supporters as well as deal with his peers or superiors . . . which might provide "voices" in a traditional deliberation process: the household, close kin, and community assemblies and the supra-village elite or matai assemblies of extended family, regional, and "all Samoa" character . . . Always there is a generalized "voice," back of his personal "voice." . . . It must never be forgotten that each elite member, in speaking publicly, has by implication his group back of him. (F. and M. Keesing, 1956:104)

Thus, though there are status differences in Samoa and no "individual" opinion, everyone shares in the leader's "voice" in some appropriate way. No one feels left out of the political process. So continual feedback to status flows in many ways through oral systems. As far as quality of information goes, this means that messages are always coming from sources whose status is known and judged, if not trusted, whereas the media information source — perhaps an advertiser who has bought television time, a news editor (D. White, 1964), a committee chairman selecting agenda, or a political censor — is likely to be a stranger unrelated to us by status or primary group trust, who is screening the information that comes to us in terms of his interest, not ours. The oral system reduces such status irresponsibility to a minimum. Everyone is accountable to what people are saying, and this always comes back to one in some tangible way.

A media system, by contrast, is able to deliver few such values. First, diffusing messages one way, they shield the sender from much feedback and give the receiver none at all. Most information comes from sources that, though perhaps credible, are in no personal sense trustworthy. There is a high ratio of "objective" factual information, compared with the prescriptions of the oral system; but even facts must be discounted for bias and possible propaganda. Whatever he gets from the media by way of information, he has little chance to respond to it effectively: He watches others perform and express opinions on mass media — *they* are expressed, he is a spectator, feeling of little account and powerless. Nor do videophones (lacking ability to transmit important nonverbal cues) nor "telethons" and other audience-participation devices approach the feedback of the oral system. Such avenues of feedback that mass media are able to provide — letters to editor, newspaper ombudsmen, radio call-in shows, information centers (Singer, 1973) — fall far short of knitting a community as a well-developed oral network does.

To sum up comparison of oral with media systems: An oral system, even without media input, has all the potentialities for balanced personal life. On the other hand, a media system, however much information it supplies, tends to deprive people of feedback and to force them into a spectator position. So drying up of oral networks would leave people with a "problem of massness," however well the media functioned. Indeed one does see a loss of oral culture — as one might call it, a "rocking chair" culture — in modern society. People linger less often to chat on front porches, around potbellied stoves, on wharves, in stations; or all day in coffeehouses, taverns, or open-air cafes. The skills of conversation and storytelling decline. Few talkers are used to being listened to. Such a lack of oral activity is reflected by the urban setting: Streets, eating places, plazas, even parks are inhospitable. There is no place to "be" — only someplace to "go." "Street people" are a problem. In such environments, there seems to be nothing to do but seek commercial entertainment or go home and watch television. So, as "rocking-chair" culture declines, one often sees people who rely rather too heavily on electronic and print input. "Talk shows" displace live talk; in the friendly bar, television or the jukebox drowns out what talk there might be. Multimedia inputs are common and easy. For example, a man might talk on an intercom or watch a video or radar screen while listening to a radio. In a restaurant an observer saw a man eating while reading a newspaper and listening to a ball game on his transistor radio, all against a background of piped music. It is commonplace for today's art to hit you with several things at once. Thus, it is possible today to live almost entirely on the communication feast provided by the media, talking into machines and enjoying transmitted messages and entertainments; some — especially old people and those confined to institutions — have to do this. But, however rich the feast, it would be a lonely kind of massness. Perhaps it is the drying up of oral networks, quite as much as physical environmental pollution, that is causing North Americans to yearn for idyllic "Apple Valleys."

Indigenous signals, largely through oral interaction, cannot be replaced by exogenous information over media, however imaginative the McLuhanesque[2] improvements.

It does seem that the world is being flooded with exogenous signals while indigenous signs are often swept away. If I might clarify this distinction: *Indigenous* signals (as classified by receivers) are familiar in origin (redundancy high); near in reference, local in range — things one experiences; communicated in personal relationships — trustworthy (though fantastic?); immediately understood without definition. The sender is known or his motivation is familiar; the signal is negotiated within one's own network, and so is continually tested and supported by consensus; and the place or frame of reference is known to the collectivity but not to outsiders. By contrast, *exogenous* signals are outside and strange in origin; wide in range (perhaps universal); remote in reference to things of which one has little direct experience ("They talk of things which seem to us like a strange language," said older Lebanese villagers of men who read newspapers — Lerner, 1958:189—90); restricted in meaning, technical, objective, likely to be irrelevant or boring; communicated impersonally; untrustworthy (though perhaps credible); and requiring analysis, calculation, or formal definition to be figured out. The intention of the sender is not known and must be divined. They are negotiated very often on one's own, though some are tested within the indigenous network ("two-step"); altogether making up the public domain of information — a vast sea of signals and accessible information. The point of this distinction is that the two kinds of signals make up very different kinds of worlds. Indigenous, arising naturally and used in a local group, rich in meaning maintained by interpersonal networks, support status, collective identity and sense of place — "our" territory. Examples are local events such as weddings, fiestas; reputations, gossip, local legend, slang, a plaque commemorating a well-known event, and familiar physical signs serving as landmarks of territory. On the other hand, the world of exogenous signals consists of images that cannot be validated by interaction (such as the personalities of celebrities), cannot be understood entirely by local consensus (for example, technical and scholarly languages, values set by an external market system, ideology as distinguished from indigenous culture, foreign speech and manners, impersonal space reference such as property survey bounds or interstellar distances). Coming via media, largely from outsiders, such images must be evaluated and discounted for their technical, propagandistic, advertising, political, and other, significance — for example, a poster announcing a political demonstration, a wall advertisement, a parade of people carrying banners, a scientific discovery announced, a contest offering prizes to the public. Such messages belong to nobody and to no particular place. Unlike indigenous signs where, even when one is manipulating the other, each knows what the other is up to, the receiver is never quite sure about exogenous messages — who sent them, why they were sent, or what went into them. It should be plain from this comparison that exogenous signals, however much they inform, are a far greater burden to handle, and contribute less to identity — either personal or collective — than do indigenous signals. Flooding the world with exogenous information could change it from one a person felt he owned to one he knew he didn't own and with which he had little connection. It could generate paradoxes like history accumulating but tradition lost, in the sense that libraries could be filled with books describing events lacking personal connection as "mine" or "ours" — happening to "some people" but not to "my people." If tradition is a sense of ownership that goes along with ideas from the past, then it is possible to gain history as information *about,* yet lose tradition as knowledge that *identifies.* Similarly for sense of place: If bulldozers and incoming strangers wipe away indigenous signs that make a recognized territory — "my old neighborhood" — it would be possible for the world to cease to be a place and become merely a modernized space within which exogenous signals can make no identifying distinction.

In this sense, the proportion of indigenous to exogenous, and of oral to media signals, becomes crucial in telling us what is happening to our world and ourselves. A fact such as six hours per day average television viewing time per American might indicate not only that an excessive amount of one kind of exogenous information was being absorbed but that oral networks were being neglected — even that the media flood was washing indigenous systems away. Could it be that while advancing into the waves of exogenous signals, people are letting go, so to speak, of indigenous networks that serve like lifelines on the beach to hold onto while wading into deep water? Such would be a poor way to enter any flood.

The media flood

In some ways media act like a net — an extension of the senses, as McLuhan observes — for gathering what we want. But this is hardly a sufficient view of the flood of information breaking in ever larger waves upon the man wading in. The exponential growth of information changing modern culture has been recognized at least since sociologists (Ogborn, 1922; Chapin, 1924; Hart, 1945) wrote about cultural lag. What's new is that the big waves are arriving not just in the open bays of scientific and technological advance but on sheltered beaches where ordinary people wade.

First, the ordeal of the experts. The output of technical, scientific, and professional information is staggering. The book glut gives some idea. Over eight billion copies of books are printed every year, mostly in a handful of advanced countries, according to a UNESCO report in 1974. In the United States alone, over 40,000 book titles per year are published, as well as (as of 1971) some 9,000 periodicals. It was estimated that in science alone approximately 2,000 pages of books, newspapers, and reports are published every *minute* in the world and that the amount of scientific information is doubling every six years (Stanford, 1971). The libraries are submerged by this "paper flood"; "keeping up" is a farce and professionals feel guilt, though they read all the time. It is a myth that facts somehow find their way to the people who need them; hopes center on improvements in the technology of information retrieval (Gross, 1964).

The flood of new technical ideas has been equally impressive. The U.S. Patent Office reported that in 1970 there were 230,000 patent applications pending and that such a backlog had existed since World War II. (The normal waiting time to process a patent is three years.)

To handle this flood of technical information, over 30,000 computers were operating, and the amount of computing power available in the United States was doubling each year (Armer, 1966). So, we get the picture of a kind of battle between print technologies and machines to process data into more usable form.

Executives struggled with ever larger inbasket loads. Photocopying saved typists time but multiplied the number of copies of everything to be read.[3] There is so much to absorb that officials rely on capsule digests prepared by underlings. In the United States State Department in Washington, official cable traffic amounted to 10,000 incoming and outgoing messages a day (Manning, 1968:162–3). The mind boggles at the number of memoranda.

Nor was it paperwork alone. Adding to the mountain of information was multiplication of vocabularies and classifications, technical and bureaucratic. Specialties subdivided into super-specialties. Those in the same specialty sometimes divided into schools that hardly spoke the same language. Beneath all this is an unavoidable fact: An almost unlimited number of classifications — starting, perhaps, with that of the question game, "animal, vegetable, or mineral? " — can be usefully imposed on reality; and of these, many can be found to have scientifically reliable relationships (for example, operant psychology); but, not speaking a common language, they do not add together but remain in separate piles. Social science seems especially afflicted with such linguistic and taxonomic proliferation. It can't all be attributed to bad English.

But the main load of information was by no means completely borne by experts and officials. The common man was being inundated, too, though he might not read a word. It was estimated in 1973 that over 96 percent of households in the United States had television sets, and that the average person peered at television over 6 hours a day.[4] Federal Communications Commissioner Nicholas Johnson reported in 1970 that by the time a child entered kindergarten, he would have received more hours of instruction from TV than he would later get in college while obtaining a bachelor's degree; an average man of 65 would have spent nine full years of his life watching TV. There was little doubt which of the mass media was reaching most Americans most effectively. Interesting findings were being made; for example, that although ordinary political appeals could not move "low interest" voters, messages resembling commercials could penetrate their defense mechanisms (Patterson and McClure, 1974).

All the news media interact, says Manning (1968), to titillate the public and increase demand for what is often the same thing over again:

The newspapers thrive more than ever because radio and TV titillate with small bits of news and make us thirsty for more detail. The news magazines thrive, often by dressing up what the newspapers have already said with spicy verbs and aromatic adjectives, because the daily and Sunday press are found inadequate. Yet while the news weeklies reach for more and more millions of subscribers, the fortnightlies and monthlies go up in circulation too, because all that precedes them is assumed — correctly — to be not sufficient to slake the thirst. In addition, more than 1,500 newsletters . . . are prospering because hundreds of thousands believe they are not getting enough of the pertinent facts from the other publications they read. Add to this the explosion of "book journalism." (Manning, 1968:158–9)

Mass media not only multiply the messages but speed up the impact of information on people, as with the thousands witnessing the actual assassination of President John F. Kennedy. Television spread rioting while it was still going on, drawing viewers to participate; it also hastened the awakening of collective consciousness among blacks (Singer, 1968, 1973). The International Telecommunications Satellite will make it possible for nations around the world to be absorbed simultaneously in an event.

At the same time, as people are brought closer — sometimes uncomfortably close — to remote affairs, they remain powerless to act on them, even to affect them in any way. So better communications could increase strains, from bad news, threat perception, and claims of people on one another, without providing the organization by which to do anything constructively about it. Nor was the sense of powerlessness helped by transitory issues, facts, preferences, fads, fashions flashing across the screen — interminable news stories repeating with equal stridency slightly varying sordid, violent, often senseless happenings.[5]

Advertising is a major culprit in the information flood. According to the American Association of Advertising Agencies, 1,600 commercial messages a day are directed at the average individual, of which he consciously notices 80. The main purpose of advertising is to implant unwanted messages into people. To do this an advertiser may spend $185,000 for a minute of prime television time, which gives him access to perhaps 50,000,000 minds (Bagdikian, 1971); the total television advertising budget in 1976 was six billion dollars (ABC newsbroadcast, November 8, 1977). It does not lessen the load on the recipient that much of this information is pseudo-distinctions among advertised brands — differences among gasolines, beers, cigarettes, and automobiles that differ in image or label but that hardly anyone can distinguish in tests or performance (Key, 1973:83). The medicinal market presents a bewildering variety of drugs masquerading under fancy labels at high prices. So the world is made to seem fuller of different things than it actually is. Boorstin (1962) commented keenly on how media spawn "pseudo-events." In the case of advertising (unless all that money is being wasted), the media are pushing the consumer to do something he really wouldn't if he considered wisely. His sense of powerlessness comes not from inability to purchase but from how he feels afterwards while surveying his unwanted goods and unpaid debts.

Mechanization merely emphasizes the ability of media to pour onto people information to which they can make no satisfactory response. Almost everyone has felt thwarted by taped telephone answers and computerized billing. A friendly disk jockey confessed that radio is becoming more and more automated: "It's almost a glorified jukebox now; everything is on cartridges — commercials, music, even announcers." Congressmen are using computerized mailings and reproducing letters from a tape system to respond to constituents in various categories (such as farmers, housewives, or Democrats), and using a mailing list to send even "Dear Mr. Jones" letters to everyone in their district. In all such automation of communication, however cleverly it simulates responsiveness, there is a certain tactlessness that cannot fail to be out of rhythm with the feelings of the one to whom the message is sent.

Intrusiveness is an especially aggravating feature of the flood of information, much of which is frankly unwelcome and comes to us whether we like it or not. "Junk mail" fills people's mailboxes, addressed from mailing lists that are sold to anybody. One housewife, saving such mail for a year, found it weighed fifty-five pounds. More intrusive is the hired telephone caller who chooses dinnertime to tell you of the advantages of an insurance policy or the need for voting for candidate X. More appalling is the thought that computer phone banks, instead of live people, can deliver 9,000 "personalized" calls per day into the home. Another aspect of this has been the sheer amplifying power of communication technology. What was called the "jukebox problem" in the 1930s has grown into a pervasive feature of life in the 1970s: Everyone has equipment, whether at home or at the beaches and public parks, by which to thrust his tastes on others — the volume of sound, stimulated by competition, thus rising. So communication intrusiveness puts a strain on the ideal of a free society: A stimulating difference of taste or opinion becomes intolerable when technology gives the power to thrust it on others — "My taste is your garbage." So alongside the slogans of "access to information" and "the right to communicate" of a free society, there began to be a new emphasis on the right *not* to communicate and *not* to be communicated to, — to disconnect, to switch off -- and the need for laws to provide safeguards to protect individuals against invasions of personal privacy (Gottlieb and Gwyn, 1972).

At the international level, direct satellite television broadcasting posed a similar problem: the possibility of flooding countries by propaganda or cultural values beamed directly into them without local consent or relay. The dispute has been carried on since 1972 in the United Nations Working Group on Direct Broadcast Satellites. In this group, the United States' position favoring unrestricted flow and freedom of information (not unrelated to commercial interests and technological advantages) was overwhelmingly outvoted by other nations. Some supported the proposal of the USSR to legally ban any direct broadcasting that threatens peace, arouses enmity, interferes with domestic affairs, or "undermines" local culture. Other nations, such as Canada and Sweden, took the middle position of requiring prior consent of receiving countries. The main issue was not quality but "foreignness" of programs felt as threat to national culture. An example was the excellent American educational television series, *Sesame Street,* which the BBC refused to screen and to which Canada, Mexico, and the USSR objected because of its impact on children; they simply didn't want them Americanized. The commercialism of American programs was also felt as a threat by France and England who, having made the decision that television would not be used indiscriminately for advertising, severely limited commercial messages. Of course there was fear of economic competition too: that a country's own products would be displaced. How the issue could be worked out was not clear in the seventies, but it was plain that the principle of absolute freedom of information was not widely accepted, even by countries that had endorsed the 1948 United Nations Organization Declaration of Human Rights. Claims of cultural protectionism and fears of cultural imperialism were keener.[6]

Such signs pointed to a new kind of saturation: The public domain of information had limits; it was not as free as had been thought; as with air, no more could one just pour in whatever he wished. Opposed to the principle of freedom of information was a growing concern for privacy that paralleled irritation at the media for commercialism, bias (Efron, 1971), bad news, poor taste, pornography, violence, pollution (Key, 1973), and so on — a concern growing with the very efficiency of the media.

Beyond that was another sort of saturation — that of attention. For many people the total time given all media could not be increased; one could only switch from channel to channel, medium to medium. Time would not stretch however attention might wander. As a result of such saturation, boredom with whatever media offered was a growing problem (for which I offer some explanation in Chapter 5) — fought continually by the designing of new programs. To the paradox of how one could be bored by so many goodies, we get a clue from the example of museum fatigue: When going from one fascinating exhibit to another — old armor, exquisite vases, Chinese jade, mummies — it is surprising how touring only one floor can make one glassy-eyed with boredom.

The odd thing is that although any one piece might deserve fascinated attention for many minutes, if one gets them all together the total impact is rather like the second day of Christmas goodies. This consideration carries to the feast of the media, jammed with things competing for attention — too much of a good thing?

Meanwhile, new developments in technology promised improvements in supplying people with even more information such as cable television supplying a wide range of selected programs, laser transmission,[7] access to computer data banks, even a communication terminal within the home — not without considerable feedback (Pool, 1973; B. Schwartz, 1973). Yet the question remained of whether people could do any better with *more* information than they were doing already.

Let us look more closely at how and why information, especially in large amounts, turns into noise.

4. When information turns to noise

Information overload

Under some conditions, perfectly good information is capable of becoming noise, in the sense that it interferes with getting the information one needs. An unalphabetized telephone directory would be an obvious example. It has long been thought that society is generating noise by its very processes of communicating information. One of the first to recognize this was the turn-of-the-century sociologist Georg Simmel (1950: 415), who described the attitude of reserve as a way people in cities protect themselves from "indiscriminate suggestibility" from too many others. Deutsch (1961:102) noted "communication overload" as a "disease of cities," in which the possible freedom of choice is jammed by "coincidences of choice" resulting from the very efficiency of communication and transport.[1] Because of the multiplicity of things needing attention, people find no time to attend to anything or anyone. He noted also the price in human meaning that has to be paid for this: loss of responsiveness to other people. A psychiatrist commented:

The technical means of communication via telephone, radio and television have become ensnarled in a gigantic traffic jam . . . indeed, there exists a positive communication explosion, a prelude to an avalanche. I have already observed in some patients the breakdown of their communication systems as a result of this overloading. We are in danger of being crushed under a mountain of information debris unless we find new condensations and simplifications to pull us out. (Meerloo in Dance, 1967:133).

Of course, what is noise depends on someone's — whether sender's or receiver's — viewpoint. Let us consider here conditions under which such a curious change occurs in the value of information.

One of these conditions I have already suggested at some length: when an individual is too alone, struggling in a sea of exogenous signals, without a group to buffer and filter information or an indigenous network in which to test it for truth, goodness, or value for earning a living or giving oneself status and meaning as a person. Too many people

47

interacting without defined status and too many facts without others to help us tell what they mean is what Simmel was talking about in praising urban reserve: If you have no group to do it, be your own gatekeeper. So massness is one of the conditions under which information overload is suffered. Stated in terms of communication this means a disproportion of exogenous to indigenous signals. Within such a context, there are many ways in which perfectly good information becomes noise.

We should not visualize an Odysseus to whom rough water ahead and shores left behind do not matter, but an ordinary man — more on the scale of Mitty or Prufrock — who, wading into a swelling sea of signals, quickly passes his depth and begins to experience stresses that can be characterized as the "battle of the inbasket" and "endless jigsaw puzzle." In communication theory the name for this limit is channel capacity.

Battle of the inbasket

Life comes to us all through a funnel in which the river of experience flows. One metaphor is the inbasket that the executive faces; it piles up with paper while he makes appropriate decisions. Some idea of the inbasket that modern executives face comes from the fact that during the eight years Dean Rusk was Secretary of State 2,100,000 cables went out of the State Department with his signature — quite an inbasket even if he merely signed them. So much information may be furnished to the decision maker that he spends a large portion of his time filtering it or searching for what he wants; further, there is danger of being diverted from his original task. He may lose sight of his goal or have it modified without being aware of it (Fogel, 1963:360). Students of management report (Raymond, 1962) that the typical executive can receive and absorb only 1/100 to 1/1000 of the available information that is relevant to his decisions. Better data processing may only flood him: Software cannot keep up with the hardware. Quite possibly your inbasket is not a computerized system but just a pile of newspapers; or, if you are a professional, journals and books with which you must keep up. If a student, it might consist of handling required reading for five courses. The effect is the same: You face the ever-piling inbasket with a sense of frustration, unable to keep up.

On the social side, there is the life of hustle. Too many things to do, too many people to see, too many sectors to cover — one becomes like a busy switchboard operator trying to cover all calls. So Linder (1970) describes the "harried" middle class, rushing through leisure, accelerating consumption often with "declining pleasures." Harried hustle shows not only that the inbasket is filling too rapidly but that things don't fit together well — you may be trying to do things that don't naturally belong to one career or style of life.

Whatever form it takes, the battle of the inbasket reaching one's limit is easily seen as a "rat race" — a Sisyphean experience. Sisyphus was a king of Corinth whose punishment in Hades was to roll a heavy stone up a hill; as he reached the top, the stone rolled down again. So it means endless, fruitless toil — exactly the definition, if one adds a little ill will, of "rat race." Unfortunately, our good friend information, endlessly piling up, demanding decisions and then telling us we didn't make it — is doing just that: helping make a "rat race."

Man is a limited channel

It all hinges on two facts that seem to be natural as well as logical necessities. They are *homeostatic needs* and *channel capacity*, both of which put limits on intake.

All living things are homeostatic (Cannon, 1939), taking what they need for their own balance, learning, and growth, while preserving themselves from too much change by using feedback as a guide to what to do next: take more of the same or seek something different? Homeostatic needs, whether for food or information, range from *deprivation* (starvation, ignorance), to *sufficiency* (comfort, well being, well educated) to *abundance* (luxury, high learning), to *overload* (indigestion, inbasket battle), and perhaps to *pollution* (poison, misinformation). Such levels depend on homeostatic needs of the organism at the time. Information hunger might be expressed by taking night courses, reading and listening to everything on a topic; overload by "turning off" and avoiding topics and persons. So the mind is in one sense a screen; shifting attention shields us from inputs that are not needed or even dangerous. Concepts are also a screen, even when not prejudiced, for logic and goals exclude irrelevance. Freud called screening of that which is morally offensive or silly a "censorship." Some psychologists conceive of "gestalt" perception as seeing a pattern and ignoring the ground. Psycholinguists such as Sapir (1949) and Whorf (1956) say it comes from linguistic categorizing itself, that a language acts like a grid imposed on ex-

perience. Aldous Huxley (1954) used the words of the English philosopher C.D. Broad to explain how the mind works like a reducing valve
on awareness:

> To protect us from being overwhelmed and confused by . . . irrelevant knowledge,
> by shutting out most of what we should otherwise perceive or remember at any
> moment . . . To formulate and express . . . this reduced awareness, man has invent-
> ed . . . languages . . . Most people, most of the time, know only what comes through
> the reducing valve and is consecrated as genuinely real by the local languages. (Hux-
> ley, 1954:23)

So Huxley argued that psychedelic drugs are justified to open this naturally closed state of mind, much as one might dilate the pupil of the
eye. So the mind, however great its intelligence and deep the unconscious, because of its homeostatic function, is not a limitlessly expan-
sive bag able to take in anything at any time or everything all at once.
Variety, problems, and change are acceptable only within homeostatic
limits.

A second basic limit on intake is channel capacity. Such a concept is
logically necessary to define overload. This, like a pipe diameter or
bottleneck, is a restriction on the amount that can be taken in or
transmitted. Rigid or not, it is always there at some point. For example,
my channel capacity happens to be small for Greek, large for music,
and limited by eyestrain for reading. The point is that however much
one likes a thing beyond a point one cannot take more within a given
period of time because of limits on the pathways through which information flows. All living systems have — indeed are — channels. All units
through which communication flows, whether living things or machines,
are regarded as channels. For example, a message may come from a human brain through a telephone wire to another brain, which in turn
puts the idea into discussion of a committee, whose recommendation
goes to an executive, whose decision solves a problem. All such inter-
mediaries are channels, each with its own capacity for handling information. At the synapse between one neuron and another, the highest
rate of information transmission has been calculated to be in a theoretically possible range of 1,000 to 3,000 bits per second.[2] Overload is
often defined in terms of a measurable relationship between input and
output of a system. The limit of a system, beyond which failure of
communication from overload occurs, is usually called its channel capacity. At the simplest level, it is a matter of transmission, that is, measur-

ing the output (message received) against the signal originally sent. The message from a channel is always less discriminable than the input signal because of a certain amount of inherent noise (any stimulus that interferes with the reception of a message). For our purposes, we must remember that noise includes not only meaningless stimuli (which carry no signal) but also perfectly good information that doesn't happen to be what we want, or that is excessively redundant (repeating what we already know and therefore interfering with new information that we need and might have obtained). Channel capacities and overloads have been determined for such things as cells, crustaceans, nerves of a cat, the retina, endocrine glands, and entire organisms, most of which were human. (See the extensive research of James G. Miller on this in *Living Systems*, 1965, 1971, 1972.)

Perhaps the most important point to remember in trying to define information overload is that whatever the efficiency of some channels (computers, cable lines, multimedia art, and so on), overload always occurs at the weakest link, which is often the human brain. The human brain has great powers of abstraction, but is severely limited in channel capacity. Experiments by G. A. Miller (1967) showed that humans have difficulty making discriminative judgments of sound, color, taste, and so on, when alternatives go beyond the "magic number seven." "There seems to be some limitation built into us either by learning or by the design of our nervous systems" that limits what we can immediately perceive without help from some device such as counting.

We are able to perceive up to about six dots (marbles, beans, dice marks, musical tones) accurately without counting; beyond this errors become frequent . . . This ceiling is always very low. Indeed, it is an act of charity to call a man a channel at all. Compared to a telephone or television channels, a man is better characterized as a bottleneck. (Miller, 1967:8, 18–25, 48)

On a job the human channel capacity may be quite low. John P. van Gigh (1976) has compared the information-processing loads of various industrial jobs in terms of the degree to which they approach channel capacity, which is defined as the maximum information processing rate or maximum entropy in bits/unit of time which can be handled through it (492). The channel capacity of workers on industrial jobs was estimated to be about 8.0 bits /second. Most jobs were found to be below this capacity in information load; though some, such as manual supermarket checking, do tax it. Variability and complexity increase the entropy (information load) of tasks.

It is not, of course, just a matter of the channel capacity of the brain. Different modes of communication have different rates of transmission; for example, Quastler and Wulff (1955) found that the maximum transduction rate of impromptu speaking was about 26 bits per second, with a mean rate of about 18, whereas oral reading reached about 35 bits.

Just as individuals do, so groups have their channel capacities and points of overload at which they lose ability to cooperate, communicate among themselves, decide together, or pass a message along. James G. Miller (1960, 1971) studied group information overload experimentally in terms of relation between input and output or performance. Overload is the point at which additional information causes a leveling or falling off of performance. In one situation, four people were required to cooperate in coordinating information that appeared on a screen. Individual *A* called out the slot in which an arrow appeared. *B* called out a letter representing that position. *C*, whose back was turned to the screen, pushed a button that registered the information he got from *A* and *B*. *D* watched some red light signals, which told whether *C*'s push was correct. If the push was incorrect, *D* told him and *C* pushed another button until he finally got the right one. The performance of such a group can be charted as a relationship between varying rates of information input and output in bits per second; that is, how much information was handled in how long a time. The performance of two teams leveled off at about 3 bits of input per second, showing the point at which overload occurred. The channel capacity was found to be between 2 and 2.5 bits of output per second. Two other findings (J. G. Miller, 1960) are of interest here: One is that the channel capacity of groups with this pattern is lower than that of individuals, though performance curves have the same shape. The second is that when overload occurs, certain kinds of behaviors (whether called mechanisms of adjustment or symptoms of failure) become frequent: (1) omitting information from the process; (2) processing erroneous information; (3) queuing − holding off some responses during rush periods with the hope that it may be possible to catch up during a lull; (4) filtering − selecting some kinds of information and leaving others; (5) cutting categories − discriminating with less precision (for example, instead of saying "I see yellow," saying, "I see a light color" or "I see a color"); (6) using multiple channels − spreading information through two or more channels, as in decentralization; and (7) escape from the task.

In small groups, various network patterns were found to have different channel capacities. For example, a "wheel" or mesh has a better capacity than a "chain" because several lines can carry a distributed load (for example, a committee dividing up an assignment); but studies also show that strain increases on the central position in a "wheel" when information increases, as measured by increased time to perform tasks, and reaches a saturation point that exceeds the ability of the individual to process information (Gilchrist, et al., 1955:119—22). So, a wheellike organization gains in efficiency by sending all its messages to one executive, but at some point it loses efficiency when the executive suffers overload.

A larger system does not necessarily handle information more easily; it may have difficulties of smaller groups compounded. Yet an organization does have a clear advantage over the individual and group, says Meier (1972:289—314), in its ability to plan for the long run and develop resources and coping responses for what previously was crisis. He describes fourteen responses of organizations, such as a library, brokerage, or health service, to communications overload: (1) queue formation, (2) queuing priorities, (3) omission of lowest priorities, (4) "chunking," (5) parallel processing or branch facilities, (6) formation of middlemen, (7) mobile reserves, (8) performance standards, (9) search for the "magic formula," (10) customer self-service, (11) reducing standards of performance, (12) breakdown or escape, (13) salvage of components, and (14) ritualistic work to rule.

Vulnerability to overload depends on how well a system is cybernetically organized. Beer notes that business firms without cybernetic control, even though computerized, easily suffer overload of facts that they cannot use for better plans and policies:

Items of fact about a business are profuse. They proliferate with every second that passes. Most of them are worthless — in the sense that they have no bearing on managerial decision. By recording them, sorting them in different ways and printing out huge quantities of tables, nothing useful is accomplished. On the contrary, managers become engulfed in a sea of useless facts . . . The manager wants information, not facts, and facts become information only when something is changed . . . The job is not to design a data-processing system at all, but to design a control system . . . New managerial control systems . . . ought to have a cybernetic validity, and . . . be more than a pooling of computer applications . . . I am speaking now of structure, which is to say organization, rather than of facts and the flow of information. (Beer 1972:31—2)

From such considerations, it should be plain that at some point information overload is inevitable for any channel and any living system. Doubtless it enters in many ways into how we feel about life and relations we have with others. Individuals vary in their capacities. But at today's levels of communication, with every bridge groaning and creaking under the traffic, it would be hard to find anyone fairly well educated and broadly concerned who is not in some way suffering from information overload. We should not confine this to cases where people actually begin to break down in their thinking or relations with others. Long before that, a sense of not liking it, of alienation, might become important. Indeed, in normative terms it might be said that information overload begins with any input past the ideal rate for digesting new information and making it part of one's philosophy. Students will appreciate this because it is a description of their education. Imagine living on an island where a boat arrives each day and brings one piece of information of significance to you, leaving the rest of the day to think and talk about it. Such might be the optimal rate of input for a thoughtful response to life. Similarly, for society, overload would begin where news stopped being pleasantly stimulating and became a source of strain on decision processes, the authority of leaders, validity of cultural beliefs, socialization of children and so on.

This leads to the question: What do you do with information *after* a channel gets it to you and you make an immediate decision? What higher meaning does the decision help build?

The endless jigsaw puzzle

As I have implied, the media are pouring on us an avalanche of bits and signals that, even if we can decide about them, surely are coming too fast for true assimilation. The more details there are, the longer it takes to fit them together into a whole. Turn to the media for advice, and you usually get more than you want — about diet, things to buy, what to see, politics — often propagandas. Turn to media for truth, and you usually get facts without meaning, rather like being handed a bucket of pennies and asked to do your own summing up. Turn to the media for depth of viewpoint, and you get triviality, entertainment, distraction, and nit-picking, which take as much time to sort out as vital issues. Most of it comes in disconnected bits that are hard to relate. (By a paradox of communication, large chunks are less of a burden than a lot of bits.) Commenting on this way that facts come at us from the media, Margaret Mead (1969) said, "This is the first age that has not had the chance to *edit*. Things are thrown on a screen just as they happen." Unfortunately, other bits have been edited, but we don't know enough about it to be able to decide what the significance of that might be.

This predicament can be illustrated by a metaphor. Imagine yourself in a room seated at a large table piled with pieces of a gigantic jigsaw puzzle. A funnel above your head is pouring more pieces on the table faster than you can sort them, let alone fit them. You note that the pieces are of different colors and textures, and do not belong to the same jigsaw puzzle. You feel that you haven't time — perhaps never will have time — to "get it together." Getting it all together is a different kind of decision than merely deciding what to do with a piece. Suppose that the puzzle you are trying to fit is the pattern, the very meaning, of your life. Then too many bits pouring in faster than one can make sense of them would mean being endlessly suspended in judgment and restricted to superficial facts, unable to develop a coherent and profound life philosophy — cheated of meaning.

The different colors and textures of the pieces of the jigsaw puzzle refer to the fact that not only does the information not refer to the same topic (especially us) but consists of different kinds of information —poetry and statistics, for example — that don't fit together by any kind of reckoning. In any case, the pieces offered hardly ever fit the particular jigsaw puzzle we are working on, which is to say it is largely exogenous and irrelevant to our personal meaning.

Some thinkers are concerned about this discontinuity. Deutsch (1966) sees eclecticism — indiscriminate receptivity and decisions incompatible with one another — as a threat not only to autonomy but to human spirit and dignity:

Dignity is nondisruptive learning . . . When we defend a man's dignity, we defend his ability to use his personality: we defend him against the imposition of an intolerably high speed of . . . changing his behavior . . . incompatible with the continuous functioning of his self-determination, his autonomous learning. (Deutsch, 1966: 240—1, 131—2)

McLuhan is not as worried but sees challenge in discontinuity:

It is worth much meditation that the news stories of the telegraph press are unified by a dateline rather than by a story line. The discontinuity among the news items themselves creates a mosaic rather than a pictorial effect. The mosaic brings about deep involvement on the part of the reader who is obliged to create his own connections. (McLuhan, 1968:vii.)

Seeing the lag of meaning behind the piling up of facts, Bertrand Russell's verdict is more sobering:

We are in the middle of a race between human skill as to means and human folly as to ends . . . Unless men increase in wisdom as much as in knowledge, increase of knowledge will be increase in sorrow." (*The Impact of Science on Society*, 120–1)

If what was piling up were facts, however small, that would be problem enough; but pseudo-distinctions, symbols that turn into noninformation, are even more defeating to meaning. For example, faddish jargon ("explicate" for "explain") adds no thoughts, may corrupt style, even threatens English as a mother tongue, says Barzun (1964:201–2), by disintegrating the public idiom to a point where it would be hard to find in half a million new words added to Webster a central group of words and phrases that everyone uses and understands; we pay for this in choppiness and crudity of feeling and thought. Fashions are also non-information when they tell us only that people are preferring something, and little about the goods. So fashion changes impose a gratuitous burden of keeping up with information one knows is trivial and will lose its validity. New marketing names multiply pseudo-distinctions:

What do you suppose Magic Moment, King Vitamin, Elephant, and Born Free have in common? They could be a soap opera, a supersized vitamin tablet, a zoo, and a rallying cry for a militant movement — in that order. In the packaged goods business, however, they are all new products. Magic Moment happens to be a woman's hair coloring . . . King Vitamin is . . . [a] new children's cereal . . . Elephant is a malt liquor . . . and Born Free is . . . [a] new shampoo.

Marketing managers have stretched their minds to crank out these product names . . . The name game . . . is driving an increasing number of firms to the U.S. Patent Office in Washington, applying and registering brand names in record numbers. An all-time high of 32,631 applications for names were processed last year, compared with 28,294 in 1968.

In the U.S. Patent Office today, there are already more than 400,000 brand names registered, a total swelling annually by 20,000 plus. (*Saturday Review*, June 13, 1970:60)

Manipulation is what so often turns information into noise, because, seeming to be true, instead of serving *you* the signals perversely serve the hidden purpose of the sender. You find yourself doing something you didn't want to, maneuvered out of your proper course much as a sailboat might be by a cross-wind or the wrong hand at the tiller. Proliferation of such symbols adds to the labor of decoding, and builds a world that sooner, or perhaps much later, turns out to be false.

As though that weren't bad enough, another defeat to meaning comes from the excessive redundancy of mass media, especially when dominated by advertising: its tendency to keep telling us the same things over and over. Redundancy is that part of a message or its context which enables us to guess what we haven't been told, or tells us what we already know — in either case because the pattern or rule of the information already exists in the receiver (more on this in Chapters 6 and 7). Useful as it often is, redundancy can interfere with meaning by becoming a kind of noise to what *else* we would like to know at that time; for example, being told fifteen times about a cigarette one didn't want in the first place. Channels overloaded with repetitive messages defeat meaning not by misleading us but turning us off in boredom.

Finally, among the unfitted pieces of the endless jigsaw puzzle come exogenous signals, already noted, that produce a burst of expectations and frustrations in developing countries — the unbalanced "want-get" ratio.[3] The trouble comes from the fact that expectations are aroused regardless of the ability of the system, or of people individually, to satisfy them. Television, for example, has made blacks, American Indians, and other underprivileged groups in North America painfully aware of a style of life they cannot share, while being urged by eager merchandisers to want it. Likewise, affluent youth have been given models of ways of life that they could not fulfill within the "nine-to-five" life-style of their parents. Travel folders lure people to parts of the world they had never dreamed of going to. Housewives watch career women and become discontented with making jelly and chauffeuring children. Everybody seems to want a piece of everybody else's action — all well and good, so long as there is progress toward such fulfillments; but should the gap widen, or merely settle into the Sysiphean experience, then dreams turn to deceptions and the world seems more false and hypocritical. So exogenous information helps destroy the indigenous meaning of systems.

The most disquieting part of this problem is yet to be considered. The battle of the inbasket and endless jigsaw puzzle are mostly due to conscious inputs. What about the unconscious inputs?

The open tape recorder

Attention is remarkably selective. Bats have an amazing ability to guide themselves in the dark by tuning in to echoes of their own tiny noises even when loudspeakers are blasting sounds hundreds of times louder in an effort to "jam" their signals (Moore, 1967:85). Humans have some such ability to thread their way through the myriad stimuli of the urban environment. One example is the cocktail party technique of "listening with three ears": tuning conversations in and out in various parts of the room. Another is flitting and hopping from one input to another, a multiple-input management strategy that might be likened to cooking on several burners at once. So Henry Kissinger has been depicted as working in a "steady babble of ringing telephones, sharp voices and electric typewriters;" while talking to a visitor, his "hand reaches surreptitiously toward magazines on the table;" on the phone, he reads while the other person talks, his mind handling both at once, putting aside the reading only when he responds (Nevin, 1969, 51–2). A busy schoolteacher might do almost as well.

A surprising liability goes with our power of selective tuning. The more we concentrate, the less we notice other things – in that sense, they don't bother us, to be sure; but concentrating does not prevent many of those other things from coming in.

One way they enter is as subliminal perceptions. Subliminal perception is described by Dixon (1971:3) as responding to stimuli of which one is unaware – in the laboratory, as determination of response by a stimulus of which the subject reports no awareness. Such perceptions bypass consciousness. If you have ever whistled (inaudibly, you thought), and had someone at quite a distance turn around, it might be that you reached him with frequencies neither you nor he is conscious of hearing. At the ends of the ranges of conscious hearing, sight, smell, taste, and touch are margins where people may feel things (intuitively, as we sometimes say) of which they are not taking, and cannot give, account. (I have not even brought in ESP.) For example, infrasound – frequencies too low to be audible, such as might come from a heating system fan or a motor – have been found to cause dizziness, blurring of vision, and nausea akin to seasickness. Tachistoscopic flashes too quick to be consciously seen have produced responses such as thirstiness. Advertising is accused of using such "hidden persuaders" (Packard, 1957; Key, 1973). They are apparently too good to pass up.

Hypnosis and hypnogogic states suggest another line of evidence: It is possible to intrude suggestions hypnotically that later act as what the subject thinks are his own motives. A familiar example is the subject who, while in a trance, is told that at a signal (for example, the hypnotist wiping his forehead with a handkerchief), he is to throw open the window; then he is ordered to forget the suggestion. When the subject later obeys the signal (though it might be snowing outside), he quickly rationalizes the behavior by saying the room was "stuffy." Again, if a person is asked to look in a store window, and then is hypnotized, he can recall many items he did not previously remember having seen. Other facts are well known about hypnosis: The majority of people are to some degree suggestible; a person can be hypnotized without knowing it; hypnotism is contagious (whole groups, or portions of an audience vicariously, can go under at once); and hypnosis can act through media such as a phonograph recording or television. Psychiatrists warn that falling asleep while watching TV can be harmful because messages act like hypnotic suggestions on the subconscious mind during light sleep.

In such ways, the mind is an almost nakedly open receptor. Now put against such unwitting perception and suggestion the startling facts found by the neurosurgeon Wilder Penfield (1952:179, 188): that our unconscious minds are incredible storehouses of practically everything that we have experienced. Stimulating the brain with an electrode, he produced total playbacks, such as a musical performance heard at age five, with the scene and feelings that went with it. As Penfield put it, recollection "retains the detailed character of the original experience" — impossible usually to recall unless as an abstraction. To realize how much we may be carrying in our inner tape recorder is staggering. And equally staggering is how much it may be playing back without our knowing it. Suppose it were playing back memories of failure, or every unkind thing we had heard said of us? Such inner noise from our own sound-track might be producing symptoms like neurosis, even psychosis.

Even without assuming playback, subliminal perceptions seem to have a gateway into the autonomic nervous system, including the track called the sympathetic, governing the defense-alarm (what Cannon [1939] called the fight and flight) system. They trigger not only alerting mechanisms such as rising blood pressure, that put the body "on the ready," but also unwitting stress reactions, because the pace of modern living overstimulates the sympathetic nervous system.

From all this, we see that the mind is like an open tape recorder into which tracks are being inserted without our knowing it. Suppose one went about in public for twenty-four hours with a tape recorder switched on, taking in everything — traffic noises, trivial talk, other people's conversations. Imagine how it would sound in playback, in what state the tape message would be. Unless information is unconsciously being sorted into patterns higher than memory packages of uninterpreted experience, the mind might become like a garbage can. At least, there seems to be nothing that consciousness can do to keep extraneous stimuli from constantly dripping in, with psychic costs hard to estimate. So the individual is in the dilemma of the unguarded input: consciously stretching out antennae to hear what he needs, but constantly intruded by what he does not want. For example, he must listen to all the traffic noise for the screech of wheels that can make him jump, because if he doesn't, he will not hear the message that saves his life. The price paid for the unguarded input is all kinds of tensions and memories from which the individual gains little good and possibly much harm. He would seem in some ways to be a victim of whatever confusion or insanity there was in the society around him.

Coping with information overload

We have seen what an enormous capacity a modern media system has for pouring information into people, much of which is irrelevant enough to be noise to them. So a burden is created of having to sort one's way through information, much of which is felt to be "garbage," knowing that the chances are small that any particular bit will apply to one's own problem. On the other hand, should one extend one's sympathy and concern, one might find oneself fretting without power to make any impact.

There are at least four sorts of stress in information overload. One is the work of decoding, which may be quite heavy with exogenous information: making sense of exotic terms, jargon, abstractions, and so on. Then there is the work of integrating new facts with what one already knows, making decisions, and fitting pieces into the jigsaw puzzle, including homeostasis.

Third is enduring whatever crisis there may be presented to beliefs and hypotheses by the new information. Being aware of conflicting feelings and ideas within is "psychologically uncomfortable," says Festinger (1957:3, 13): People will "try to reduce dissonance and achieve consonance." For example, they will avoid situations and information that contradict what they believe, and seek evidence to confirm decisions already made, by "selective exposure" to views that support their own position.[4] If challenged they will react homeostatically; for example, by rationalization. If they belong to a cult whose prophecies have failed, they will talk all the harder and all the more optimistically to persuade people to join (Festinger, Riecken, and Schachter, 1956). If they are doing rather unpleasant dirty work that they were not forced into, they will compensate by talking enthusiastically about it to themselves or others, perhaps finding something interesting in the experience to make themselves feel better about what they have already done. (Behavioral results of cognitive dissonance are reviewed in an excellent summary by Zajonc, 1960.) Essentially, what we have here is information that doesn't fit together well accepted into the mind. It would not be hard to translate the want/get gap into dissonance between what we have and what we think we should have. Another way of looking at it might be inner noise from cross-channel interference of parts of our minds.

Fourth is the stress of irrelevance, which Berlyne (1960:288) holds is an unpleasant, strongly arousing sort of conceptual dissonance. It runs against our training and expectation that conversation will follow threads and that thoughts belong to categories. Not only is conceptual dissonance unpleasant, but it is a denial of information. "Irrelevant thoughts correspond to signals that are statistically independent of important events and consequently bear no information about them, leaving high uncertainty undiminished. So in all cases, we have the makings of intense arousal."

Who suffers most from information overload? Granting that channel capacities vary, it would be people highly exposed to conflicting information, overprivileged in this as in other ways, such as well educated people trying to keep up, professionals, and university students carrying five courses at once and perhaps a dozen different subjects in a year in addition to whatever is coming through the mass media.[5]

There are various ways of coping with information overload. All involve some kind of snail's tradeoff, as I would call it — reaching out tender antennae at the risk that one can't cover oneself before something hurts.

We naturally practice *selective perception* in some way. It remains the classic defensive strategy against information overload. *Specialization of work,* for example, provides a partial shield against information overload by restricting what one must know to a narrow sphere of expertise or formal responsibility. Education of the "generalist" (Royce,

1964:165) is another way of avoiding overload, as in the "Great Books" movement: trying to study the best in a mounting pile of the transient and trivial. But is not generalizing another kind of specialization, in higher abstractions rather than the specialist's details?

Another common response to information overload is esthetic or moral *insulation*. A connoisseur may try to create for himself an island of taste, sifting his environment adroitly to pick out the best and avoid the rest. A moral kind of insulation is found in "positive thinking," Coueism, or "psycho-cybernetics" (Maltz, 1960), which reinforces good thoughts and refuses to think about bad news and suggestions. A sterner moral insulation is that of the monastic, who shuns the "world" altogether. Compromising with this are moralists who try to follow the advice of St. Augustine; as I recall Dwight L. Moody, the evangelist, put it, to live in the world, but not be filled with it. If the water gets into the ship, she goes to the bottom. Sectarians join together to form an island of moral consensus. So insulation acts as a shield against the information overload of modern society.

Another way people defend themselves from too much information is commonly called prejudice. A great deal of research shows how this happens. An example is failure to see a joke if it is against one's own point of view (Cooper and Jahoda, 1947). Studies show that audiences are self-selecting: "People tend to see and hear communications that are favorable or congenial to their dispositions," and expose themselves more to chosen opinion leaders than to the mass media (Berelson and Steiner, 1964:101–4, 529–33, 551). Voters don't seem to want information on issues they are deciding about: They listen to views mainly of those on their own side, they avoid propaganda and media that might change their opinion, they make up their minds before campaign argument begins; only a minority welcome new information from cross-pressures (Lazarsfeld, 1944; Kriesberg, 1949). Identification with a political party, found Campbell and his associates (1964:76), "raises a perceptual screen through which the individual tends to see what is favorable to his partisan orientation"; and the stronger the party bond, the more selection and distortion of what one sees. Faced with people who do not agree, the tendency is to draw together with one's own kind and communicate with those who reinforce one's own values; for example, a liberal will seek other liberals and tend to avoid conservatives (Lazarsfeld and Merton, 1954). It was no surprise that psychologists Neil Vidmar and Milton Rokeach (1974:36—47) found that prejudiced people watched Archie Bunker, the bigot of the television series "All in the Family," more often than those rated low in prejudice. From such things, we see how powerful is the tendency toward selective exposure, protecting stereotypes from new information. And, in the face of unrelieved dissonance in the world, does not clichéd thinking — to turn to banality in entertainment, commentary, and religion, and to welcome nostalgia and fantasy in place of facts — sometimes seem a blessing? Boredom, apathy, and jading need another look as forms of insulation against information overload. People turned off from what they have had too much of seem apathetic to those who want to arouse them. But this may be a kind of defense. This is illustrated in the following not altogether couth remark from a lady fed up with communication overload (Klapp, unpublished data): "I have often found myself becoming tense, anxious, frightened, and so on, from information bombardment; rather saying 'screw it all,' my whole being throbbing with ennui (if that is possible)." This was Simmel's (1950:410, 414) point about the sophistication of the blasé attitude being a kind of psychic callus: "He reacts with his head instead of his heart . . . An incapacity . . . emerges to react to new sensations with the appropriate energy. This constitutes [the] blasé attitude." Helping produce such apathy in audiences is what might be called the "wolf, wolf" syndrome of the media which, continually shouting alarm and claiming concern, use up their credit for getting anybody to do anything.

Poorer responses to information overload are ways of coping, but these are less than adequate. One is illustrated by the "bottom drawer technique," explained to me by an executive who said, "When messages come in, I put all I don't immediately want to answer in that bottom drawer. If no further word on the subject comes within a month, that's where they stay." Such a technique doubtless cuts decision load for the individual but produces a mysterious lag in organizational response. Another less than adequate way of coping with information overload is to blame some particular element for the stress that is actually caused by many problems. Certain villains may be chosen, such as smut merchants, agitators, communists, even the news media themselves for so much "bad news" (a survey of fifty-three editors and public officials by the Associated Press in 1969 agreed that trust in the press declines "when the public is frustrated by the enormity of unsolved problems and this is one of those times.") Even paranoia — seeing oneself as persecuted by enemies — is a way of coping with information overload by simplifying and integrating[6] details into one big conspiracy, of which one has the honor to be the victim, thus dramatizing one's own importance. Indeed, one might feel called on to become a crusader (Klapp, 1969:257—311), a public savior. A letter to the editor of the *Christian Science Monitor*, after deploring pornography in movies and television, ends by asking, "When are we going to wake up to the fact that we have got to unite in an effort to forbid and suppress such broadcasting?" Many kinds of hostile outbursts, backlashes, and repressive legislation may so be due to the scapegoating response to the strain of information overload.

It should be plain that all such responses, adequate or inadequate, involve a tradeoff at some point at which one stops scanning the range of information and takes a risk. "Skating on thin ice" is always part of the price of closing off excess information. The expert accepts this as a calculated risk, knowing that there is a tradeoff between scanning and concentration, that depth of expertise means shallowness in that in which one is not expert — and one makes little progress in getting the larger pieces of meaning together. The anticommunist crusader might also be called a kind of expert at finding what he is looking for, at fitting certain pieces of information into his particular jigsaw puzzle and ignoring the rest. The expert, however, constricts conscientiously, knowing the tradeoff and being willing to pay the price; whereas the crusader and fanatic may constrict without knowing the price they have to pay. In any case, *scan-and-zoom* — the cameraman's technique of sweeping a field, then coming in for a close-up — is a basic strategy for handling large amounts of information, always involving a tradeoff between more of everything and more of something in particular. So it always runs risks of taking in too little or too much. On the too much side, scanning is like holding one's hat aloft to see if the enemy is there — it may draw howitzers. Scanning human relations sensitively requires the snail's tradeoff: disclosing oneself to reach others.

When coping with overload, everyone scans at his own risk. But a great help is to get others to act as scanners, and to do the same for them. A habit of quick notes and clippings sent to people we know are interested in a particular topic will vastly increase the efficiency of all who share the network, without adding to the overload of irrelevancy.

Use of students as "slave labor" in graduate schools is, of course, a device to draft scanners, reducing information overload of professors. As a cooperative tactic, this is one of the most powerful ways of coping with information overload: when communities of people — not necessarily in the same place — keep one another posted through mail, phone, personal contact, video tape, even by computer, and thus help to overcome the powerlessness of the "battle of the inbasket" and the hunt for the missing piece of the jigsaw puzzle.

Electronic media and computers — as McLuhan (1964) called them, extensions of man's senses and brain — do much to increase the range of scanning. Such mechanized systems are a natural ally for modern man in facing information overload. Scholars draw on vast data pools and retrieval systems, feeding information to computers and reading printouts. Students carry pocket computers, speedread a thousand words a minute, and scan six books at a time. Many are using computers even for homely tasks. In 1970, *Life* magazine featured a computerized family, who had bought an $8,000 calculator and were enthusiastically applying it to all of their problems — grocery bills, income tax, even the children's homework. The *Handbook for the Home,* the 1973 Yearbook of the United States Department of Agriculture, announced the coming of the home computer terminal to plan meals, keep tab on family spending and credit, report on the whereabouts of members, and relieve Mom and Pop of many managerial duties. Yet the fact remained that at some point, however much data is gathered, however rapidly, and however complex the calculations, someone must finally decide what it all means and what to do about it. Here the channel narrows again to its "weakest" part: man's brain facing more facts than ever. The crunch remains. Can it be lessened by the strategy of futurism in education and planning (Toffler, 1970)?

All such coping responses, however hopeful, are of little help in the peculiar problem of the open tape recorder: There is no known way to consciously manage *unwitting* influences. The scanning tradeoff cannot be advantageous if one does not know what and how much have come in, when to close to more of that, and when to scan for something different. In such adverse situations, there may seem no strategy more effective than the old-fashioned one: avoiding situations when one intuitively feels too many "bad vibes," taking all or shunning all in monkish, sectarian, Puritan, or ethnocentric insulation.

Whatever troubles individuals have in coping with information over-load, society has more because it is unwieldy, because the tasks are larger and organization poorer.

Societal lags and the absurdity of systems

There are three large consequences of information overload on social systems. They are decision lags, consensus lags, and meaning gap and growing absurdity.   ①   ②   ③

Decision lags

From the 1930s on, a growing anomaly became visible in advanced so-cieties: Increasing knowledge was not reducing social problems as might be plausibly expected, but information and problems were mounting hand-in-hand. Sociologists (Ogburn, 1922; Chapin, 1924, 1928; Hart, 1945) noted that lags, as they were called, were growing exponentially, but hoped that with more knowledge and better prediction people could catch up. At the same time they could see uncomfortably (as in textbooks like Elliott and Merrill, *Social Disorganization*) that lists of social problems were getting longer. More and more people were feeling the thrust of technology and its side effects such as pollution, popula-tion crowding, and mobility weakening roots and multiplying the im-pact of people on one another. Ogburn's student Phillip Hauser (1969:3) characterized the "manifest confusion and disorder" of a "chaotic soci-ety" suffering a "social morphological revolution" (population explo-sion, population implosion, population diversification, and accelerating change) that threatened its viability. There was a growing sense of ill co-ordination in the midst of communication, widening gaps between problems and solutions — such as crime increasing nine times as fast as population; ten percent of the population expected to occupy mental hospital beds, and America ranking twenty-third among nations in infant mortality rates. Survey after survey, commission after commission, reported on crime, poor housing, lack of health, unemployment, vio-lence in media, drug abuse, and so on, without appreciable effect ex-cept to increase the amount of printed information. It seemed the more we knew about such things the farther behind we got. Toffler (1970) drove the shock home to millions who had slept comfortably with cul-tural lag. The world energy crisis of 1974, compounded by the Arab oil boycott, pointed up the failure of information to solve problems: It had been foreseen for at least a decade by scientists giving full warning that the supply of fossil fuels was running out. Four years earlier a book had been published with the title *The Energy Crisis,* by Lawrence Rocks and Richard Runyan. Why had the country been so late in developing an energy policy? editorials asked. Even the Arab oil cutoff could have been foreseen, said a *Time* essay (December 10, 1973); but instead the nation kept building highways, overusing electricity, and "with remarkable consistency . . . doing the exact opposite of what was required." Such lags produced a crisis of confidence in leadership of advanced countries like Japan, England, and the United States. In January, 1975, the Harris Poll reported that only fifteen percent of Americans felt their government was dealing effectively with problems — the lowest level of confidence in government recorded since poll-taking began.[7]

By the seventies, so many problems had erupted that the very idea of progress was thrown into crisis. A world Gallup poll (December 4, 1969) found that in advanced countries only a minority of people thought the world would be a better place in which to live in ten years. People were unable to adjust their thinking to facts like big automobiles being obsolete, growth meaning pollution, and hard work not being needed in an age of automation and labor redundancy. What the crisis of progress proved was that the encoding mechanisms of society — by analogy the ship's compass, helm, and chartroom — had for some inexplicable reason failed although information about an approaching iceberg had come onto the radar screen.

In short, countries with advanced technology were about as far behind in dealing with social problems that had been predicted as much as half a century before as they would have been had they received no warning at all. It seemed as though the piling up of social science information had little or no effect in hastening the solution of problems. Indeed, with the rapid growth of problems and information about problems, it almost seemed that for every step forward society was losing two steps.[8] Sisyphus provides an allegory not only for the executive struggling with his inbasket but an information-overloaded society.

The reason for the anomaly of information mounting hand-in-hand with problems, I have argued, is not only that information is not applied; but that, accumulating past a point, it becomes *part of the problem.*[9] Information awakens people who have not had enough of it to new opportunities to make trouble (such as oil embargoes, guerilla tactics, chemical synthesis of dangerous drugs), whereas to those who have had too much of it, it becomes noise diverting them from decision and consensus.

Consensus lags

There were several layers of difficulty. The first, we have seen, was practical decision, such as simply finding what to do technically. But beyond that was consensus formation — getting people to agree about what to do in such matters as policies and laws. Time is needed to communicate, persuade, educate; rigidities in institutions and habits make it hard to respond in new ways; one might have to build a political party to support policies no current one accepts.

Consensus lags give trouble at three levels in most public problems. First, science and scholarship fail to keep up, by theory building and research, with the flood of raw data from the environment, perhaps because of retrieval problems, overspecialization, lack of funding for research, or inability to develop unified theory that coordinates new information with old. Science and scholarship feed their already lagging output into a second level of decision making, government and administration, which have their own reasons, such as bureaucratic rigidities and political goals, for being out of touch with the scientific community, for failing to use theoretical information effectively even if it is available. Flooded by crises and popular pressures, operating largely without the benefit of scientific theory or even indicators, government and administration are slow and inept in developing policies, and by piecemeal or repressive measures may actually make problems worse, feeding back into the mounting crises. Below these two decision levels is a third level, public opinion, which exerts some effective pressure on government and administration, but is on the whole apathetic and uninformed, tends to avoid cross pressures, and is hard to mobilize — yet it sometimes rises to veto group action (for example, paralysis of policy by vocal minorities who lack the power to get what they want but have enough leverage to block experts or even a majority decision). A case in point is, perhaps, the fate of water fluoridation measures in American community politics. When fluoridation was put into effect quietly, there was no trouble; but when put to a referendum, angry opposition, even paranoid elements, often defeated the proposals (Crain, Katz, and

Rosenthal, 1969). Such cases illustrate sources of lag that seem to be built into the formation of democratic consensus.

A great deal of lag in decision and consensus is due to homeostasis, which operates at all levels of living systems. That is, even if technical information is available for solving a problem (for example, a plan for efficient mass transportation to reduce use of automobiles), and the *communication time* required to clear or make channels, diffuse information, and educate the public is not long, there will still be homeostatic resistance from individuals and groups who want to preserve their own ways of doing things, defend their own structures, and persevere in their own goals. So one saw resistance to the change in habits required by the energy crisis, such as car pooling, waiting for gasoline, using mass transit, not driving on long vacation trips, turning down the thermostat, wearing more clothing indoors. Habits are the essence of individual self-conserving patterns. Similarly, groups tend to preserve themselves. Suppose a group of medical doctors were efficiently informed of a better type of treatment. However good the communication had been, we should still expect them to be slow to adopt it if it required radical change in the structure of practice — for example, some form of socialized medicine, or giving more relative status to nurses, paramedics, and technicians. "Keep things the way we like it" is the whole thrust of homeostasis. No different would we expect the response of other groups to be, such as labor unions, teachers associations, churches, even radical political parties, if their own structures were threatened by information. Even scientists as a collectivity act homeostatically, if we may so judge intolerance toward experiments like those of J. B. Rhine on ESP, or toward theories like those of Immanuel Velikovsky (to which controversy a special issue of *The American Behavioral Scientist* under editorship of Alfred de Grazia was devoted in 1963).

Closing to unwelcome rates and kinds of change is a normal homeostatic response of all living systems, and will be explained at length in Chapter 7. The idea of channel capacity expresses the limits of variety beyond which information overload occurs. But, whatever is meant by the channel capacity of a social system[10] must take into account homeostatic responses of all groups and their gatekeepers and opinion leaders who intervene between the source and destination of a message. Every group, for example, maintains a boundary, perhaps by gatekeepers; fosters consensus; rewards members' loyalty; and decides what is relevant, and what they will do or not do to cooperate, act on a commitment, or pass a message along. Such "bottlenecks," resistances, and constrictions engender societal lags to information overload. However, far from regarding them as something to be gotten rid of, they should be seen as the normal selectivity of living systems — more alarming if absent.

With such factors operating, the notion of society rushing eagerly into change is nonsense. Most people are thrust or dragged into it. It is more accurate to say that people want to keep on doing what they have done satisfactorily, including the fact that some keep on doing things that change the environment for others. Democracy and liberty need such homeostatic controls as rules of the game, umpires, tolerance for dissent, and the sturdy moral fiber that helped the Minutemen resist tyranny. The nice balance needed for liberty is expressed by the metaphor of the surf rider: He doesn't move forward by falling off his board but by keeping balance in change.

So homeostasis helps us to understand the paradox of information overload: that speeding up communication does not necessarily speed up effective response. Indeed, sometimes quite the reverse is true: The faster messages pour in, the more confused and resistant our responses become. Not only is this from the Sysiphean strain of keeping up and sorting out, but when too much new information threatens, homeostatic responses take over from learning and creating, and people become more concerned with preserving themselves and their groups and spend more time opposing change than trying to understand it.

Meaning gap and absurdity of systems

There is an even slower horse in the race with change than homeostasis. It is the meaning of it all. Computers can speed the processing of data, but give us little help in reading the meaning of the printout. Meaning has a reputation for arriving late — indeed, the highest meaning, wisdom, is also slowest to arrive. Beckett has his characters "waiting for Godot," leaving the audience in doubt as to whether Godot will arrive. If each new bit of information was like a "yes" or "no" answer in a twenty-questions game, life might have the excitement of following the clues of a detective story. But bits don't add up, each new fact is unrelated to the proceeding — that is the character of information today.

We can see this in education. As a university teacher, I can say after twenty-five years of experience, that the average instructor teaches as much as he can of his own subject without the faintest idea of how it all adds up in the student's mind with the other subjects he is taking. Nor is there any testimony from most graduates that they have reduced the meaning gap when they finally put on their cap and gown. On the contrary, they enter careers realizing that changes have made nonsense of institutional values such as the idea that all must work (in a looming age of cybernation and guaranteed incomes), or that economic growth is good. The conventional wisdom seems absurd, but the new wisdom is yet to be found.

A meaning gap is not merely inability to come to a decision or policy, but failure to agree on what a policy should be for. For example, a group of engineers might have plenty of expertise to build a bridge, yet might be doubting where to build the bridge, whether to build it at all, or even whether to be engineers. For the latter kind of question, their calculations are of no help. So I would define a *meaning gap* as an inability of people in the same society to agree on purposes and values even when they share the same factual information.

This is the trouble with the piling up of information: that it does not automatically make it possible for people to agree about purposes and values, and may, indeed, generate an increasing sense of absurdity. Our review of the problem of information overload helps us to see the source of such absurdity. First, it is plain that the enormous heap of information has not led to proportional solutions to problems; rather, lags occur wherever channel capacities are exceeded, and problems seem to multiply along with information. Second, in many cases information has exacerbated tensions and increased wants without increasing the means of satisfaction — thus producing a growing want/get ratio of frustration. Third, the world communication explosion has not increased human consensus as optimists of the Enlightenment, such as Concorcet, had fondly hoped — the one world dream seems as far away as ever. Fourth, accumulating information has led to loss of integration — wholeness — in life outlook, and surely has not increased wisdom. Indeed, it bears no discernible relation to that neglected quality. Such paradoxes flout what we might normally expect of information: that it should bring people together, make sense of the world, and finally hand us the crown of wisdom on a gold platter of happiness. No such thing!

Much of the trouble centers on the fact that, unlike information, which can be generated and multiplied almost mechanically, *meanings*

seem to require natural processes of indigenous communication networks, including the slow growth of languages, beliefs, traditions, we-
feeling, and connections of status — all of which might be called
"roots." Such indigenous nets support the individual, help him to realize his own meaning through feedbacks that are complex and may require time to complete (even ancestral debts), and help him to understand his world through gatekeepers and opinion leaders. It should be
noted that there are two essential cycles of feedback necessary for
meaning. One is input of discursive information, the basis of decisions,
theories, techniques and practical adaptations. The other essential cycle
is of nondiscursive feedback, through roles, gestures, and silent signals
such as body language, which tells how others feel about us, how we
feel about ourselves, and supports social feelings such as sympathy,
friendliness, trust, sincerity, and tact, on which role-playing depends.
Such feedback charges the batteries of social sentiment and makes
people feel alive to one another. Without enough of it, people feel a
sense of emotional shallowness and emptiness. Yet it is quite possible to
communicate too well, by overloads of irrelevant facts, news, and such
discursive information, while neglecting or losing the nondiscursive signals of social feeling and concern. This is what we mean by a mass society, increasingly crowded with people who are poorly related to one another in indigenous networks, loaded with information from many
sources yet not knowing what or with whom to think of it. We have
noted in this chapter how the flood of exogenous information through
media has often been at the expense of the very indigenous networks
where meaning should be generated. Meanings do not hinge on single information decisions but on a complex process of interactive support
that always takes longer and that cannot keep up with the information
flood.

So society suffers a meaning gap, between input of factual information and the construction of common meanings, especially shared values, "we" feeling, and a sense of togetherness. The faster new facts pile
up, the worse does the meaning lag become. Society may be unable to
construct meanings fast enough to give its members a sense of living in a
common world in which they can believe.

Such paradoxes and absurdities — problems multiplying along with
information, channel capacities exceeded, want/get frustrations, loss of
meaning in indigenous networks, increasing conflict, lack of wisdom —
seem quite enough to make social systems look hypocritical and hollow,

even without bringing in factors like ill will, prejudice, and class exploitation to explain why people feel deprived. Under such conditions, politics comes to seem a charade, which tries to convince the public that something useful is being done while everyone can see that things are worse. It is this feeling of the senselessness of events and information crowding the media, more, I say, than powerlessness, that is the heart of alienation. A person can feel powerless, yet life remains meaningful — as might be illustrated by the Basques struggling however futilely against Spanish domination. But how much more absurd to have power — for example, command of a B-52 carrying an H-bomb — yet feel it is senseless! In such a way modern man goes along, aware that many assumptions of the life of affluence no longer hold, but not knowing with what to replace them. He has only the growing sense of absurdity, and the knowledge that the way we have been living is increasingly invalid and out of joint. A few in despair, here and there, turn to small-scale solutions — experimental communes or gurus, for private answers — because they can make no sense of the larger system.

The paradox of the meaning gap generated by information overload is that ever more facts pile up the credibility of which is unquestioned, but the overall meaning of the system is lacking and its rhetoric is rejected as hypocritical. The whole is less than the sum of the parts.

This is the way in which information overload contributes to the alienated feeling of being in a "rat race" — to be involved with so many facts that don't add up, so many problems that are never solved, so many contests that no one wins. For those who are not aware of such loss of meaning, perhaps the appropriate comment comes from the fencer who, after eluding a stroke, taunted his opponent, saying, "Ha ha, you didn't touch me!" to which the other fencer replied, "Maybe not, but don't turn your head suddenly."

I hope I have brought into plainer view how information overflowing channels can create jigsaw puzzles that do not come together, overstuffing us with facts while starving us of meaning. The price of information overload is living in the front of one's mind.

Information does not merely sit there, a resource waiting to be used. It is intrusive. Thousands of unsolicited messages are thrust past our defenses, putting us in the predicament of the open tape recorder. So it is no surprise that too much information can become alienating noise, making the public domain of information seem like a lot of garbage.

Sociologically, the heart of the trouble is not in sheer amount of communication but in too high a proportion of exogenous signals. Indigenous ones are familiar, comfortable, reinforcements of the world we know, and therefore are easy to handle. It is another matter with exogenous signals, which are troublesome to interpret and analyze, and tell of a world we may not know except through representations from people we do not know, and who sometimes may be deceitful or threatening. So the burden is greater and chances of being right are less. Not only that, but the quality of exogenous signals is much in question, as we shall see in following chapters. Exogenous signals are capable of washing away indigenous networks and disintegrating the familiar world. The trouble is that people don't dance enough to their own music.

So study of information overload carries a strong argument for renewed concern with homeostasis — societal as well as individual. Where does blame for destroying homeostasis lie? Not, I think, primarily in the power of technology to change material circumstances and of media to flood us with messages. The real culprit is *modernism*, the uncritical assumption that everything new is good. This assumption needs to be reevaluated in the light of information overload. Things should be scrutinized for qualities other than whether they are bigger, faster, cheaper, or more powerful. The "invisible hand" of the economic market cannot be counted on to automatically balance social systems. The same goes for the "free market of ideas" that liberals assumed would select the true and drive out the untrue for the progress of mankind. They had no idea, apparently, of the possibility of information overload, that a point could be reached where society could get too much even of facts. We know it isn't so that if a certain amount of fertilizer is good for a garden, twice that amount will be twice as good; or that if praising another person will make him like you, praising him twice as much will make him like you more. Why should it be different with information? Stresses of overload show that the liberal ideal of openness to information is valid only within a certain range of input: a stimulating amount of information that people are able to use in a meaningful and creative way, the limits of which are set by the system's ability to balance itself at new levels. But for a society exploding from conflicts, stresses, and identity problems, and suffering from a sense of absurdity, "more of the same" seems hardly the prescription. In such a setting modernism is a pep pill for a Mad Hatter's tea party.

We have seen how too much information can create a crisis of noise, when variety, fragmentation, and irrelevance place a burden on decoding resulting in stress and lags of decision, consensus, and meaning formation. So, contributing to the crisis of noise, information overload helps trigger closing to preserve a living system — individual or collective — from entropy, as suggested in Chapter 1.

Some hypotheses about social noise

After describing information overload as a crisis of social noise, it is appropriate to try to state hypotheses about the occurrence of social noise. Under what conditions does it occur? What are the characteristics and positions of those who suffer information overload or other forms of social noise?[11]

I begin with broad hypotheses that presumably apply to several levels of system, then move to some that are more specifically about characteristics of individuals who suffer social noise and its location in networks and social structures.

General communication milieu

Some hypotheses concern the general milieu of communication in which people live:

1 Whenever communication increases in rate or variety, so does the likelihood of social noise.

2 A system with alternative (redundant) channels suffers less from social noise than do systems with few or limited channels.

3 "In a channel there is always a progressive degradation of information and decrease in negative entropy or increase in noise or entropy. The output information per unit time is always less than it was at the input. A system never completely compensates for the distortion in information flow in its channels." (J. G. Miller, 1972:2)

4 The greater the variety of signals, messages, persons, purposes, viewpoints, cultures, mixing, the higher is the potential for social noise.

5 The more signals are manipulated, the more social noise results. (Chapter 5)

6 The larger and more complex the system, the less chance there is for overload by social noise of the system *as a whole* because

of diversity of channels, adjustment processes, and deciders. (J. G. Miller, 1975:501)

7 "The probability of error or overload of an information channel is a monotonic increasing function of the number of components in it." (J. G. Miller, 1975:366)

8 Social noise is high where markets are highly developed, bringing diversified products and competitive pressures to buy and make economic decisions.

9 Social noise is high where technological innovation is rapid, forcing adjustment and new skills (whether of work or leisure) on people.

10 The more highly developed a media system and the greater its output, the more chance of overload by social noise.

11 The more illiteracy and/or the more people are absorbed in oral networks, the less is the chance of overload by social noise.

12 The more difficult signals are to encode and decode, the higher the social noise. For example, in groups whose linguistic code is elaborated rather than restricted (Bernstein, 1954), individuals may be expected to experience more social noise because of a greater burden of explaining themselves and their words, adding to the volume of explicit communication and coding difficulties.

a The more different and various the codes that must be translated, the higher the level of social noise — for example, multilingual interpreting and international money exchange.

b The higher the ratio of exogenous to indigenous signals, the higher the level of social noise.

13 The more technology makes information-processing easier (computers, cash registers, dial telephones, cassette recorders, and so on), the less is the overload of social noise.

Individuals' characteristics

In any position in a system, chances of noise overload are greater for individuals with certain characteristics. Many of these are biological and psychological. For example:

14 Tolerance for social noise decreases with age.[12]

15 Tolerance for social noise decreases with strain, tension, and fatigue.

16 Tolerance for social noise varies with personality traits such as rigidity bigotry, authoritarianism, and introversion (Extroverts

seem to need and seek higher arousal from interaction than do introverts [Eysenck, 1967, 1972; Scitovsky, 1976], and therefore are less likely to experience noise overload).

17 Persons with identity problems have low tolerance for social noise, because good redundancy played back as identity (Chapter 6) is weak versus cross-pressures.

18 Tolerance for social noise varies with commitment to status-role.

    a Persons who are generally alienated, as in ways described by Seeman (1972:387), have low tolerance for social noise.

    b Persons with low commitment to roles are more responsive to social noise — for example, people in some bureaucratic jobs;[13] or in "holding tank" status, such as conscripted military forces, those in involuntary retirement, public work projects, and refugee camps, and welfare recipients, prison inmates, ghetto dwellers, high school students, and some categories of university students.

19 Tolerance for social noise varies with circadian and other biorhythms.

20 Tolerance for social noise varies with mental functioning and health. For example, neuroticism, because of high inner noise, adds to the burden of external social noise. (Chapter 4)

Locations in structures

Sociologists are especially interested in hypotheses about the location of noise overloads in structures that might affect people to some extent regardless of individual characteristics.

Location in the urban setting is one of these conditions. Cities vary in information load. R. Meier (1962:132) estimated that in a metropolitan area like San Francisco people receive about 10^8 bits per capita per year, 100 times as much as in a place like Addis Ababa (with less literacy) where the load is about 10^6 bits. The larger cities are and the closer they are together, the greater the flow of information between them (Stewart, 1950).

21 The larger the city, and the closer one is to its center, the higher the load of social noise.

22 The larger and closer cities are together, the higher the load of social noise in routes and channels between them.

More specific hypotheses about the location of noise overloads follow:

23 The load of social noise is high for those whose intake of information is large and for whom a high proportion of which, from media or direct experience, is unfiltered by personal networks.

24 The load of social noise is high for gatekeepers and opinion leaders whose function is to transduce information rapidly or continually to a group depending upon them. (Examples: airport traffic control, international news service, military intelligence, orthodox rabbi of immigrant group)

25 Groups whose norms and leaders are authoritarian react more negatively to lower levels of social noise than do groups whose norms and leaders are liberal.

26 Those with access to and responsibility for large stores of information are more prone to noise overload. (Examples: researchers, librarians, book sales clerks, book buyers, news reporters, advanced students)

27 Professions processing information rapidly are more subject to noise overload. For example, doctors process information faster than do farmers (Katz, 1961); scientists are more likely to suffer overload than are technologists, who get most of their knowledge from textbooks. (Marquis and Allen, 1966)

28 The more bureaucratized a position is, the more routinized, specialized, and less discretionary it is; therefore it is less subject to overload of social noise.

29 Professions requiring much public exposure or contact with large clienteles experience more noise overload than do professions with minimal public contact and small clienteles. (Examples: public affairs, show business, medical practice, lecture tours)

30 Positions with high feedback tend to incur noise overload. A complex relationship between feedback and noise overload is expected because, although feedback decreases error, it also adds to information load, so at some point feedback can help bring about overload of information and other sorts of social noise. (Examples: heckling, press conference of U.S. President) In other words, error reduction by negative feedback and error increase from overload of noise are at cross-purposes, so to speak. The hypothesis is as follows: Without feedback the error rate is high; negative feedback reduces error but also increases information load; at some point information including negative feedback turns to noise, and stress and error increase.

31 Agencies and persons handling urgent problems are subject to social noise overload.

    a Those that handle emergencies and crises are prone to temporary overloads. (Examples: hospitals, the Red Cross)

    b Those who take on others' problems, such as counselors, psychiatrists, and pastors, are more prone to overload.

    c Those who take on a wide range of problems without specialized skills are more subject to noise overload. (Example: troubleshooters)

32 Those whose position is marginal between parties whose purposes or cultures conflict are more subject to overload of social noise. (Examples: labor arbitrators, marriage counselors, foremen, positions in the Bureau of Indian Affairs)

Some hypotheses express the general proposition that certain communication patterns and certain positions in networks are more subject to overload of social noise.

33 The more central (Bavelas, 1946) a position in a network, the more chance of social noise overload. For example, centralized deciders of four-person groups were found to be more vulnerable than other members to information input overload, especially at beginning of tasks (Mulder, 1959).

34 Certain communication patterns suffer more or less than do others from social noise. For example, in five-person groups, circles were found to be more accurate in solving problems with high semantic noise than were chains, stars, and pinwheels (Christie, Luce, and Macy, 1952).

35 The more echelons and the larger the span of control, the greater is the chance of noise overload in the decider.

36 Social noise is lower when networks are dense[14] and uniform[15] because members reinforce one another with good redundancy and cohesion (Chapter 6); and social noise is higher when nets are sparsely connected and diverse. (Example: A neighborhood of Portuguese Catholic fishermen in San Diego, California, experiences less social noise than do typical neighborhoods in the same city.)

Conclusion

Most of these hypotheses require considerably more specification to be verifiable, and some may even seem to be contradicted by evidence now in existence.

Besides deducing sorts of persons or locations in structures that could be expected to suffer from social noise, the problem should be attacked inductively, that is, by sorting out individuals or groups who suffer high social noise, then discovering what sorts of statuses and structural locations or relationships they have.

Responses to social noise — closing or otherwise — also need to be spelled out and studied. I shall describe some in following chapters.

Before that, though, let us look at some more serious sorts of social noise: entropic communications that generate conflict and disorder and spread negative feelings such as suspicion and ill will.

5. Entropic communication

There comes a time when a signal system fails to warn, unite, and encourage the community — not because it has broken down but because it is delivering too many signals that in net balance are entropic, producing feelings like ill will and panic. Such signals may build up until society reverberates with bad vibes like a gigantic echo chamber. Communication becomes entropic when the message flow has worse consequences than silence.

At such times, closing of communication is often an intuitive, even unwitting, natural response: Damp such vibrations; cool it; don't answer; don't call the kettle black; don't listen to or pass on malicious gossip, pass on smiles instead; turn off bad news on the media. Is this always an ostrich policy? The clam says no.

During crises, the media sometimes close by adopting a constructive news policy without having to be told to do so. They do so in various ways. In almost any country during war, the press avoids spilling military secrets and giving comfort to the enemy. Tact is a sort of self-censorship, which the British media have notably shown in such matters as war secrects, possibility of libel, publicizing criminals, and fictional violence — yet they remain free. In the United States, the media pay at least lip service to not advertising certain products to children and to holding down violence on television during family-viewing hours. Not only do media tighten up during emergencies, but they take it on themselves to assist and guide operations and serve isolated communities. Ham operators join such efforts, staying up nights to make a relay in touch where other lines have failed.

Yet there can also come a turning point, as in tragic drama, when bad vibrations build up unchecked by prudent closing and parties plunge down destructive courses, as in the conflicts that raged in the Middle East, Ireland, and Spain in the mid-70s. Or a panic spreads until credit and confidence are shattered and enterprises ruined. In the 1950s and early 1960s in the United States, the hysteria of Communist witch-hunts, defamation, and blacklisting drove teachers from their jobs, forced ministers from their churches, and put performers and writers out of work. It also led to a cold war mentality and to the domino theory, which helped mire the United States in the Vietnam war. Did not Fascist Germany and Italy go through such a tragic course in the 1930s? Such downturns seem due at least in part to entropic communication. Indeed, is it not possible that defunct civilizations — Roman, Egyptian, Mayan, Incan — were ruined by the rot of entropic communication?

Of course, few intend to bring about the fall of anything. They just do not see such tipping points soon enough. The value of studying entropic communication is to identify it early enough to hope to check its part in tragic escalations. This is no Pollyanna policy of false assurance, for indeed the universe seems tilted toward entropy. All too often spasmodic responses — slamming the gate after the horse is gone, a run on the bank triggering failures, fleeing the sinking ship, pouring water on an electric fire, authoritarian crackdowns and backlashes — are too much or too little too late, and only feed the escalation. Nor is the fault always in spasmodic closing. Cannot a sanguine policy of openness, instead of purging hostility and allaying suspicion, sometimes open a witches' brew? I do not claim to know where such dividing lines may be, but try to look at cases where communication is plainly entropic. The boundary may not be marked but the countries are surely different.

The great slide

We all know some version of Murphy's humorous law: that things go from bad to worse; jobs take more time than they should; if you fix the lock the door will fall off; it never rains but it pours. Oddly enough, many scientists agree. One of the most respected laws in physics holds that there is a tendency for disorder and trouble — entropy — to increase.

So it is easy for the world to seem a dangerous and evil place, a perilous path for John Bunyan's pilgrim. This is because of the sense of entropy within us. All know it, even the child: His blocks tumble down more easily than he can build them up. All know the creep of disease, age, despondency. This is why religions fore-arm and reconcile us. In short, we all sense that the universe is tilted toward entropy.

The Second Law of Thermodynamics says that disorder, confusion, and shuffledness are more probable than order; and that, even if there is a decrease in entropy in some part of the universe, it is always more than compensated for by a larger increase somewhere else. Increasing entropy is, as Sir Arthur Eddington put it, time's arrow. No way has been found to circumvent this law — not even Maxwell's ingenious demon.[1]

Such a tilt may have been what St. Augustine was trying to symbolize by the earthly city and its precarious peace,[2] and what Freud may have meant when he wrote in later years of a death instinct. Be that as it may, the going is rarely easy and, if entropy is irreversible, the odds are more often against us than for us.

Nevertheless, as biologists point out, life has a capacity to create beachheads and strongholds of order against entropy, even if not to win the last battle — on this earth at least. And so communication creates order, yet noise continually degrades it, just as entropy threatens life and progress.

In the face of such a tilt, wisdom is not pessimism but knowing when and what to do — whether to close or to open — to slow the slide and avoid the worst collapses of what ever good and meaning man can achieve. It is turning the tiller before the ship gets too far off course into a current. In terms of communication, it is reading the signs of entropic communication and checking it before an irreversible escalation occurs.

What sorts of communication favor entropy and so accelerate the great slide? This chapter explores six ways, aside from sheer overload. They are:

1 mass contagions, in which negative feelings and images spread and reverberate by reinforcing feedback, and therefore damage the social fabric and deprive people of self-control and responsibility;

2 bewitchments, which destroy integrity and responsibility;

3 villain images, which make entropy visible by personification and stir hostility and conflict;

4 modeling noise, in which information given by heroes confuses norms and breaks down order;

5 manipulation, which degrades information and, when perceived, destroys trust; and

6 social traps, in which vicious circles of reciprocal feedback hold parties in entropic situations.

Let us look first at negative contagions.

Contagions

By the metaphor of his play, *Rhinoceros*, Eugene Ionesco warns of the dangers of totalitarianism to men who fancy themselves immune. He remarked that in the course of his life he had been much struck by the power of contagions of opinion in which people allow themselves suddenly to be invaded by a new doctrine, a fanaticism. The hero of his play is astounded to see his friends turning into rhinoceri: their skins thickening and hardening, gloves and shoes becoming hoofs, foreheads sprouting horns, dispositions becoming stupidly ferocious. He cannot understand why men would want to bellow with the herd. But anyone who has read historical works like René Fülop-Miller's *Leaders, Dreamers and Rebels,* or Gustave LeBon's old classic *The Crowd*, knows that among humans there are herd-like reactions, some called mobs and mass hysterias, others fashions and fads. One trouble with such contagions is that in them men's *view* of things can change, the old standards no longer apply; new things look better. Such fluctuations of public mood are like an emotional weather, watched closely by politicians, investment analysts, and manufacturers of fashionable merchandise. And one of the most alarming phenomena that Ionesco's play shows is that people deny the power of contagion even when it is upon them.

Many mass contagions were working in North America during the 1970s. Some were versions of the "doomsday syndrome." One was a widespread fear of environmental pollution, triggered by Rachel Carson's *Silent Spring* (1962), which led to an "organic" or "natural" food movement that put out a literature defining as dangerous more and more foods and beverages that people had taken for granted because of contamination by pesticides, fungicides, gasses, fertilizers, chemical additives, cholesterol, hydrogenation; and by nutrients that had been removed, as in refined sugar, rice, and bleached flour. Seeing the food environment so full of dangers, people tried to avoid "processed," sought and paid more for "organic," and tried to grow their own foods. The net effect of alienation from an adverse food environment was a kind of nutritional puritanism, in which people became anxious, selective, fastidious, even guarded and suspicious toward foods and their sellers. So the *Los Angeles Voice* (April 26, 1974) denounced the "great milk conspiracy" and the "big lie" of the Federal Drug Administration's claim that nutritional deficiencies do not exist in the United States. An association, Organic Merchants, was formed and published a covenant guaranteeing not to sell consumers unsafe foods. Members of the movement gathered to hold classes and exchange information about sources of pure food. So we see that such nutritional puritanism is a kind of natural closing in mutual defense against an environment perceived as inimical.

Another version of the "doomsday syndrome" was expectation of a "fall of Rome," described, for example, by Ambassador College, Pasadena, California, in *The Modern Romans, the Decline of Western Civilization* (1971) as collapse of institutions and demoralization of character in a mad craze for pleasure, selfishness, and militarism toward political and economic disaster. Before that, a book called *The Last Days of the Late, Great State of California* (Gentry, 1969) became a bestseller, predicting an earthquake in which San Francisco, Santa Barbara, Los Angeles, and San Diego were to disappear into the Pacific. Preachers led their congregations out of the state, and many who remained rushed to buy survival kits. Another earlier "doomsday" contagion was the atom bomb fallout shelter panic in 1962–3, which set thousands of people to digging underground shelters which turned out to be rather expensive wine and mushroom-growing cellars. Economists in the 1970s also picked up the "doomsday" theme, predicting disastrous depressions and inflations, Robert Preston's *How to Prepare for the Coming Crash* (1971) having 300,000 copies in print, advising people to stock gold, food, and firearms, and retreat to remote hideouts to save themselves.[3] More scientific studies, such as Grosser et al., *The Threat of Impending Disaster* (1964), Meadows's *Limits to Growth* (1972), and Commoner's *The Closing Circle* (1971), had similar apocalyptic overtones, especially when picked up in paperback titles like *The Doomsday Book, Can the World Survive?* (G. R. Taylor, 1970), and *How to Live in Our Polluted World* (May Bethel, 1970).

Conspiracy theories also abounded. Views were elaborated on how many guns were pointed at John F. Kennedy, Robert F. Kennedy, and Martin Luther King. Inquiries persisted, sharpened by suspicions that information was being suppressed. Revelations continued of illegal activities of the Federal Bureau of Investigation and Central Intelligence Agency. While such suspicions were fanned among liberals, the far right wing continued to suspect what the Reds were up to.

Such a popular mood helps explain the revival of the devil's popularity. A signal — and perhaps a trigger — was William Peter Blatty's bestseller, *The Exorcist* (1971), which sold 4,000,000 paperback copies in its first six months, and nearly 10,000,000 copies in 31 printings by 1974. As a film it was expected by Warner Brothers to gross 180 million dollars, breaking the previous record of "The Godfather" (155 million dollars). It depicted a twelve-year-old girl who became possessed by Satan, and committed blasphemies and obscenities in the midst of supernatural phenomena such as moving furniture, walls evidencing rapping sounds, her bed rising in the air, the temperature of the bedroom chilling to zero, and a man being hurled out of a window to break his neck. Other books on the devil, such as Anton La Vey's *Satanic Bible*, and *Soundings in Satanism* (Sheed, 1973), sold widely. This was a part of a wave of interest in the occult — witchcraft, fortune telling, spiritualism, voodoo, alchemy, astrology, the tarot, the I Ching, palmistry, graphology, and so on. Such things led film critic Hollis Alpert (1974) to conjecture that the devil had eclipsed God in popularity.

Controversy over the significance and effects of *The Exorcist* approached furor. Fundamentalist churches saw it simply as a vindication of their views. Baptists scheduled meetings to discuss its Biblical message. Jehovah's Witness literature quoted the Bible on Satan, the "evil mastermind behind the scenes . . . manipulating human affairs, drawing all mankind irresistibly toward disaster." The media reported other cases of people possessed by demons and requiring rites of exorcism. Billy Graham (1974) warned people to: "Stay away from the movie . . . Anyone who exposes himself to the Devil, even in a movie, is exposing himself to real danger. . . . Meddling with demons can unleash supernatural forces that man alone cannot handle . . . Everyone is vulnerable." The Catholic Church approved the film. Pope Paul, in an audience in November, 1972, called on the world to resist the devil, "the evil and crafty deceiver who knows how to creep into us," regretting that modern scholars showed so little interest in the "mystery of wickedness" under the influence of which whole societies as well as individuals can fall. The Archbishop of Canterbury, Michael Ramsey, concurred that there are genuine demonic powers in the world, but judged that the wave of claimed cases of possession by the devil was mostly "a lot of fiddlesticks," containing elements of "superstition" and "morbidity." A rabbi called it "an unhappy and even tragic reversion to medievalism," and regretted that it would make many people believe in exorcism and demonic possession. There were also observable physical effects: Psychiatrists reported people becoming clinically ill and entering hospitals for mental treatment after seeing the film; a theater operator reported ten people per day fainting while leaving "The Exorcist." Among Catholics there were also misgivings: Jesuit Father John O'Neill reported that after seeing the film he was unable to sleep for several nights; Dominican Father Richard Woods, a specialist on occultism, reported twenty-three cases of people who thought they were possessed by the devil after reading the novel. By the spring of 1975, a surge of demon possessions and exorcisms (described in terms such as "boom," "tripled in the last five years," "thousands every year," "surging interest") was reported by spokesmen of various churches, including Baptist, Lutheran, and Catholic. What we learn from such scanty evidence is that the image of Satan does have powerful suggestive effects on some people, as well as the power to arouse the interest of millions.

So the "Doomsday syndrome" seemed to be working hand in hand with conspiracy theories and belief in the devil to provide a picture of a world in which people were becoming helpless before evils too big to deal with, and giving a sense of moral as well as physical danger.

Such contagions need to be viewed against a background of earlier hysteria well known to Europeans and North Americans, such as the dancing manias and speculative fevers described by historians (Hecker, 1837; MacKay, 1841); the witch hysteria of Salem, Massachusetts, which killed over a score of innocent people, including a dog hanged for collusion with the devil, and which involved some of the most educated people, such as Cotton Mather, in the persecution; the great "Red Scare" of 1919–1921 in the United States, which caused hundreds of aliens to be deported; and its offshoot, the Sacco-Vanzetti case (Allen, 1931). Other cases well known to social scientists are "devil baby" rumors; the "phantom anesthetist" of Mattoon, Illinois; the "windshield pitting" epidemic in Seattle in 1954; the "phantom slasher" of Taipei, Taiwan in 1956; the white slavery conspiracy in Orleans, France in 1969; and the "June bug" hysteria among textile workers (Kerkhoff and Back, 1968). A worse side of mass contagion is found in waves of suicide, such as those triggered in Japan by lovers leaping into the crater Fujiyama, or in Europe by Goethe's novel, *The Sorrows of Young Werther;*[4] and recently the spread of rioting (especially in over thirty U.S. cities in the "violent summer" of 1967), skyjacking, kidnapping (twenty-two kidnappings within six weeks of the kidnapping of Patricia Hearst were reported in the United States), assassination, bombings, terrorism, guerrilla tactics, or a "poisonous atmosphere" of hatred and violence such as those pervading Northern Ireland and Palestine in 1975 and 1976, and which continues even today.

Of course, mass contagions can be benign, too. They are tolerated in the "spring madness" of university students. Fads are welcome in market booms and sale of fashionable merchandise, and help make songs and shows into hits.

Rumor, of course, is an important vehicle of contagion, consisting of stories uncritically accepted and repeated in endless chains. Tension increases suggestibility and rumor flow (Shibutani, 1966). Its contribution in spreading malice, damage to character, prejudice, and incitement to riot is well known.

But words are by no means the only signals spreading mass contagion. Much of it consists of an uncontrolled, largely unwitting, flow of nonverbal signals. Studies of "body language" (kinesics, proxemics, and possibly subliminal perception) are widening the spectrum of communication of which we are not ordinarily aware. Professor Ray Birdwhistell (1970) has labeled over one hundred messages from eye movements alone, with other signals coming from mouth, nose, forehead, and eyebrows. In Birdwhistell's system posture, arm movements, and body proximities are also significant; touching someone is especially "touchy." The country is practically helpless in preventing spread of contagion in such ways.

From such phenomena of communication we are hardly justified in concluding that "hysteria" affects "crackpots" only. Contagion *can* involve the normal; "bad" messages are catching; "it can't happen here" is false assurance — Ionesco's point about the German experience. And if badness can be catching, it is not just because of the power of contagion, but is also because entropy — not the devil — is strong within us. Any artist knows that it is all too easy to imitate the bad.

Contagions make us aware of a vast flow and leakage of anonymous, therefore irresponsible, communication that can easily become entropic. When such currents are flowing, the environment seems inimical: The quality of life seems to deteriorate, the media seems polluted; "moralistic" minorities talk about censorship or boycotts; people become aware of danger lurking on the streets, the calculating stares of pickpockets, hustlers, and muggers. Being so aware, they give off similar vibes. Entropic communication gets mixed with whatever was wrong in the first place.

Monitoring rumor flow and other such indicators of negative contagions of ill will, hysteria, and so on, is needed to make an early warning system.

Bewitchment

Bewitchment is loss of self-control and destruction of personal integrity as a result of outside management. Unlike mass contagion, it is typically a relationship of two or of a leader to a small, close group. When a bewitched person does wrong, it is hard to understand, from *his* character, why he did it and difficult to hold him accountable.

The power of some persons to bewitch others has been recognized from prehistoric times. Every folklore tells of sorcerers and their spells. Merlin beguiles King Arthur. Devils bind victims into pacts to do their bidding (Rudwin, 1931). Tribal cultures institutionalize shamans who go into trances and put others into them (Laski, 1961; Lewis, 1971). Notorious figures like Rasputin and Charles Manson, and victims like Patricia Hearst, merely highlight and dramatize the sort of thing that happens in countless Svengali-like relationships uncelebrated in biography or fiction.

Of course, bewitchment can be benign. Love and obedience make people slaves to others. When leadership uses such a power constructively, it may be called loyalty, morale, commitment — or healing.

Faith, too, shows a dimension of bewitchment, as in the devotion of willing martyrs and the social pressures that help them (Riddle, 1931). Strong cult leaders often hold despotic sway over their followers. In a case personally known to me, an American girl fell under the influence of the prioress of a Russian Orthodox convent while traveling in Greece, became a disciple, repudiated her family and friends, including her boyfriend, and refused to return or even to speak to them again. Who is to judge whether a person who leaves his family and career to follow a cultic leader does right or wrong? After all, Christianity recruited in such ways.

Brainwashing has come to be used for group effects that would be called bewitchment or hypnosis in dyads. Several thousand American soldiers who were prisoners of war in Korea returned with startlingly changed political convictions (White, 1957; Biderman, 1963). Army psychiatric reports and other accounts of Red Chinese methods (Lifton, 1956; Schein, 1961) explain the sorts of group pressures used. After that, proselytizing methods like those of the Children of God sect or the Symbionese Liberation Army in California came to be called brainwashing.

But, whether group or individual, and whether malign or benign in judged effects, the fact remains that something like bewitchment does occur, in which humans are so under the sway of others — hypnosis, if you please to call it so when dyadic — that they can no longer be said to be individually responsible for their behavior: Their wills are not their own.

How far the power of suggestion and hypnosis goes in explaining this remains to be settled. Psychologists have long recognized the tendency of normal people to accept and obey uncritically. Hypnotism is the most spectacular sector: Everyone knows that it can be used to cancel pain and produce hallucinations; as an entertainment, audiences are hypnotized, sometimes in groups of forty or more; one often sees people deny they have been hypnotized, then at a snap of fingers fall into a trance. Well-known experiments (Sherif, 1936; Asch, 1952) show how individual judgment gives way to social influence. "Immoral" suggestions will also be obeyed: Milgram (1963) showed a surprising man-in-the-white-coat effect in which people were willing to give dangerous, even presumably fatal, shocks to others simply on command of the experimenter. Doctors at a convention of the Association to Advance Ethical Hypnosis in 1973 expressed concern that television was putting millions of people into a genuine hypnotic trance night after night, with effects of the screen dramas of crime and violence that could only be conjectured.

The danger comes from two facts about hypnosis and suggestibility. One is that when a person is relaxed, his conscious mind distracted, his emotions aroused, messages can be implanted in his mind, many on a subconscious level. The other is that much of the power of suggestion comes from the fact that we are moved by *the image itself*, and are not affected by verbal qualifiers such as "do" or "do not." So a warning like "cigarettes may be dangerous to health" would have little effect on the message of the image of a fashionably dressed, good-looking smoker puffing his way through all situations. Such effects of suggestion put us in the predicament of the open tape recorder described in Chapter 4: Bad can get recorded in the microgrooves of our minds right along with good with a sort of idiotic fidelity, whereas conscious decision governs only a small sector. We can only hope we do not act on such images in an idiotic manner.

To sum up: Mass contagions, bewitchment, and hypnosis show how suggestions can: (1) invade us without our being fully aware, (2) change us in spite of our will, and (3) create their own vision of reality, making things look different at the time. So they increase irresponsibility. When tension, group pressure, and other factors increase suggestibility, it is no surprise that many who thought themselves immune, who "come to scoff" may "remain to pray." I have not even mentioned possible influences through extrasensory perception.[5]

Now with such influences of contagion helped by the entropic tilt in things already mentioned, it is no surprise that a "poison pen" or "Typhoid Mary" of communication could damage an entire community. Seeing this, we may get a clue as to why popular imagination has been so intrigued with, and folklore and drama so busy painting, villains as troublemakers.

Bad guys

Many villains (characterizing events in villainous terms) indicate a high level of entropy in a social system. The traits imputed to villains reflect the sorts of disorder society is suffering. Also, by personifying trouble, the villain makes entropy more visible and inclines people to attack and conflict or spasmodic closing. Controlling, expelling, or projecting the villain outside reduces the entropy within.

Now, in the light of the tilt toward entropy and facts of contagion and bewitchment, let us consider villain images as indicators of entropic communication. My theory is that when there is a downturn, there is more hysterical contagion and more tendency to characterize events in villainous terms, for example in demagogic rhetoric (Lowenthal and Guterman, 1949) and rumor. In other words, my theory is that entropy triggers closing, but that villain-casting helps triggers to become visible by embodying entropy in personal forms. In such times, rhetoric becomes florid and vilifiers get busy and are listened to so that villains are more likely to appear in public dramas and imagination. When people are so characterized, the world becomes more "paranoid" (a problem of all contagions — and this applies to some extent even to fashions — being that the very criteria of reality change). Yet, once the villain has been cast, it is possible to close against him.

A demon is a wrecker singlemindedly devoted to increasing entropy. A pure villain has few redeeming traits to make people sorry for him; as the *Song of Roland* describes a Saracen, he is all compact of evil and as black as melted pitch. Fictional characters sometimes come close to being pure villains. One such is Iago, who, seemingly out of sheer spite, stirs up tragic suspicion in his friend and master Othello. Another is Ibsen's Hedda Gabler, who enters the scene to destroy the lives of others — first her former lover who, with the inspiration of another woman, is pulling his life together for creative literary work. Bored with her world, she toys with them ("I want the power to shape a human destiny"), deceiving her friends, driving the man to drink again and to lose his precious manuscript, then supplying him with the pistol with which to shoot himself. Then, as consequences close in, she shoots herself, remarking, "Everything I touch becomes ludicrous and despicable — it's like a curse!" What makes her such a villainess is that so little reason can be found for such malice, beyond boredom and a kind of dog-in-the-manger envy.[6] When understandable motives for evil fall short, the villain enters.

The general mark of a villain is that his motives seem gratuitously wicked, discontinuous with normal ones, and hence unpredictable and incomprehensible. He seems to come from nowhere to intrude his dirty work into an otherwise tolerable state of affairs. Where he enters, things become a shambles, either all at once or pulled thread by thread.

I have studied types of villains in popular imagination and folklore,[7] and find certain patterns (such as traitor and outlaw) generic, possibly worldwide, and others (such as loan shark) culturally local. Some of the main categories are order-destroyers, oppressors, strange outsiders, and sneaks.

The first category, order-destroyers, includes such types as the following: the *outlaw* (known perhaps as desperado, bandit, two-gunman, tough guy, vandal, public enemy, terrorist). Less violent, but no less subversive, is the *flouter* (sometimes called profligate, debauchee, reprobate, harlot, Jezebel) who seems to thumb his or her nose at decency by scandalous misbehavior (his ideal end, as depicted in Hogarth's "The Rake's Progress," being shame, poverty, disease, delirium tremens, and death; but, if he gets away with it and becomes the talk of the town, he teaches that others can happily do the same, as shown by rogues like Volpone, Casanova, Don Juan, Falstaff). Another order-destroyer is the *troublemaker* (also known as bad apple, smart guy, upstart, sorehead, agitator, rowdy, rabblerouser — personified in Shakespeare by Cassius, Lady MacBeth, and especially Iago) whose entry into a peaceful scene stirs up conflict, disturbs status, "rocks the boat." People feel that if he were not around things would be all right. The *rebel* aims to overthrow social order for something he believes to be better (as a bad guy popularly conceived of in terms such as Bolshevik, subversive, mutineer, or anarchist).

Oppressors, the second category of villains, abuse superior position and power, so they flout the ideal of fairness and justice. Often they are entrenched in positions of authority, for example Aegisthus, Pharaoh, Nero, Josef Stalin; or are persecutors such as Adolph Eichmann, Simon Legree, and Cotton Mather. Ideally, an oppressor should be proud, powerful, cruel, unfair, and relentless. Other types often conceived as oppressive are the authoritarian, bigot, or censor, the figure so sure he is right that he does not hesitate to impose his ideas on others.

The third class of villains consists of strange outsiders from beyond the pale, whose foreignness threatens group unity and introduces entropy into "things as they should be." The *intruder* (crasher, meddler, invader, foreigner, barbarian) pushes in neither knowing nor caring about the social rules; people ask, "Why doesn't he go back where he came from?" The *suspicious isolate* (creep, prowler) is one whose detachment, segregation, and queerness arouse fears about whose side he is on or what he may be up to. More alarming is the *monster*. Even Judas acts from certain low but familiar motives, but there is a point at which doing evil passes comprehension and produces a "creepy" feeling we associate with werewolves and vampires. Then people talk of a monster (pervert, degenerate, sadist, psychopath, Bluebeard, Jack-the-Ripper, fiend, demon, witch, ogre, Marquis de Sade, Richard Speck, or Ilse Koch, the "witch of Buchenwald").

Last in the rogues' gallery come undercover operators who might be called *sneaks* because they specialize in deception and treason. They keep wrongdoing secret and give misleading information. Besides the *traitor* (turncoat, Benedict Arnold, fellow traveler, double-crosser, informer, Uriah Heep, Iago, Delilah, Mordred — "false heart must hide what the false heart doth know"), there is the *sneak attacker* who strikes from behind in a cowardly fashion (sniper, backbiter, mudslinger, black-hander, poison penman, assassin). In legend he stabs the hero in the back, shoots him in the heel, or poisons him while asleep — as Sir Lancelot says, "A good man is never in danger but when he is in danger from a coward." There is also the *parasite*, who saps society with a hidden advantage or by claiming something he is not entitled to (chiseler, racketeer, boondoggler, freeloader, sponger, leech, grafter, fat cat, profiteer, tax-dodger, moocher, extortionist). Undercover operators also include *corrupters* who exert a demoralizing influence (drug pusher, briber, Lady MacBeth, Don Juan, Fagin, Rasputin, Charles Manson, the evil governess in Henry James's *The Turn of the Screw*). Corrupters may display an innocent surface, their ability to attract and entrap enhanced by ready favors and sticky charm (they may be thought of as a sort of spider, or a sorcerer casting a spell). In primitive societies such influence may be thought of as defilement or pollution that threatens disorder to a social system (Douglas, 1966). All sneaks reduce the reliability of information.

Why do so many unpleasant characters continue to show up? It must be admitted that there is a certain redundancy in the way villains repeat in plot patterns of folklore and in crime and horror stories. The answer seems to be that, from a functional point of view, they can be negentropic; they do something to earn their keep. One service is dramatic-ceremonial: to keep alive moral vigilance, and, by their defeat in public events like court trials and on the stage, sustain faith that all will turn out right, that "crime does not pay," thus reaffirming the "collective conscience," as the sociologist Durkheim was first to note. A second function of the villain is to provide an occasion for the affirmative entrance and service of the hero, whose mission is to put things right. In this way, the villain and the hero are like partners in a ballet, with opposing but complementary steps, repeating their duet in an endless performance that demonstrates how entropy is overcome. Yet a third function of the villain is informational: He is brought back to tell his story about what kinds of people are to be feared and about the nature of evil. Though we should be surprised to find many people like Benedict Arnold as bad as they are painted, there is real information in characterizations such as traitor, oppressor, even monster; and some villain concepts (chiseling, gouging, ripoff) can show a state of affairs accurately enough even when persons are not named or known. So the villain, for all the entropy he brings and symbolizes, is not entirely useless.

And to such functions I suggest be added the use of villains as social indicators — they tell what is going on in a given social setting. When there is much exploitation, deception, and so on, villainous terms will be used to characterize environments even when persons are not named: "everything is a hustle," "dog eat dog," "chiseling." Villain images are rather like antibodies whose presence in large amounts indicates disease — in the case of society, downturns toward entropy and likelihood of closing, followed perhaps by backlashes, rioting, crime waves, terrorism, suicide,[8] even war.[9]

So the number and kinds of villain images in communication should be monitored by periodic content analysis, such as the studies of violence in media by George Gerbner and associates[10] and the Surgeon General's 1972 report to Congress on television violence (Rubinstein, 1974), so that society can begin to cybernetically read and respond to its own entropic states, as a patient does with a thermometer.

Having suggested that villains be used as indicators of entropy, we should not lose sight of the two-sided character of such concepts. On the one hand, the villain concept is functional, albeit in a primitive way, because it is a structuring against entropy and helps organize the fight against evil. But, on the other hand, just because it so functions it can help escalate violence, feuding, civil war, hysteria, and so on. So the dilemma is that recognizing villains leads to conflict, but that failing to recognize them at all can also be entropic, and can lead to a sort of paralysis of conscience and will to stand against evil.

Because of this two-sided significance, villains sometimes indicate the spread and threat of entropy and at other times its control. The hypothesis of opening and closing helps explain how this could happen in social change. I speculate on the basis of my research that the definition of villains — how many and what kinds — depends on which way society is turning and how far it has gone in the cycle of opening and closing. A society in the midst of a swing will be uncertain and ambiguous about heroes and villains, opposite aspects both being visible. For example, an innovator may seem both a pioneer and a rebel, a culture hero both a rule maker and rule flouter, a law enforcer both a defender and an oppressor, a moralist both a man of principle and an authoritarian. When the cycle reaches a peak or a trough, the definitions of heroes and villains become clearer because most people have one mood, opening or closing, and little sympathy for its opposite. At such a time, because the villain stands for what most people dislike, he may be said to be most functional. His recognition helps swing society the other way, to do the opposite sort of thing. If the villain is an opener, people move toward closing; or if a closer, the reverse. So it seems that Senator Joseph McCarthy went too far during the era of the "witchhunt" for communists, was censured by the United States Senate, and became for many a persecutor. (I have analyzed such dramatic reversals of role in *Symbolic Leaders*, 1964.) The peak of a swing occurs when society has

reached a saturation, of which heroes and villains are presumably indicators.

A hypothesis, therefore, is that in times shown by independent indicators to be opening, content analysis of public communication will
show that a higher proportion of heroes will be openers and more villains will be closers (authoritarians, oppressors, and the like); whereas
at times indicated to be closing, more heroes will be closers and more
villains openers.

Modeling noise

Modeling noise is another sector of entropic communication in which
information given by popular models confuses norms and damages the
order of a system. Here the question is not what the bad guys are up to,
but what kind of guidance the good guys are giving. Are models supporting ideals generally recognized by the society as desirable, or is
their influence detrimental? As most people would understand such a
possibility, detrimental models are those teaching that the way to get
ahead is by courses that are dangerous, desperate, dishonest, or despicable.

Modeling is some sort of imitation[11] by which society sustains needed roles and character traits. The most admired models are called heroes,
who not only provide guidelines but hold up to honor high achievement.[12]

Of course, all public modeling is not by heroes. Many ordinary people have positions in the public eye that are sensitive because of modeling functions — for example, clergymen. Or consider an American President's wife. Long after the President's assassination, Jacqueline Kennedy's conduct disapppointed those who expected her to continue as a
saintly, grieving widow. Similarly, Mrs. Ford caused a national flap
when she told reporters, as almost any American mother would do, that
if her daughter had a premarital affair she would advise and counsel her.
Such a tolerant code did not seem to apply to the First Lady, however
many other mothers used it.

Of course, all who get in the public eye via the media are not held to
such standards. Indeed, one wonders if any standards at all are applied.
This is where the problem of modeling noise comes in. Media obviously
publicize some people more than others, and make them into heroes of
a sort, if only because of "publi-ciety" (Amory, 1960). The glamour of

people with such status in the media, along with the impact of best-selling novels and the like, constitute a considerable modeling problem. Pornography is but a small part of this. The general question is: What if bad examples (judged by whatever standard) become as prominent, numerous, and influential as good examples? Does society go into a sort of moral slide once the uplift of heroes is gone?

Not enough information in terms of content analysis and audience research is available now to answer such a question, but even a cursory look at contemporary models is hardly reassuring. The first fact, denied by no authority of which I am aware, is the *mediocrity* of people glamorized by the media; this is the age of the antihero, as is commonly said. It is unlikely that the characteristics of a sample of television celebrities, for example, would be on average in any way superior to those of a hundred people taken off the street. Equally glaring is the sheer amount of violence, fear, ill will, cruelty, dishonesty, and other negative content[13] in the media. Surveys show, for example, that in the United States eight out of ten television programs portray violence. Such systematic mayhem shrinks to proper proportion the performance of those rock music groups who augment their music by displays of mindless aggression — smashing guitars, antagonizing the crowd, hacking dolls, affecting satanism, and so on.[14] Sensationalism and showmanship for the sake of publicity, rather than real depravity, are reasons for some of this. But no one denies that real desperadoes, terrorists, drug abusers, multiple murderers, swindlers, and so on, have been glamorized by the media until they were more famous than a Supreme Court justice or a Congressional Medal of Honor winner.

What it plainly adds up to is that public modeling in modern society is indiscriminate: However silly or obnoxious a person is, he can become a celebrity; practically any kind of behavior is publicized; "bad news" gets more play than good news; and entropic content gets much of the spotlight. A result of such chaotic proliferation of models is that there is little or no reinforcement of kinds of character society wishes to emphasize; the public gets a kaleidoscope rather than an icon, a lottery rather than guidance. Traditional pictures of the saint and great man look quaint indeed against such an array. Put in terms of communication, the noise is louder than the signal.

If the models before the public eye were classified so that villains could be distinguished from heroes (as in Western movies in which they wore black and white hats respectively), there would be less modeling noise because negative models are aversive and do not call forth the identification and sympathy that heroes do. Where villains are easily recognized by traits like cruelty, unfairness, crookedness, and treachery, in contrast to the hero's kindness, fairness, honesty, and loyalty, there is little attraction to them and the hero gets the biggest hand at the end of the play. But it is another matter when those who are supposed to be villains display picaresque charm, like Volpone, Don Juan, Becky Sharp, or Shaw's charming Devil in *Man and Superman.* Similarly, in real life bandits like Bonnie and Clyde, the Symbionese Liberation Army, Pancho Villa, Jesse James, and Billy the Kid, become romantic and are sentimentalized in story, ballad, and film. Nor does it help the distinction to see the media indiscriminately glamorizing the chronic alcoholic, philanderer, smart operator, white collar criminal, false good fellow, tough guy, basically nice lady guerrilla, gentlemanly Mafia godfather, ruthless espionage agent, or a secret agent like James Bond who kills more people than the bad guys do.[15] Such corrupted heroes (Klapp, 1962) make far more modeling noise than outright bad guys.

Such features — mediocrity, the overemphasis of negative content, and the indistinguishability of good guys from bad guys — make the modeling of modern society seem almost chaotic. Such dubious models, instead of encouraging and uplifting, merely add to the bombardment by creating negative self-images (violent, suicidal, sick, anxious, pained, pill swallowing) which are already so heavy from sources such as advertising and "bad news." Proliferation of models blurs identity, and adds to the frustration of the wish: "If such as they can be famous, why not I?" Corrupted heroes discourage playing according to rules when so many prizes go to evaders and flouters. One wonders whether an oversupply of villains and a shortage of real heroes, a state of affairs in which the wrong qualities seem to be rewarded, does not put a society into the predicament deplored by Karl Menninger (1973): that of a kind of paralysis from being surrounded by evil, yet it is a situation for which "no one is responsible, no one is guilty, no moral questions are asked . . . [and] we sink to despairing helplessness." At least, modeling noise raises the question: How can a nation form a favorable identity while feeding back such images to itself? We need, of course, to know more about such questions as whether people are in fact *identifying* with bad models and just what the *behavioral* effects of such phenomena may be.

Manipulation perceived

We all know that part of the overload of information that adds little to knowledge and meaning is messages designed to manipulate people. Perhaps it is inevitable that parties in a market will manipulate information given to competitors and customers. Industries such as lobbying, public relations, advertising, and, of course, politics are devoted to it. The truth is that we do not know how much of contemporary information is manipulated, nor that less is manipulated in a free than a managed society — we know only that there is less concentration of control.

Manipulation is getting someone to do something without letting him in on the secret. That is, a manipulated message is one in which information is withheld to achieve a strategy not possible with full disclosure. If the total information of a frank message is H, then what gets through after a manipulator withholds the purpose, meaning, and facts (M) is $H - M$. Misleading information inserted in the message increases the loss M. So manipulation necessarily degrades information of messages, thereby increasing their entropy (from the receiver's viewpoint, noise).

Not only does manipulation deny information, but it also increases entropy because control by manipulators means that people are unable to reach their own goals — the world is strangely thwarting.

People don't mind being manipulated as long as they are not aware of it or if the results are pleasant, as when a magician baffles an audience by sleight-of-hand. Yet for a cooperative group it is not so amusing. Imagine a fishing fleet that keeps in touch by radio. If all give out the best available information, all will arrive at the best grounds. The catch of the "early bird" lessens after the others arrive, but in the whole season all catch more. Suppose, however, that the first skipper on the scene manipulates information — withholding, delaying, distorting, deceiving. He may gain for a while, but others seeing his larger catch will sooner or later know he has been cheating, and at their cost. They may punish him or decide to cheat themselves. Either way, the result is that in the long run the manipulator is penalized, whether punished alone or as part of a cheating group.

Is not society rather like this? Universalizing rules like those of Christ and Kant help us to realize that there is a point at which too much cheating becomes negative sum. Sociologists call it anomie. It seems to me that this is the danger of manipulation: that it degrades information to the point at which the benefits of knowing it turn to detriment. A crisis of noise, as I would define it, is entropy from communication so high that participants are inclined to close, quit communicating, and reject signalers as unfriendly. This is what I think manipulation is doing to contemporary society.

Under what conditions can manipulation produce such a crisis? One, I think, is when information becomes so untrustworthy that an individual realizes that his world has become unreliable. The chart and beacons are so inaccurate that he cannot steer his ship but finds himself arriving where he had not intended to go, almost as though there were another hand at the tiller. Would he not then reject the chart? The condition producing such a crisis would be revelation of deceit by a trusted authority or network.

It seems to me that on both counts modern society has been suffering greatly. On the one hand, contemporary literature has made the public painfully aware of ever greater amounts of manipulation. Books and articles have appeared with titles like *Moneysworth*, or "The Consumer Jungle: How to Survive in It"; *Seeing Through Shuck* (Kostelanetz, 1972); "The Fake Factor" (Herzog, 1973); *Man the Manipulator* (Shostrum, 1967); *I Can Sell You Anything* (Wrighter, 1972), which offer to "spill the beans" about weasel words, deceptive claims, visual gimmicks, emotion-charged symbols, and psychological tricks used by Madison Avenue advertisers. Herbert Schiller, in *The Mind Managers* (1973), depicts an educational, commercial, and military combine (EDCOM) that manipulates minds to support the status quo. Since Packard's treatment, subliminal persuasion has received new public attention with Wilson Key's *Subliminal Seduction* (1973). Television writers (Loring Mandel, 1970) complain of artistic work altered by "knowing or unknowing hands," which results in omissions and "lying about what life is really like," and blame commercial control of media for a "weekly inundation of crap." Crusades to protect consumers and voters were mounted by groups such as Common Cause and the Nader organization. The Federal Trade Commission tried to restrain phony testimonials and endorsements in TV commercials.[16] Admired entertainers freely admitted trying to "con" their audiences. John Lennon of the Beatles said:

We know we're conning them, because we know people want to be conned. Let's stick that in there, we say. That'll start them puzzling. I bet Picasso sticks things in.

I bet he's been laughing about it for the last eighty years. Beethoven is a con, just like we are now. He was just knocking out a bit of work, that was all. (Quoted by Hunter Davies, 1968:82)

On the political front, elections have become an image-building, promotional operation in which candidates are sold in much the same way as are products. Even "selling the Deity" is "big business" (Fiske, 1972). All seems to be con. It is hard to find a public message that has not been rigged or jiggled by somebody.

On the other count, many cases can be found in which trust has been damaged by revelation of manipulation. The collapse of the Penn Central Railroad, in which executives were accused of diverting over a hundred million dollars into private investment schemes, auditors of filing false financial statements, and bankers of not informing their customers about the true financial condition of the railroad, was the largest business failure in U.S. history. Also damaging trust during the era were government war-making initiatives without Congressional, let alone public, approval; the Bay of Pigs fiasco, which revealed a secret invasion of another country; the confidential "Pentagon Papers" released by Daniel Ellsberg and published by the *New York Times*, which showed collusion by military and civilian officials to mislead Congress and the public about reasons for committing American troops to combat in Vietnam; and the Cambodian incursion, which upset a sector of the public enough to provoke the Kent State massacre.

A case like the Watergate scandal, though belabored and hardly savory to recall, has some use as an exemplar of how revealed manipulation can produce an entropic crisis in government. What "struck a nerve" in the public was not mere legal facts, such as burglaries, bribes, or the large number of persons close to the president self-confessed or convicted of felonies, but a *drama* showing operations called "dirty tricks" which officials tried to cover up, and the news scenes gripping the public day by day that portrayed a group of men concerned almost solely with manipulating the public and with playing a Machiavellian game against their enemies. Transcripts of conversations published daily revealed efforts by White House staff to withhold information from the public, to edit and manage facts so certain impressions would come through the shields of executive privilege and national security. So the melodramatic impression was exactly that of conspirators huddled about a candle-lit table — government by a cabal to which even party leaders were not privy. Such disclosures showed how far manipulation had permeated the system; the highest officers merely played the game harder with more impunity.

Unquestionably, a public impact was the moral melodrama in which bad guys were trying to get away with something and to hide it by manipulation of information, and for which they were caught and to some extent punished. The question here is whether such a melodrama reduces entropy (the sense that order is restored when villains are caught) or increases it by creating the sense that evil is loose and bad guys are "getting away" with it. It could, of course, work both ways, with some of the public feeling that exposures had "cleared the air" so that trust could return, and others convinced that it had muddied the water and let off too many offenders.[17]

Even though the results were so mixed, social indicators showed that the public was dispirited and demoralized more than it was comforted by disclosures such as those connected with Watergate. Various opinion surveys, as reported in the press, showed results such as the following. A survey by the University of Michigan Center for Political Studies (August, 1973) found that distrust in government had grown since 1958; and, if the trend continued, threatened to generate widespread cynicism and discontent. A Gallup Poll (May, 1974) revealed that, according to college students (over half of whom cited Watergate or the President's leadership) distrust of leadership was the nation's number one problem, though the general public was most concerned with runaway inflation. The Louis Harris Poll reported in October, 1975 that the popularity of elected officials had dropped to an all-time low, and people were unwilling to support politicians' rhetorical promises or appeals to fear.[18] Loss of confidence was also reflected in the difficulty the White House had in recruiting high-caliber staff. The Republican Party reported low voter turnout in California primaries; according to a survey by pollster Mervin Field (June, 1974), their members were shocked and resentful. Business, too, suffered loss of trust: A Gallup Poll (July 2, 1973) showed that big business had the lowest vote of confidence (26 percent) among eight institutions (the other seven being labor unions, 30 percent; television, 37 percent; newspapers, 39 percent; Congress, 42 percent; the Supreme Court, 44 percent; public schools, 58 percent; organized religion, 66 percent). Norman Jaspan Associates (Jaspan, 1974) reported increasing business crime. They uncovered $100 million in business thefts in 1973; corporate and employee dishonesty had reached an all-time high; thefts and kickbacks amounted to

$10 billion annually, adding as much as 15 percent to the cost of goods and services. From the press came news that 7,500 college students had evaded loan obligations by declaring bankruptcy in the preceding ten years, with the rate rising sharply in 1973 and 1974; and even, in May, 1974, news of a "Watergate" among Boy Scouts, which involved falsified enrollment figures.

Social traps

Finally in this review of entropic communication, I would like to mention social traps, pockets of entropy in which influences are so strong that individuals are drawn in and held in spite of distress, areas strewn with "wreckage" but seemingly impossible to avoid, like the Bermuda Triangle. Much of the trouble comes from vicious circles of communication in which parties are held by reciprocal feedback.

Two American couples boarded a cruise ship for Europe. They looked forward to a happy vacation together. On the way, to while away the time they played poker. One man began to lose steadily. Instead of stopping, the reluctant winners continued the game to give the loser a chance to win back some money. By the time they arrived in Europe, the unlucky couple had lost so much that they bitterly announced they could not afford to travel and returned by the first flight to the United States. The winning couple had offered to cancel the debt, but the loser felt honor-bound and in a pique insisted on paying then and there. They parted with hard feelings and never spoke to each other again.

Social traps are situations in which feedback becomes entropic, and relationships and rewards sour before people are able to recognize and avoid trouble: Gratifications induce them into the trap, but the price turns out to be too high. Yet stimuli are coercive enough to hold them even when loss is perceived. As examples of coercive stimuli, many people find it hard *not* to rush for a bargain or a seat on a train, answer a ringing telephone, startle at a scream, laugh with others, listen if they hear others talking about them, sleep while their child cries, refuse a dare, or give when refusal will make one look like a cheapskate. When social networks produce reciprocal feedback of coercive stimuli with too little payoff, parties become locked in. They become prisoners of one another, one might say. The largest may be called ghettos, cultures of poverty. But many other kinds of situations have such features: con games, duels of honor, parasitic friendships (flatterers, leeches), causes involving "brainwashing" or martyrdom, milling crowds, escalating hostilities, even a dull party or ceremony. Freud called traps of parent-child relationships "Oedipus" and "Electra"; Somerset Maugham described love slavery in *Of Human Bondage;* the Greeks wrote of tragedies like those of Atreus, Oedipus, or Orestes; entire families, even communities, of soured relationships are described in fiction like that of Eugene O'Neill, Thomas Wolfe, and William Faulkner. Sometimes social traps are just called bad environment.

Is it possible for a *whole social system* to be a trap? Some (Marx; Marcuse, 1964; Henry, 1964; and Freud, who blamed culture itself) say so. Anthropologists have found cultures in which everyone suffers from costly envy, paranoid suspicion, ghost fears, and so on. Habits, norms, sanctions, and boundaries can make escape difficult while negative outcomes are likely. Where violence is honorable and feuding a habit, death for many is unavoidable. Where military operations are so vast that people who do not hate one another must fight, conscription proves a painful social trap. Is the modern system a sort of greed-machine, as Tawney (1920) held, where operators are honored for how much they can take? If so, it is no surprise to find manipulativeness engrained in a "rat race" (with the tendency of Machiavellians to win,[19] and with the biggest ratraces at the top, among the affluent — precisely where one finds white collar crime and alienation).

Social scientists are pinpointing mechanisms of social traps. Some offer no way out from a dilemma between two or more losing outcomes. A rat race, for example, may offer a choice betwen being a failure and feeling badly about playing to win, or the "double bind" between making money and losing friends or keeping friends but losing money. In parent–child relationships, Gregory Bateson (1972) analyzes how a "double bind" generates schizophrenia: A child can't win love whether he approaches or whether he withdraws from his mother.[20]

A common mechanism of social traps is a *vicious circle*, a relationship among two or more parties in which positive coercive feedback encourages all to go on doing more of what led to the trouble in the first place, a familiar example being someone's rudeness calling forth another's, which in turn confirms his own and leads to new discourtesies. Conflict-oriented personalities easily fall into such traps, as when a friendly argument grows into a row. Positive feedback can reinforce good things too (such as generosity or fun) but there seems more of a tendency for this pattern to be trouble-producing: flirtation disrupting marriage, social drinking leading to an alcoholic binge. The problem is not recognizing dangerous positive feedback, or misreading signs as positive when they are really telling one to stop (as in continuing to give medicine to a patient who is already dying of an overdose). So it is in many collective interactions: milling mobs, market panics, hysterias, escalating arms races (Richardson, 1960), or riots such as that at Attica Prison in which rebellion turned into a massacre of prisoners. From small beginnings, "mutual causal processes" can bring about startling changes in entire systems (Maruyama, 1968:304).

In some social traps, individual short-run payoffs encourage collective disaster.[21] Although all would prefer the general good, each in his own interest must choose a course of action that ruins all. Such was the "tragedy of the commons" (Hardin, 1972), in which English herdsmen ruined the common grazing land of the community by allowing their herds to grow, none having incentive to limit his herd as long as others let theirs expand. They were "locked into" a race to use the resource before others exhausted it; freedom thus brought "ruin to all" (p. 349).

Conclusion

In this chapter we have looked at some darker parts of the noise spectrum: sorts of information that are polluting even in small amounts. The main sorts of entropic communication considered were contagions of reverberating negative feeling, bewitchments reducing integrity and responsibility, the high level of villain-images personifying entropy and triggering hostile responses, the demoralizing impact of models, manipulation that deprives people of control over their own lives which destroys trust when revealed, and vicious circles of entropic interaction. Of course much research is needed to spell out such consequences. But modern society seems to bear a heavy burden of entropic communication. Staggering might not be too strong a word. My theory is that too large amounts, in forms such as hysterias and vicious circles, become a crisis of noise that can wreck a society just as many feet tramping with the same beat can destroy a bridge. Even in smaller amounts, such communication can trigger closing at various levels, from ingroups to nations.

Yet this book is based on the idea that swings can be redemptive when unfavorable intake is remedied by movement in the opposite direction. In this case, a crisis of noise is expected to trigger closing in or-

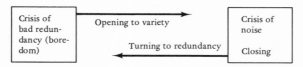

Figure 2. Opening and closing swings

der to cut down entropy and gain redundancy. Feedback from indicators of entropic communication should help people to realize when the situation is serious so society can respond more promptly for its own good.

The whole picture is yet to be delineated (see Chapter 7); but, as suggested in Chapter 2, it is oscillation of the general character depicted in Figure 2. This chapter has focused on the right-hand (noise) end of that model.

Because entropic communication is a trigger of closing, backlashes, and other spasms, it can be used as a predicter of general and perhaps specific kinds of behavior such as vigilantism, moral crusades, or law-and-order crackdowns — and even of such individual behavior as terrorism and assassinations, where contagion is known to be a factor. Whether or not we can do much about all this, monitoring entropic communication could be part of an early warning system. With such a system, we might hope not to abolish the "great slide" but to avoid precipitous slopes and the worst falls, which get us to the bottom faster than we wish. Before a tipping point such as irreversible conflict, we might call the sources of good will into action, as a big bank does funds to prevent a market depression.

Where is the leverage for reducing entropic communication? Looking at problems such as contagions, modeling noise, and perceived manipulation, I do not think that a democratic society has any special advantage. Indeed, a democratic society may be at a disadvantage — in contrast to a society where information is controlled. For example, if manipulation degrades information, the entropy produced by many manipulators must be more than that produced by one party: A scramble of strategies gives rise to bewildering, equivocal signals from many sides. If one party is manipulating information, it is possible to divine the hidden strategy, whereas when N parties are manipulating, the difficulty is multiplied N times. Therefore, it is small comfort to have a democracy manipulating information. Nor is manipulation likely to be reduced in a society given to intense commercialism.[22]

However bad the state of public information may be, censorship is precluded in a free society. But ethical standards and a voluntary constructive communication policy, acknowledging public interest to be foremost in the use of public media, can do much to restrain entropic communication. Half of ever so tiny a loaf is better than none. If media are spreading negative contagion, manipulating messages, and holding up models that are really advertising the villain's stock-in-trade, education and science can do much to sharpen awareness of this. If a country is to continue to have freedom of expression, sooner or later it must adopt a voluntary constructive communication policy to check entropic trends that can bring on closing reactions that will destroy freedom.

We have looked at the negative side long enough. The purpose of closing is not just to avoid entropic communication but to reinforce good redundancy within social boundaries for the sake of integration and identity. What is good redundancy? Why is it needed? The next chapter takes up the mood of nostalgia, the yearning for a lost past and ethnic roots, which builds a case for redundancy, an unappreciated quality of life, whose presence is indicated by "that good feeling" of resonance. Through ingrouping, people try to get more redundancy. The chapter will hold that redundancy feels good because identity — individual or collective — is based on playback of valued parts of one's past, as in ceremony. Trouble comes from the fact that modern society, by its very variety and disconnectedness, is unable to give enough of such reinforcements. So many people today live in crosswinds without a strong cable of redundancy to tie to. Such need, called "nostalgia," requires us to reconsider what is meant by progress.

6. Good redundancy: identity as playback

A steady flow of signals helps an airliner get to the landing field when visibility is low. Without such feedback telling the ship when it had departed from the beam, it could not correct course. So with our lives: We need feedback reminding us where we have been, what we have done, who we are.

Such feedback includes redundancy – the good kind, which makes identity and communication possible. Indeed, one might define identity as a kind of playback of the best of oneself while one moves on to new possibilities. The identity of any living system rests on its ability to keep information and play back memories for its own guidance and self-awareness. So redundancy has two sides: the kind we want to forget (dealt with in previous chapters as overloads of irrelevance, banality, and bad vibes), and the kind we need to remember.

Unfortunately, however, people usually think of redundancy as something you don't need.[1] Tell a man on the job that he is redundant and he will expect to be fired. Such redundancy is not even a useful spare, like a fifth wheel: It is clutter, the point at which one throws even good things away. We have clutter because our affluent society accumulates so much. The garage must be cleared of stuff from the spare room to make way for overflow from the living room. Treating souvenirs as junk is part of the price of having to make way for so much more. We have a throwaway society – as Joseph Wood Krutch (1965:14) said, a "civilization of the disposable."

But let us pause in our urge to throw away. As the Old Testament teaches: There is a time to lose and a time to get, a time to cast away but also a time to keep (Ecclesiastes 3:6).

Lost past

Many people have the feeling of a lost past, of something good thrown away that they must find or recover before it is too late. A New En-

108

glander laments the loss of his boyhood town as he knew it. Explaining why few people commit suicide in the place where they were born, he says:

Too many of their ancestors are watching . . . Surrounded by sights, sounds, and people totally familiar to him, the man who lives where he was born is rarely alone . . . It is difficult . . . not to derive pleasure from something each day of his life. A tree he saw planted — now sixty feet tall — the first patch of grass that gets green early in the spring, a bunch of boys playing baseball in the same lot where he once played baseball. The town or village native knows many secrets. He knows, for instance, who lived in what is now a funeral parlor . . . where the old road went before the new one was built . . . Considered one by one, these secrets have little value. Taken as a whole, however, they can be as priceless as life itself. Furthermore, the man who lives where he was born, when he hears a train whistle or a church bell or the voices of children as they are let out of school, can in the merest of instants, relive his entire life. Sounds that are inaudible to most ears can make him young again . . . People need the familiar just as they need food. Most people would truly rather see the same places, the same things, the people every day of their lives than be exposed to the new and different. (Eddy, 1966:108)

A man living where he was born lives in a state of constant outrage

against those who are confining his childhood memories in concrete pipes all in the name of flood control. He resents the miles of plywood he sees snaking over the land. "Where are the trees on which I carved my initials?" he asks. As he looks about his birthplace, he feels the bulldozers crush him as well . . . He sees growing numbers of people as a skin disease. Secretly, he longs for a plague to stop every bulldozer dead in its tracks. Only his ever dwindling supply of secrets sustains him. Perhaps it would have been better if he had moved. (Eddy, 1966:110)

It is easy to see such a man as an old fogey standing in the way of progress. But did he not suffer some injury from the wiping away of the symbols that made *his* environment meaningful and *his* kind of identity possible? Was he not, in a sense, robbed of identity?

Such feelings doubtless help explain a mounting struggle to preserve the past, described by Constance M. Greiff in *Lost America* (1972). In 1975, the National Trust for Historic Preservation reported a rise from 14,000 to 87,000 memberships since 1968. There was enthusiasm for the quaint and antique. People rushed to antique stores to buy old wind-up phonographs, butter churns, pieces of farm machinery, ancient cash registers, old bottles — almost anything left over from a bygone age. *Time* (May 2, 1969) commented on the rise of "instant nostalgia": " . . . the urge to buy old objects . . . They are relics of a slower, more peaceful world, and each comes replete with a history . . . The soaring popularity of yesterday's hardware is also a meek rebellion against today's slick throwaway products." Similarly, "The Forsyte Saga" and "Upstairs, Downstairs," television series showing Victorian ways, enjoyed extraordinary popularity throughout many replays.

Another dimension of the same kind of feeling was the reaffirming and the rediscovering of ethnicity as a form of historical continuity with ancestors. There was a surge among "unmeltable ethnics," said Michael Novak (1971): reclaiming folklore and languages, voting ethnically, and doing such things as wearing "Kiss Me, I'm Italian" buttons. An advertisement in the Los Angeles *Times* asked:

ARE YOUR CHILDREN JEWISH? Do they know about Masada? . . . About Martin Buber? Do they know about black Jews and Mountain Jews? About the part Jews played in the discovery of America? . . . The Encyclopaedia Judaica belongs in the home of every Jewish parent who cares . . . David Ben Gurion said, "It is the duty of every Jewish parent in the English-speaking world to have a copy of the Encyclopaedia in the home, for the benefit of the next generation."

Indians resisted highways and buildings on tribal hunting grounds and burial places. Some blacks asserted ties with ancestors in Africa. Activity in genealogical sections of libraries over the country indicated that many WASPs were no less busy seeking stronger ties of some kind with their past.

Mobility, of course, plays a large part in generating such an urge for reconnection. We would have less trouble keeping roots if we lived where our ancestors lived. But for most of us, of course, that isn't so. In a mobile society life becomes a frantic nest-building, wall-to-wall carpeting of place after place, with a car in the garage awaiting one's next move (in America, such moves usually occur about every six years). The anthropologist Levi-Strauss (1969) compares the sense of the past among moderns with that among primitive peoples: Primitives have no recorded history, yet live in the sense that things have always been that way; there is a strong sense of rootedness in ancestral connection. Moderns are just the opposite: They have abundant history, but little tradition or connection with their people's past. Hence, though historical knowledge may be greater than ever, there is less personal connection, whether through lineage, the teaching of a guru, or whatever. In this sense, among shelves of historical books, a modern might lose his past.

Whatever the gains in progress, one can't throw the past away without costs. Roots-hunger and pangs of nostalgia indicate that loss of a past is painful.[2] The reason, as I hope to make plainer, is because it is a symbolic disruption that deprives us of important kinds of redundancy. Being a part of ourselves, these kinds of redundancy hurt when they are taken away — and feel good when restored.

Uses of redundancy

What are the services of redundancy? Let us consider them under two broad headings: playback of information making us who we are, and collective identity.

Identity as playback

A test of good redundancy is resonance that is warm and joyful. Everyone knows the good feeling that comes from contact with an important part of one's past — photo albums, school yearbooks, remembering good times together, reunions, candles on a cake, a letter to a teacher from a student who remembers her. Such things bring back warm memories and sentiments. The function of souvenirs is to serve as triggers for reliable playback of such good redundancy. Returning to a familiar place may do this. An Englishman writes:

I . . . have chosen to maintain myself somewhere approximate to the scene of my birth in the belief that by tearing oneself up by the roots the central taproot is likely to be severed so that one withers upward. I live only fifty miles away from London, where I was born. Whenever I go there I always feel a curious sensation, half physical, half emotional, of elation, a great warmth, as the train crosses the River Thames into Charing Cross Station in the center of that vast city, my native village. I cannot account for that. But I am grateful. (Richard Church, 1969)

Why is it not boring to see the same scene every day? The answer must be in the functions of symbols, memories. Granting a desire for the new, we must also recognize gratification from the old and familiar. Researchers at the University of Michigan, headed by Dr. Robert Zajonc, planted nonsense words (such as "Kadirga" and "Iktitaf") in student newspapers. They found that, by a wide margin, the readers liked the words they had seen most often, even when they had no idea what they meant. Similarly, familiarity is very important for the enjoyment of music. It takes time for people to get accustomed to new compositions; they then perhaps go through a fashion cycle of popularity and waning interest. However old, some keep the capacity to give that good feeling. Popular orchestras keep a "memory book" of tunes likely to be request-

ed by sectors of the audience. One age group may resonate to songs by
Irving Berlin ("Always," "A Pretty Girl Is Like a Melody," "Alexan-
der's Ragtime Band"), another to music and songs of the Swing Era
(Cole Porter, George Gershwin, Duke Ellington, Benny Goodman,
Glenn Miller). So Time-Life Records, advertising an album, "The Swing
Era," invited the public to recall "How It Was to Be Young Then."
When listening to the songs of one's own vintage one has the feeling of
being restored to oneself, alive again in a time when perhaps one was
most alive. Fortunately, there are overlapping bands of memory, maybe
folk songs or classics, in which all of the audience can join without
waiting for "their" tunes.

I am not implying that familiarity is all that makes us like such things.
But in familiarity there is one special capacity that the unfamiliar cannot have: to give the good feeling that comes from resonance.[3] Resonance is tapping one's foot with the beat, moving one's body while
watching a sport or dance, hearing an old joke and being ready to laugh
at the punch line because one knows what is coming. The good feeling
comes from putting ourselves in, responsively vibrating in heart or body
because we, too, know how and like to do it. Another way of putting
this is that the good feeling comes from reinforcement.

Then, returning to the question of what it is in the past that hurts
when lost and feels good when restored, I have suggested that it is redundancy as the capacity of signals to give us back part of ourselves, to
restore meaning to us. But, unfortunately, there are two kinds of redundancy. Good redundancy warms the heart, restores us, gives us something we need, makes us whole, and is therefore wholesome. Bad redundancy cheats in some way — that is, filters out or overemphasizes some
parts of the message at the expense of others: and what it delivers is felt
as irrelevant, sterile, boring. So that kind of redundancy hurts in its
own way. By contrast, good redundancy feels warm and deep because it
does something for us in the way of welcome reinforcement.

What are these services? Let us look more closely at ways in which
redundancy is the basis of *continuity*. Without it, our thread would
snap, individually and collectively.

It is plain enough if we define redundancy in the broadest sense as
predictability or patterning, as does Gregory Bateson:

(1) The physical environment contains internal patterning or redundancy, i.e., the
perception of certain events or objects makes other events or objects predictable for
the animals and/or for the observer. (2) Sounds or other signals from one animal

may contribute redundancy to the system, environment plus signal; i.e., the signals may be "about" the environment. (3) The sequence of signals will certainly contain redundancy — one signal from an animal making another signal from the same animal more predictable. (Bateson, 1972:415)

The goal of information, says Bateson (130—1), is to create redundancy — that is, pattern, order — out of variety. In this sense redundancy is predictability (by us) on the basis of any regularity in the universe. It refers to such things as repetitiveness of a pendulum, the constancy of laws like that of gravity, or the persistence of blue eyes in a blue-eyed population. It is the sameness in which a difference can make a difference. In the broadest possible sense, redundancy is no less than the lawfulness of the universe, on which we count, if we know its signs, to go on doing things in the same old way.

The social role of redundancy, then, is to surround us with familiar cues assuring us that things are, and will continue to be, what they seem; that people are known and reliable; that debts will be paid, money is good, and so on. Our social world in this sense *is* redundancy. So redundancy is a conserving mechanism, what William James called the great flywheel of habit that keeps society going. Our everyday interaction is virtually a bath of redundancy.

For the individual, this boils down to the requirement that there not be so much change in his environment that he cannot keep his inner tape record up to date: He must play back relevant memories as a map by which to guide himself. Lacking such ability to play back in such a way as to correspond to what is happening in the present is like remembering the wrong words or notes for a song — the individual sounds out of tune and his world dissonant, crazy. Lack of enough redundancy would produce a confusion like that of switching road signs, as the British did in World War II in hopes of baffling invaders. For the world to make sense it must have a certain amount of redundancy.

Such a definition makes our case for the uses of redundancy almost too strong. Conceived in such grand terms, to oppose it seems almost like defying gravity.

The narrower sense of redundancy, as a characteristic of signals — not of the entire world — is good enough for our case. In this sense, it is that feature of a signal that tells us what we already know — whether by repeating information within a message or a series of messages coming from several channels, or cues in the context telling us what we may assume about the source and intention of the message. So redundancy serves as a kind of *insurance for messages:* that they will not be lost or the memory tape erased. It may be deliberately added to messages to overcome error and noise, as when a check states the number of dollars as well as the word for that number. Because we usually do not need all of this repetition, it is in fact useless much of the time. If our memory is good, we do not need a grocery list, still less a reminding call from our wife. The more careless and noisy communication is, the more redundancy is needed; J. R. Pierce (1961:143) says, "It is only because of redundancy that anyone can read my handwriting." A general rule is that the more likely a signal is to be lost, faded, garbled, or misunderstood, the more it should be repeated and amplified. Redundancy can be also increased by multiplying channels or preestablishing understandings about the message. Much of our knowledge of English grammar and spelling is built in so that we need not discuss it with other English speakers; indeed, Birdwhistell (1970) says that without such internalized automatic rules we could not communicate by language at all. It is widely agreed that most languages have about 50 percent redundancy; perhaps this is an ideal mix for life in general, speculates Colby (1958). By such services to communication, redundancy makes messages more widely available in a population, so contributing to viability of a species, says Birdwhistell. Nor need we play down the role of colloquialisms — clichés, slogans, aphorisms, jokes, even stereotypes — in making man-to-man understanding quicker. Even in art, for all its search for the new, says Anton Ehrenzweig (1970), the destruction of cliché and convention would at some point mean loss of ability to communicate — or to create. Especially in music and the lively arts we have already noted that redundancy helps resonance. What, for example, would Ravel's "Bolero" be if its length were reduced by half? In sum, redundancy seems as important to communication as is new information. Without either, there is no message.

Within the historical time dimension, redundancy provides further service to continuity, not just by spreading messages but by recycling information from the past back into the present circuit: from memory (and the genetic codes) into decision and learning; and from generation to generation as culture. Such redundancy is like money in the bank: *symbolic capital.* Fortunately, recycling carries on without our paying much attention to it. For example, a study of the games, speech, and rhymes of school children in Britain showed that the children repeated local patterns hundreds of years old, even though newcomers moved in and adults forgot what they had played as children (Opie, 1959). Likewise for much of what adults do in daily life, like hat-tipping, or the use of any number of words, gestures, manners, and taken-for-granted notions, which William Graham Sumner (1906) called the folkways. The identity of any social system rests on such redundancy: It must repeat what it already knows in order to continue to be the same system. Naturally, the old have a greater stake in it because their memory banks are fuller. For them, a large change in culture is like devaluing a currency: They are left holding the equivalent of worthless paper. The moral of this is that a society should lose redundancy with the same concern for the potential for risk as when it changes a currency, knowing that at some point a meaning-crisis might snap continuity.

The best part of redundancy is *wisdom*. Gems of experience and meaning give us deep answers to big problems without our being continually shifted by every new bit of information. In the face of meaninglessness and a world seemingly going to pieces, wisdom gives a renewed sense of order -- assurance that things make sense after all. Wisdom is subtly recognized as a kind of gold among facts and opinions that are dross. An anonymous document called "Desiderata," photocopied and pirated in uncounted thousands of copies, shows how people try to hold onto such a morsel. (I am not, of course, claiming that everything that circulates widely is wise.) If Plato is to be believed, wisdom is rare and found only among people in middle years or later, though by no means in all of them. How it is acquired is something of a puzzle: Surely it is not a matter of formal education; primitive peoples have it, according to Paul Radin, who showed the high thought of unlettered philosophers; nor is it just an individual acquisition, much being imbedded in folklore like proverbs, tales, and hero myths (stories like Oedipus, and even Cinderella, have evoked endless reflection about their deeper meanings). There seems no question that wisdom is a precious form of redundancy. Perhaps we need to be reminded of this in a world where, Jonas Salk (1973) says, so much power is in the hands of the unwise that there is real question of whether the wisest will survive.

For all of this the keenest appreciation of the value of redundancy comes, I think, from returning to the point that its loss is really an identity problem -- that without it we cannot fully appreciate who we are, or have continuity as persons. Souvenirs supply memory, and memory of "who I was at all preceding moments" becomes "who I am." In this sense, identity is the staked out, recallable, *reclaimable* part of our stream of experience. To lose all of the past, as in amnesia, would be to lose ourselves. Souvenirs and ceremonies earmark certain parts of the past as especially memorable, to be recalled as needed. Only in its capacity to be replayed as part of the self does any information serve identity, as the concept of who we are. Otherwise it merely enters the stream of forgotten experience. So, good redundancy is the stuff of personal identity: Information about the kind of person we are must be played back to us for us to decide either to go on doing the same thing or to do something different. Our social self (as distinguished from innate or unconscious qualities which may not be expressed) is the meaning of oneself to oneself and others, a concept formed from the responses of others to us from the moment of birth, as explained by the well known theories of Charles H. Cooley and George H. Mead. We may have a conception of ourselves that is not shared (for example, as potentially the world's greatest tennis player), but our *social* identity is proven by the fact that we can negotiate it, as with a coin, with others: People confirm or challenge, accept or reject us in day to day experience. Crucial identities are bestowed by social rites, tests, and certificates. In any case, social identity rests on a pragmatic relationship, success in dealing with others on the basis of the identity claimed. Should people deny such identity, refuse to treat a person as he expects, it is a severe crisis, as when an insult shocks dignity. Social forms and clichés ("by your leave," "your honor," "in your judgment") protect dignity and assure that we will not rub people the wrong way. Even impersonal red tape (for example, the manner in which a female nurse invites a man to take off his clothes) helps by its redundancy to maintain — at least not to challenge — the kind of identity we wish to keep. In sum, identity is not a quality fixed in us by birth, like blue eyes, but a fragile mechanism, with which it is easy for something to go wrong. Its equilibrium needs constant support from a proper environment — the support of both new information, the variety that helps us to grow, and reinforcing redundancy, the sameness that keeps us the same.

In the matter of reinforcement or change, every person has a channel capacity that limits how much new information, ambiguity, noise, and bewilderment he can accept. When he feels a strain from noise, he needs more redundancy in the signals he relies on, just as the homing beam helps an air pilot in a fog. People who ask for more redundancy in a noisy world are sometimes called traditionalists, conservatives, even bigots or "rigid personalities" by those who do not mind a higher noise-to-signal ratio. Yet, it is a mistake to suppose that everyone does not have a limit to variety tolerance, some point at which he needs more redundancy, or at which he feels risk to what redundancy he has. Few people welcome continual, large changes of information that would require them to form new views, even new identities. Radical changes of identity — conversions, amnesias, and psychoses — do occur, but usually (most of the time fortunately) these are once-in-a-lifetime experiences.

It should now be plain why loss of the best of the past — which I call the loss of good redundancy — is very much a reason why modern society suffers so many identity problems. Best-selling books with titles such as *Modern Man in Search of a Soul, The Divided Self, The Supreme Identity,* and *The Magic Power of Self Image Psychology* show people's concern with finding themselves. There is a vast uncertainty about goals, the fitness of careers, the fitness of mates, the rightness of judgments, the right thing to tell children. "Who are you?" is becoming a fair question that might be asked of a housewife, an autoworker, a businessman. Such questions would not be so common if there were more good redundancy. Our mobile and changing society constantly violates the sense of identity because it puts low value on continuity and on the good redundancy necessary in signals to have identity. Identity problems coming from symbolic disruption are sometimes called "future shock," but one should bear in mind that it is not sheer encounter with the *new* that is so disrupting as loss of enough of the old to keep a *balance* — a lifeline, one might say, to tie to the pier when too many waves rock personal continuity. Gypsies wander the world without losing identity because their lifeline is strong.

Collective identity

All that has been said about the services of redundancy to continuity — expectable pattern, insurance for messages, symbolic capital, wisdom, identity — and the need to reinforce redundancy, applies to collectivities as well as to individuals.

The fact that any human group, or an entire society, can have an identity may strike some people as odd (perhaps recalling that old dispute about a "crowd mind" started by Gustave LeBon). But there need be nothing mystical about collective identity. We need suppose nothing more mysterious than symbolic communication among individual minds. For example: "He went to London, I went to Berlin, together we went to Paris" — *that* memory shared is our collective identity, and here are the photographs to remind us. Of course, a strong group may have a whole album of such recollections with arrangements to emphasize them. It is more complicated if a million people do things for centuries, but there is no reason why they cannot share those memories by communication.

On this sort of thing the identity of any social system rests — not on just the likeness of people and the ways they act — but on shared redundancy (what we already know and wish to have repeated and remembered about us). Recycled, replayed like a phonograph record, it gives continuity to collective identity. So one might see a Buddhist church in Southern California repeating the ancient Japanese Memorial Day Festival, Obon, featuring dances in colorful kimonos to the beat of the taiko drum, rejoicing for souls that have been liberated from suffering. This dramatic spectacle is said to have been repeated for 1,300 years, a visible display of collective memory.

All people do not have equally strong collective identity, nor do their identities revolve about the same groups. But where it is strong it is felt as really there, distinct from individual identity. For example, a young Japanese diplomat who had spent much time in the United States said:

What I want to know is how Western or how Japanese I really am. I go along thinking I'm Western, or American, and then all of a sudden I'm called upon to perform some typical Japanese family function, and I find that as the eldest son I respond just as a Japanese eldest son is supposed to — which is of course not at all like "American" behavior. I can even stand off and listen to the words that come from me instinctively, as it were, and am amazed at them. But there it is. At other times, I think I am Japanese only to discover that I can't laugh at the same things . . . I can share certain forms of humor only with Westerners or Westernized Japanese. (Bennett, 1958:84)

His Japaneseness, then, is distinct from his Westernized identity (which may or may not be collective). Most people have some concept of "we," or of self-as-belonging — perhaps to a team, church, community, at least a family — distinct from his personal identity ("I," "me," ego). A person may have a strong "I" and a weak "we," or vice versa. If, however, he is to have a *bond* with others, he must share a sense of "we" with them, even if so diffuse as to be merely a sense of humanness.

Loyalty, of course, requires stronger stuff. To stick to others, to devote oneself to them — even sacrifice the "I" — one must feel strongly about "us." The collective image may be very warm, and the pride in it fierce, as illustrated by this incident told by Jan Yoors (1967) while he lived among gypsies. Four gypsy boys had gone to town and came back to their camp wearing new suits that they had bought from a tailor. They strutted about to show off their new style. At first nobody paid much attention, but soon a reception occurred that was not what the boys had hoped. Everyone seemed to admire the garments, praising their elegance and asking the price. One came up to finger the wide lapel of a new jacket. In a flash he tore it off, and another boy's collar saying, "May your clothes rip and wear out, but may you live on in good health and fulfillment." The boy reflects:

The men returned to the fireside without any further hooting, taunting or mocking. The incident was never mentioned again, and it might never have happened, except for my torn lapel, which I proudly wore as a badge of my Rom-ness. Needless to say, the lapel was never sewn back on again. (107)

In this act, the gypsies were referring to some collective image of what a gypsy should be. Their style was to wear one outfit only, usually torn and dirty, until it decomposed. They had no conception of dressing up for a special occasion. So the rebuke to the boys was not just to "take them down a notch," but a defense of gypsy identity: They didn't look like gypsies any more; they needed to be reminded *who* they were. If group pride is strong, people will submit to far more than having costume dictated. "Miracles" of morale — such as the stand of the Spartans at Thermopylae, Masada, Kamikaze missions, or the "road of a hundred days" built almost bare-handedly through the mountains by Greek villagers — come from it. "We must, we can do it," is often enough to generate effort an individual might not make for himself.

Most modern peoples have some sense of national identity, however attenuated. Greeks, for example, describe themselves as egotistic, obliging, sly, competitive as drivers, witty, and unsystematic (Vassiliou, 1967). Turks have a different list of traits by which they describe themselves. If someone listed these traits to you — thrifty, parochial, kind, patriotic, stubborn, proud, canny, fond of drink, dour, hot-headed — you would have little difficulty guessing that these are terms Scots apply to themselves. Likewise, the terms phlegmatic, unflappable, reserved, conservative, proud, tenacious, fair play, and stiff upper lip identify the English as they speak of themselves. Such conceptions show that even nations, made up of millions of different kinds of people, can have a sense of what they are like as a people — paradoxically, as individuals' conceptions of their own personal identities may differ. Even North Americans — a very conglomerate lot — can recognize themselves as Americans or Canadians by such lists, though it has been suggested by the historian Allan Nevins (1968) that Americans are held together less by memories of what they have been than hopes of what they will be. In such a case, however, images of the future would have to be played back to give a collective identity. Even if people don't share much notion of what they themselves are like or have done, they can usually agree on heroes — whether legendary figures like Ulysses or historical personages such as Beethoven, Shakespeare, Lincoln — who, adopted by a people as "ours," serve, one might say, as group superselves. A superself is not an average man, but rather represents what people think they *ought to be.* Admiration of him is really the people's pride in themselves — like Odysseus at the prow of his ship, he provides a journey for all who ride with him. What this means and how long collective memory of a hero can last are illustrated by an incident recounted by the archeologist Schliemann, who visited the island of Ithaca where Ulysses is supposed to have lived. In the Field of Laertes, he sat down to rest and read from Homer's *Odyssey.* The villagers, having heard of his arrival, crowded around to ask him questions. He answered by reading to them from the *Odyssey,* translating it word for word into their dialect:

Their enthusiasm knew no bounds as they heard the melodious words ring out in the language of their forefathers of 3000 years ago. They grieved at the terrible sufferings that King Laertes had endured on the very spot where we were gathered, and shared his exultant joy as he found again, in that very place, the beloved son whom he had not seen for 20 years and whom he had mourned as dead. Their eyes filled with tears, and when I had finished my reading, they came up to me, men, women, and children, and embraced me, saying: "You have made us very happy, we are very, very grateful." (Lessing, 1966:46)

The opposite of such affectionate ownership of a collective past is alienation, toward which we move as we lose our sense of place, past, people, and heroes with whom we can identify. Total alienation might be illustrated by one of Samuel Becket's (1967) homeless men, who have no sense of belonging at all. But alienation is not just rootlessness; it is being turned off, embittered, as in this reproach by a poverty-stricken urban Mexican to his own people:

Mexico is my country, right? And I have a special profound love for it . . . But regarding the Mexicans, well, I don't have a good impression of them. I don't know whether it is because I myself have behaved badly, but it seems to me that there is a lack of good will among them. The law of the strongest operates here. No one helps the ones who fall; on the contrary, if they can injure them more, they will. If one is drowning, they push him under. If one is winning out, they will pull him down. (Lewis, 1961:232—3)

This man has soured we-feeling, because his love of the land is mixed with mistrust of his fellows. Perhaps that is not far from the view of many in modern society, where noise and banality drown out the good signals of togetherness.

Just as a man would lose his notion of his ancestors if there were no pictures or stories telling of them, so all collective identity is kept alive and grows by communication flow. Cut off, one would be in a predicament like that of Robinson Crusoe, whose "we" was fading, at least until his grateful encounter with Friday, who could give him live feedback. To have a "we" one must have some kind of talk about "us," whether in the form of stories, or images created by artists and poets, or gatherings about the photo album, or readings from history and biography, or ceremonies like Christmas and Yom Kippur. Only by such reminders can people remember who they are, as illustrated by Schliemann and the villagers. Not just special occasions, but also daily life should provide us with an input of "we"-relevant information in forms like greetings, encouragement, tokens of reciprocity, group outings, nightly campfires, or just plain chat about what we are doing and how we feel about it. Ritual is a device that society has developed to regularly repeat vital "we"-relevant input in ways that have been found to be most emotionally effective — drinking from a common cup, firing salutes, taking oaths, fasting and other ordeals, raising flags, lighting candles, reciting creeds together, ancient dances, dramatic reenactments such as the Landing of the Pilgrims or a Passion Play. All this — whether done by priests, storytellers and other custodians of collective memory, or just by anyone as he feels like it — makes up a *network* of feedback for "we"-related information, which is all one means by collective memory.

As I said, to bury such stuff in books that people don't read is to lose collective identity. We must decide as a society how we feel about feeling together, and with whom. Is boredom preferable to concern and common cause? We must decide how much we want of ritual and its languages: "You are not alone, we are together;" "Don't worry, things will work out all right, something is working for you" (perhaps magic); "Congratulations, you made the grade;" "We hold this to be right and self-evident;" "Crime does not pay;" "That is ridiculous, don't do it;"

"I owe you, you owe me;" "We are like brothers;" "Honestly, I'll really try and never quit;" "Help us, Supreme Power, don't harm us;" "We are cleansed, born again;" "Aren't we proud of ourselves!" — the ritual of pomp. Such messages, however mystical they may seem, speak for meaning and togetherness. Groups that endure take precautions to emphasize them by regular ceremonies because they are too important to leave to chance.

Such are the uses of redundancy. Because personal identity and social continuity and togetherness hinge on it, we must decide how much we want of this unappreciated commodity to put in the balance against the race of change and alienation of modern living.

Lack of reinforcement

There are signs that modern society suffers from symbolic poverty. That is, symbols that are supposed to be rich with meaning are flat, shallow, lacking in juice. They give little spark to imagination and feeling. Perhaps analogy with a battery is appropriate: They are run-down — or, as we may say about souvenirs, heirlooms, and relics, they have lost sentimental value. Much the same might be said of anniversaries, Christmas cards, and the like; and of prayers and ceremonies of almost any kind. University graduation, for example, is a negligently attended, dull affair compared with what it used to mean. It seems that modern man is often denied ceremonials of identification that intensify his awareness of himself as a person, a member of a group, or participant in mystiques such as a sense of rebirth, or of living in the "eternal present" of the deeds of gods and ancestors ritually reenacted as in primitive societies (Eliade, 1954, 1958). And, as already noted, the sense of attachment is weak, to places where one has lived and of which one knows the meaning, though people are rallying to protect historic places, fearing their ties with the past will be sundered if certain landmarks are removed. (An anthropologist, Victor Turner, [1967] explores the remarkably rich symbolism that a tribal people, the Ndembu, attach to a certain tree as a kind of cosmic mother symbol.) The historian Carl Bode (1959) notes how rich were the sentiments of the American Civil War period — so warm that they seem "sentimental" now. Tragic drama is supposed to be an intense emotional experience, yet studies (Krutch, 1929; O'Connor, 1943; Klapp, 1958) suggests that the modern response to it is weak. How strong should social sentiments be to support the claim that they are up to sufficient levels? The Greek villagers weeping to hear Schliemann's recitation from Homer may set a mark hard for us to reach, if, indeed, we care to.

Another measure of symbolic poverty is the ratio of new things to old. Fads, fabrications, designed products, even copies of old originals, in general do not make rich symbols. Consider new sanctuaries: How can a structure that looks like a launching pad for a rocket compare in meaning with an old cathedral? Can suburban developments with names like Sun City or Golden Oaks create an environment as rich as the old towns from which many of their dwellers come? The fact seems to be that too much newness *is the same as* symbolic poverty, because meaning, like a patina, is built up over a period of time by appropriate interactions. Symbols cannot simply be invented, because the interactions that make them cannot be invented. So new things, however finely finished, have a kind of barrenness, too much of which destroys good redundancy. Such signs suggest that some important sentiments have been allowed to drain away heedlessly, as a battery might run down.

If the analogy is appropriate, then there are two general causes of symbolic poverty: Either the circuit — the connection that generates meaning — has been broken, or the circuit is intact but not enough of the right kinds of current (signals) are flowing. Perhaps the channel is clogged or polluted with too much noise in relation to signal, as suggested in Chapters 2 through 5. In either case — broken connections or poor signals — there has been information deprivation. And the kind of information needed is that which would be reinforcing.

Any social form we wish to keep requires reinforcement. We can see how it would be with language if words were not repeated with the same pronunciation and meaning, or if so many new words were introduced that it taxed memory to learn them and we lost time in errors of pronunciation, spelling, definition, and so on. If this went too far, we would call for dictionary-makers or someone to rescue us from not just debasement of language but from impending chaos in communication. For learners it is especially important to follow the right rules. Native speakers can withstand more abuse of their language, but even for them there comes a point at which usage is harmed by too much of the wrong.

As with language, so it is with the rest of social life. One couldn't have a ball game if people were busy arguing about what it meant to say "foul" or "out." Most messages must flow smoothly to allow time for other things. So it is no surprise that basic education consists mostly of redundancy — things such as the alphabet, multiplication tables, the Constitution. Adding another hydrogen atom to the formula for water would hardly be appreciated. Who wants variety in driving on one side of the road?

Manners and morals have also been a place where redundancy is more stressed than variety — we are taught not how to do it differently but how to go on doing it rightly (though one of these does not rule out the other). There's no point in having men and women decide when they reach the door who should go through first. Here redundancy is a lubricant that smooths relationships. So for all *rules of the game:* One must be continually reinforced to learn them, and reinforce others to keep playing consistently.

The harder the rules, higher the standards, or sterner the moral lesson, the more reinforcement is required. Not only the sheer difficulty of being very good, but the fact that the payoffs may be remote and intangible (to society rather than to the individual) make this so. So examples like the patriotic martyr Nathan Hale, or the boy who put his finger in the dike, or the youth who wouldn't tell a lie even if truth meant punishment are not easy to maintain even under the most favorable circumstances. Examples like the following seem so astounding to us that we wonder how they could be viable at all. A Japanese son describes his father's hara kiri:

My father called me, and told me that he felt under compulsion to join the spirit of General Nogi, and that he wished me to assist him in the act of hara-kiri — if assistance became necessary through his failure to perform it efficiently. I was to stand beside him, slightly to his rear, with his great two-handed sword upraised, and strike off his head if all did not go well. I remonstrated with him, because he was yet a comparatively young man, only fifty-one. But he said that he had followed General Nogi through many years of fierce battle and he was resolved to follow him in death. I watched him bathe, put on his white kimono and prepare the place of his ending. Then he took up his gold-hilted *wahazashi,* the short sword, and wrapped a snow white cloth about its hilt and the upper part of the blade. Slowly he thrust the blade deep into his abdomen on the left side, and then cut across to the right side, turned the blade and cut upwards. His face was very white and tense, and his eyes closed as he pushed the blade home. I watched closely for any signs of weakness, for that would have been the signal for me to decapitate him, but there was none. He was a great warrior and a true samurai. (Clear, 1943:103—4)

To the son, the payoff here was pride. Where tradition and group reinforcement are strong, even such stern lessons can be taught. The early

Christians encouraged an extraordinary number of martyrs (Riddle, 1931). Such stern models receive insufficient reinforcement to be viable today, maybe because nobody wants them; but, if needed, there is the question of how they could be maintained.

Even less demanding character models get too little reinforcement. A glance at the mass media assures us how little danger there is of anyone being overwhelmed by moral examples, even of the minor virtues. If one searched among the character models presented by the media, even among those presented as stars, it would be hard to find many who could pass muster as a good man, let alone a great person or a saint. The mediocrity of popular favorites has long been noticed, and it is almost unnerving that a similar judgment applies to elected representatives. Yet, suppose the media do provide a model of honesty, kindliness, or thrift. It is immediately offset by dozens of contradictory models — one might call them modeling noise — many extolling the very things regarded as vices yesterday. Over it all hangs the dictum of self-indulgence so emphasized by advertising. What character models are the media reinforcing, if any? It might well be a man who is self-centered, gluttonous, sex-obsessed, hedonistic, manipulative, and violent, with a mind attuned to triviality.

But the dearth of character models is not, of course, a peculiarity of mass media. It is startling to ask oneself how many persons among one's friends one would rate as unquestionably better than average morally. The fact is that we are not in the habit of making such judgments. But suppose one did know someone who was an especially good character model. It is unlikely that he would have much impact, for even if his advice were asked, he would be reluctant to give it.

The trouble is that in modern society (for all the influence that peers are supposed to have) the rule is that we don't set people straight by direct response. We may gossip, but we do not usually tell a person to his face that he did wrong or needs advice. We make no response that helps him to clear up errors, especially in moral matters. He is let to go on his own way, stew in his own juice. Indeed, in many sectors of business and politics, people no longer make moral judgments at all. And this rule about not being a meddler is paralleled by the feeling of people that they don't need support, let alone advice on how to live. The fact is that people do not realize how much they need reinforcement. A man might imagine, for example, that he could associate with heavy drinkers all the time, yet not have his own habits influenced; or work in a business where most employees were stealing and not be tempted himself. The notion of freedom in our society exaggerates independence of signals from others, thus giving us the feeling that we are steering our own ships even when we are like barges being towed down a canal.

Such reluctance to pass or receive moral judgments is a familiar part of the liberal position, bound up with not being authoritarian, with not casting the first stone, and above all with minding one's own business. But at some point, to deny others not only information and feedback that might set them straight, but also what they have a right to know — your judgment of where they have erred — becomes for others a moral vacuum, and for oneself a moral paralysis. In most cases, the only negative feedback people get is that others are silent (clam up). It isn't that people don't have moral opinions, but that they don't feel free to express them or doubt their validity (the very word "moralistic" discounts a judgment). That there may be an about-face in the thinking of some people today is indicated by the fact that Karl Menninger, the dean of American Psychiatry, asks *Whatever Became of Sin?* (1973), and recommends a larger dose of personal responsibility even if it carries uncomfortable guilt; we should be all the better for it, argues Menninger. When "amorphous evil appears all about us" and "no one is responsible . . . we sink to despairing helplessness" (188).

Moral despair aside, even in casual daily relations there may not be enough redundant feedback of the easy kind, as expressed in smiles and neighborly greetings such as "Good morning" and "Nice to see you, how are you feeling?" to assure people that everything is all right and that they live in an environment of good vibes. *I'm Okay — You're Okay*, the title of a bestseller by psychiatrist T. A. Harris, indicates that to sustain mental health, people need more reinforcement in daily living. It seems that many simply do not get enough redundancy from their environment.

And in the midst of this shortage of good feedback, we see what kind the "bad guys" are getting: appallingly low rates of reporting, arrests, convictions, and sentences for crimes. Criminals are told that they have an excellent chance of getting away while law-abiding people learn they have little chance of seeing justice done. The United States Government and Federal Bureau of Investigation reported that between 1969 and 1971 crimes of violence (murder, rape, robbery, and aggravated assault) went up eighty percent. In 1971, 5,955,200 crimes were reported to the police. Only nineteen percent resulted in arrests. Of those arrested, only five percent were convicted and sentenced. Of those who went to jail, a large percentage, which included murderers, rapists, and child-molesters, were released long before they had served out their sentences. It was estimated that at least twice as many crimes are committed as are reported, and only one-half of one percent of all the crimes committed result in convictions and punishment.

All of this adds up to a discouragingly low level of good redundancy. ,Put simply, the odds are quite low that a person will be supported — whatever his view or position — at the time and place where he needs it, especially in moral matters. As with clean air, our society is unable to give enough feedback.

Instead of food reinforcement, what a person usually gets is something quite different, which can be summarized in various ways as a lack of feedback:

1 silence: nonresponse, indifference
2 surface agreement: a pseudo-consensus in which a person is unable to tell if there is real resonance with his view
3 difference not resolved by feedback or information:
  a massive repetition of message, whether by media or people, without response to the person's view and unrelated to his needs
  b manipulation, in which his disclosure is used by those who do not share his view to promote their own aims — probably involving him without his consent
  c a Babel in which few are supported or even know whether they agree or disagree
  d shifting topics without resolution, or mobility so high that those from whom one might have learned are gone
  e squelch or put-down by group or individual pressure

In a world of such deficient feedback, a person skates on thin ice much of the time, unsure of where he is in relation to others. To illustrate, a television actress tells of her dating experiences:

You can go out every night with a different guy, but after a while you're bound to get tired of it, because all the running around you're doing is in a circle. Really, you don't get anything. You don't get to learn anything about people. You'll find six months of it is a very long time. After that, you're asking yourself, "What's going on? What's it all about?" ("Pleasures and Pains of the Single Life," 1967:37)

Plainly, she wasn't getting good information through such channels; but compounding the trouble was disconnectedness, a prime characteristic of a highly mobile society. Even in the most crowded places, one may find people living side by side with no meaningful connections among them, total strangers who might as well be miles apart. People are disconnected not only from others but also from places, traditions, ideas, even from themselves. Facts about American mobility are familiar to almost everyone: The average time spent in one home is about six years; thirty-two percent (almost sixty percent of all persons in their twenties) of the population change homes within three years (U.S. Census Bureau, 1974); eight percent of the population is away from home on any day; about one-fifth change addresses at least every year; some six million persons live in mobile homes (which aren't as mobile as the name implies); a substantial part of the unemployed are "street people" without homes at all, "losers, left hanging in a weary state of disconnection" (Baumohl and Doberman, 1973). An American might meet as many people in one year as the average person a hundred years ago met in a lifetime, yet be lonelier: People are not together long enough; they are too busy to communicate; they do not listen to one another; and thus knowledge of others is blurred by the very numbers one meets. In such mobility, people easily get the feeling of aloneness and forlornness so stressed by existentialism; they cannot find answers to emotional questions, find their insight into others dulled rather than deepened, and perhaps finally seek group therapy. To such lonely ones, also, a cult with firm faith and loving fellowship may seem like a beach to a shipwrecked sailor, and the counterculture an island blooming with greenery and fruit. Sociologists such as Westhues (1972) find lack of reinforcement a prime cause of emergence of a counterculture that one can believe in and feel one belongs to.[4]

Such disconnectedness, together with the inconsistency of what messages one does receive through channels whose lack of feedback has been noted, compounds the difficulty of getting enough good reinforcement in modern society. One is led to wonder how a society generating so much noise while offering so little reinforcement can hang together. At some point loss of redundancy seems to call for a metaphor stronger than a leaking battery, perhaps that of bleeding.

There is yet another source of symbolic poverty to which we have not given enough attention.

Banality as noise

All too often it seems that what *is* reinforced in modern society are clichés and artificiality, a sort of redundancy often called banality.[5] We encounter banality almost everywhere — in "motel modern" style, endless miles of paving, streams that have been straightened, houses that look like cookies from a mold, in what has been called the "Doris Day" kind of beauty,[6] and in the choice of Howard Johnson in ten miles or Howard Johnson in thirty miles.

In surroundings, banality comfortably encloses us in small talk, soft canned music, vapid speeches, political clichés, complacent clatter, monotonous stimuli of one kind or another. Lacking surprise or enigma to challenge curiosity, the situation becomes flat and is perceived indifferently because nothing is expected.

But banality can be felt as a denial of information. Then it arouses boredom.[7] It is a deprivation when it supplies neither new information nor good redundancy that we want. We are often in the predicament of having not enough good redundancy and far too much bad redundancy!

It is important, therefore, to distinguish these cousins who look so much alike. They have in common the fact that they repeat messages. The difference, then, must be in other features such as the content, style, or context of communication. Let us contrast good and bad redundancy. The main point is that good redundancy, though repetitive, brings us the news we want to hear: that things we care about "are the same." So it is relevant, warm, and reassuring. Banality fails to do this because in one way or another its repetitiveness acts as a filter that deprives us of information. Therefore it is like noise.

Four features distinguish banality: (1) *Exact* repetition, of course, makes communication tiresome because it gives no new information. Except in scientific and technical procedures, where precision is important, we would rather have some variety, a live drum beat rather than that of a metronome, or a slightly different handmade pot than a machine-made one. The main fact here is that exact repetition cuts off all the other things that might have been said, such as how people feel. It acts as a filter either by interfering with good signals or by simply leaving them out. In the vocal signal of a telephone it makes the human voice sound flat and metallic; it turns a fine-grained photograph into a cartoon. Boring sameness can come not only from signals monotonously *alike* but from random (Gaussian) noise which is highly *variable*, but equally lacking in new information.[8] When there is too much such noise, the environment becomes "low fi," as R. Murray Schafer (1973: 33) describes the modern soundscape.

At the same time, we note that monotony is not always boring. If one is concentrating on something interesting (art, reading, making love, and so on), then the monotony of the *rest* of the environment thwarts no information need. Again, a monotony causing a resonance within us, as with a drum beat, Ravel's "Bolero," or a hypnotist's words, may lead to mounting intensity, even to ecstasy or trancelike concentration. Perhaps this is what a religious mantra is supposed to do. (2) The second distinction is that good redundancy is relevant to us, but that bad is indifferent and does *not respond to our needs* (this can be epitomized by repeated billing by a computer, bureaucratic impersonality, or a wedding anniversary card received by a divorceé). So good redundancy is reassuring us that some relation or value important to us is the same, whereas banality either repeats some value we care little about, or else its insensitively reiterated message seems hollow, falsely reassuring, even hypocritical. (3) Banality comes from situations such as pushbutton living that *reduce personal output* to a point at which one becomes a passive receiver, or at which signals are so uniform that they require little attention. Such conditions depress the alert give-and-take that makes life interesting. (4) The last distinction takes note of the fact that *emotional* information seems to need and bear more repetition than does rational, of which more than one or two repetitions are boring unless the information is not clear. Just because good redundancy carries such a load of important emotional information, and partly because it is obscure, it needs repetition for reassurance, as in ritual. By contrast, banal messages are emotionally shallow and their rational news cannot keep us interested.

Such characteristics — exact repetition, irrelevance to needs, passivity of receiver, and shallowness — describe how the band of information of redundancy can become too narrow, not rich and alive like a drum beat, to serve as a natural part of living resonance.

In art, kitsch is the term used for the sort of banality found in poor imitations and sentimentality (Dorfles, 1969). This emphasizes the point that widespread banality is a man-made systemic product, as in mass-produced clothing or as in the media which because it packages and filters information in certain ways, has become a vast pump of banality

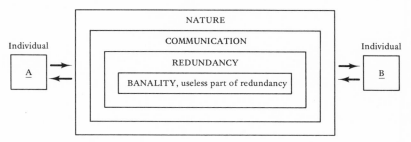

Figure 3. Banality in communication

into modern life. In short, nature is never banal, although man can be in communication and cultural products. Figure 3 may clarify this. If communication is like blood circulation, then banality is like cholesterol clogging channels; or by another metaphor, it is like paraffine in gasoline lessening the efficiency of an engine. Though tolerable at low levels, overproduction leads to an enervating, sterile environment — a sort of emotional flatlands. People feel defeated by clichés, romantic artists and poets like birds in a plastic cage. But the trouble with banality as a communication product is that it is so inert and boring that it builds up quietly without waking people into protest. They stay in what R. D. Laing (1967:12) calls the sleep of alienation, "of being unconscious, of being out of one's mind ... the condition of the normal man." The mind *can* live comfortably within a cage of restricted sensibilities. Banality is the jailer who quietly closes the door.

If such is the distinction between good and bad redundancy, then having an interesting and resonant society depends not only on variety but on increasing good redundancy without overloading people with banality, which turns them off and adds to the alienation of the plastic society. Good redundancy repeats what people need, so it can be reinforcing and therapeutic. Bad redundancy repeats what people don't need, overcrowding circuits and interfering with signals they do need, cutting out highs and lows, the rich tones of life. The environment becomes poorer, and so does society.

How reinforce redundancy without overloading people with banality? The solution lies in distinguishing redundancy that feels alive and good from that which is formalistic, shallow, or artificial. For example, sometimes a traditional wedding properly done will give this feeling, at other times a ceremony designed by the couple themselves, which takes place in bare feet under the trees or beside a swimming pool will give the best feeling. Good redundancy evokes a resonance and warmth, as in a folk dance, making people feel so good they want to do it again. It *doesn't* turn highbrows off. Of course the distinction is not going to be easy; further study is needed.[9] Different kinds of systems have different needs for redundancy.[10] And the time (position in the opening and closing cycle) doubtless makes a difference.

With cousins so much alike, it will not be easy to exclude one and welcome the other. But this does not make it any less true that more banality cannot be a cure for the ills of banality. This leads to a critique of modernism.

Critique of modernism

The fallacy of modernism lies not in just its rush into "future shock" but, as it ignores the difference between good and bad redundancy, in its presentation to us of a plastic society which it calls "progress." It does so by assuming that traditional redundancy is bad and newness is good (the future will be better than the present, the present is better than the past — it is our duty to catch up), while thoughtlessly accepting change that is often more banal than the tradition it replaces. Along with this come overdoses of variety for which people have not been reinforced enough by good redundancy. Opening floodgates of variety and banality at the same time threatens to overwhelm a society with entropy.

Faddism shows such a possibility of indiscriminate opening, having reached epidemic proportions of a disease that at least one writer, Christopher Booker (1970) has called neophilia, or a compulsive keeping pace with what is new. In such a state, frenzy passes for vitality, and people suffering already from change frantically scan the horizon, looking for they know not what, seizing anything that looks like "it." Guru-chasing, an effort to transcend banality, is part of this, as will be described in Chapter 8. But the turnover often resembles that of fashions, which do not give lasting satisfaction and may bring in as much banality as they replace. One is forced to conclude that whatever people are seeking in fashions they are usually not finding, but instead playing a sort of Russian roulette with what the future is bringing. Beyond a point, faddism as indiscriminate openness could destroy any life-style, and make it harder to proclaim social identity. It could become *style-*

lessness which would no longer identify the individual (whatever one did or wore, no one would notice), and life would become like a madhouse where everyòne was equally peculiar. To put the matter in terms of redundancy, if style is a continuing statement of oneself, then what too much faddism could do is break down the basis by which people can declare themselves: When anybody can be anybody, nobody can be "somebody."

If redundancy is as important as I have said, then losing too much of the good, or getting too much of either bad redundancy or variety, could have dire results for individual identity and social resonance. So it seems to me ancient debts are coming due, mankind faces a reckoning. Much of what we have thoughtlessly called progress has increased the world's entropy. Suddenly the position of the conservationist has become stronger.

If one recognizes redundancy as a store of identifying sameness in society and the individual, it becomes plain that the very ideal of openness — that openness is always better than closedness, that the more change and information the better — should be reconsidered. Since the eighteenth century, liberal theorists like Karl Popper (1952) have held that an open society is better than a closed one, and similarly for the open mind, according to Milton Rokeach (1960). Closure, whether in terms of censorship, conservatism, or bigotry, is always bad. Always the cure is *opening* doors of change and communication, never closing them. Yet how, in the light of our study of redundancy, could this always be so? Are there not times when slamming the gate or staunching the wound is necessary? Yet some writers talk as though the trend to openness could just go on and on. Warren Bennis and Philip Slater (1968), for example, see the world of tomorrow not in terms of restored redundancy, but as a "temporary society" in which people are separated from permanent groups that give them ready-made values and identity. The work of society will be done by task forces of strangers with various skills who deal with problems as they come up. No longer will there be bureaucracy with its routines. What rules and we-feeling there are will have to come from volatile relationships on the job. People will be interchangeable in most relationships, except perhaps for marriage which will have to bear the brunt of supplying a sense of togetherness, as mates will increase emotional demands on each other. But, for all this adaptability and freedom, it will not necessarily be a happy world: Part of the price, in this society that has given up the value of permanence, will be personal ambiguity, alienation, shallowness of relations, and meaningless-ness. Paralleling this, psychologist Louis Zurcher (1972:181—6) sees the emerging personality of tomorrow as a "mutable self," without fixed social identity, oriented toward continual change, to whom. adjectives such as the following might be applicable: mercurial, ephemeral, proces-sual, chameleon-like. I am sure there are times when we enjoy people like this and want to be that way ourselves. But if I were to pick out the ten people I wish to spend the rest of my life with, not more than one would be like this, and the rest would probably be busy trying to hold this elusive character down. In a world with such minimal redun-dancy, there would be, to my way of thinking, a dismaying fluidity and turbulence, which would be comfortable about as long as one enjoys bathing in big surf. One couldn't imagine people choosing that as a place to anchor.

So it is for society, which to hold to itself and be worth living in must keep enough redundancy in the signals people hear. Resonance is the great social gift of redundancy, making it possible for people to dance and feel together. Identity is the gift of personal redundancy, sustained by a reasonably redundant world.

To keep the right balance, opening and closing are both needed. Closedness is needed to conserve good redundancy and the identity and resonance it sustains. Opening is needed to get the most of the best information. But one cannot be limitlessly open without suffering in-tolerable entropy. By opening and closing tactically, society can move to higher levels of synergy. What is involved in this game is stated in the next chapter.

7. Theory of opening and closing

In his poem, "The City of Yes and the City of No" (1966), Yevgeny Yevtushenko tells of rushing like a train between two worlds, his nerves strained like wires. But it would be a mistake to read this merely as a longing to escape a closed society. Rather, it is tension between loyalty and wishing to burst from his City of No. In a broader sense his problem is shared by all of us. We all live in the City of Yes and the City of No.

This chapter treats a pattern displayed by living things: opening *and* closing, not one without the other. At the social level it is a matter of communication flow: when, how, and with whom people interact; whom they keep out; the boundaries of groups. In such flow, there seems to be a sort of pulse in which people are more or less inclined to say yes or no. Sometimes ingroups tighten, communicating less outside and more within. Sometimes networks loosen, and people talk more to different kinds of people, fashions spread easily, and the new is more welcome than the old.

Popular moods such as nostalgia, romanticism, and ethnicism seem to reflect such a pattern. What I shall suggest is that every society, indeed every living thing, needs a balance between openness and closedness which varies according to the system. If it opens too far, it will feel a strain to come back to more good closing. If it closes to a point where redundancy is felt as banal and stifling, it will, however snug the joys of togetherness, yearn to open and let in more fresh — even cold — air. Popular nostalgia is a signal that opening has gone too far. Doubtless it is the same kind of feeling as that with which a cub returns to its mother, a bird to the flock, or a traveler to his hearth: the wish to shorten lines of supply and communication with one's own kind, to cut down entropy of noise and strangeness.

Let us look at ingrouping in this light.

Ingrouping

The rise of Archie Bunker as a popular favorite in North America was a rather large signal of a changing mood about ethnicity. The television

135

drama, "All In The Family," made fun of Archie, a lower middle-class WASP, whom ethnic minorities taught lessons in more or less kindly ways. But there was another side to the lesson: Much of the audience seemed to enjoy Archie's outspokenness and the opportunity to have it all out in the open. If half the message was a bigot "put down," the other half was the bigot asserted against ethnics who would not stay in "their place."[1] Either way, the show highlighted ethnic difference.

Earlier signs of what was happening had come from the black nationalism of the Nation of Islam under the leadership of Elijah Muhammed, described by C. Eric Lincoln (1961) and E. U. Essien-Udom (1963). Later the "soul" movement asserted the uniqueness of blackness, rejecting assimilation or even success according to white middle-class ideals as "Uncle Tom," viewed as a kind of betrayal of one's race. Parallel claims in the name of "Brown Power" and "Red Power" were made by Chicanos and American Indians respectively.

By the 1970s, some 70,000,000 American descendents of Irish, Italians, Spanish, Greeks, Armenians, and Slavs were asserting themselves as "unmeltable ethnics," according to Michael Novak (1971), against the "hypocrisy" of the "melting pot" as WASPs conceived it. Their feelings were expressed in words like the following from an Italian-American (Novak 1971:46): "Well, if anybody ever asks me my nationality, I'm always proud to say I'm Italian instead of — like so many people say — they're Americans. I don't see myself superior to anyone — don't get me wrong. But I think deep down inside that Italian is best." The same outspokenness was seen in Novak's statement about himself (53): "I am born of PIGS — those Poles, Italians, Greeks, and Slavs, those non-English-speaking immigrants numbered so heavily among the working men of this nation." Yet he deplored his "shallow knowledge" of his "roots," and regretted that he had been instructed by his parents to imitate Anglo-Saxons and to say "American" rather than "Slovak" when asked his nationality (54). But a "tide of resentment" was beginning to overwhelm the descendants of immigrants, and a "new politics" that stressed ethnic consciousness rather than the melting pot was emerging in challenge to the WASP view (270—2). A survey by the U.S. Census Bureau in 1971 showed that about 60 percent of Americans still maintained their sense of other-nation or racial heritage (including about 28 percent who identified themselves with an Anglo-German background, 18 percent who could be called Roman Catholic-Mediterranean — including Irish, French, Italian, and Slavic — 11 percent black, and 5 percent Spanish-speaking). A study by Mark R. Levy and Michael

S. Kramer (1972) held that the ethnic factor was becoming crucial, indeed might hold the key to America's political future. Courting the "ethnic vote" became a larger consideration for politicians. Lapel buttons proliferated with slogans like: "Kiss me, I'm Italian," "I'm Black and proud," "Dress British, think Yiddish," and "Swedish power." Nor was it so different in Canada, though the melting pot had never been stressed. "Archie Bunker for Prime Minister" posters were sold in department stores. The Minister for Multiculturalism, Dr. Stanley Haidasz, said in regard to the resurgence of pride in cultural identity that people were standing in line to join cultural organizations. *Time's* "Essay" of September 3, 1973, summed it up, announcing "ethnicity is in." So, as it happened, were genes coming back in, in the form of the notion that heredity was important in group differences in intelligence and performance.

Along with emphasis on ethnicity came higher values on tradition, and nostalgia was big business (as noted in Chapter 6). Writers were concerned with "roots," feeling that vitality came from connection with ancestors as well as from new insights. It was prominent among American blacks searching for a tribal past, but can be seen in the following statement by a Canadian novelist, Margaret Laurence (1973: 203-5), who explains that real liberation comes not from turning one's back on his ancestral past but by knowing and using it:

For me the past is extremely real. I can't believe that all of life is contained today, and the past goes back a long way . . . Not only as far as one's own parents . . . but the grandparents and the distant ancestors, and a great deal is passed on . . . People change from generation to generation, but they don't change totally . . . I do have a very strong sense of a kind of tribal society.

Such turning to the past is recognition of the importance of redundancy in obvious and more subtle ways. The obvious way is that heredity *does* count. The subtler way is that, aside from genes, residues of the past carry through many generations by *communication:* as concepts, gestures, emotional tones (often called temperament), styles, and accents (I remember a speech teacher telling me that I had traces of a German accent, although that language had not been spoken in my family for several generations). The new emphasis was concern with keeping such things, a product of the feeling that redundancy was not merely useless baggage but a valuable resource necessary for living, working, creating. Closing to it was not regression but a move forward.

Separatism shows another gain from closing: generating the collective will to go it alone. One saw this in black nationalism, already mentioned; or in the thousands[2] of radical communes formed to try out new life styles, and composed of people who had dropped out of conventional economic, political, and religious activities. This phenomenon is described in the magazine *The Modern Utopian*, or in sociological studies like Rosabeth Kanter's *Commitment and Community* (1972) and Keith Melville's *Communes in the Counter Culture* (1972). Such groups, I say, generate the collective will to become an autonomous society and decide for themselves how they will live and how organize to do it. In such light might be seen the nationalist movement among French Canadians of Quebec during the 1960s, which sought to revive French language and culture, to break away from tradition and especially from English influence, and to modernize economically. From the "quiet revolution" emerged the Parti Québecois, which was militant in promoting French language and urging political (nonviolent) separation from the rest of Canada, though the majority of Quebec voters continued to reject such an extreme move (Astrachan, 1973). It should be plain that such separatism, generating the collective will and organization to go it alone, is more than mere nostalgia or emphasis on ethnicity. Going back and gathering with one's own kind is only part of such closing: More important is a synergy from within, a surge of collective vitality that enables the group to create, develop, and carry on with a new sense of togetherness, which is a loss for the larger group but a gain for the smaller one — when successful.

Nevertheless, it cannot be doubted that much closing, lacking the positive thrust of separatism, is merely defensive. "Backlashes," for example, seem to express the negative side: refusal, shutting out, closing *against*. So, in 1972, small towns in Alberta, Canada, renewed the fight to restrict the Hutterites, a growing religious sect, from buying more farm land. This growing group, with their Anabaptist beliefs and unique communal style of living, had failed to integrate with local communities, and indeed were so successful with cooperative buying and farming that they aroused a sense of threat among surrounding farmers and merchants which led to efforts to restore statutes that had formerly restricted them — a backlash for which the motive for closing ranks was mainly defense. There was little of the warm feeling that goes with ethnic and religious nostalgia. The same explanation applies to efforts by whites to prevent minority children from being transferred to white schools, as described by Lillian Rubin in *Busing and Backlash* (1972),[3] and to the "seething intolerance" of "long-haired" and Chicano styles in Taos, New Mexico, described by Melville (1972) as a three-way antagonism. As a "long-haired" commune dweller put it: "The locals aren't smiling . . . You may have heard stories of violence in Taos — believe them. This is not the place to come if you're not known here, have long hair, white skin, or black skin, or dress a little different" (142). Such backlashes are closing in self-defense with a feeling of antagonism toward the group causing the threat, closing in which warm feelings of revivalism or nostalgia (or such good redundancy) may be lacking. Rather, there is in backlashes a kind of spasmodic quality, a tightening of muscles and a striking back.

Such defensive closing shows the "keeping out" rather than the creative side. When closings are defensive, the prime questions are: By whom, and from what? Sheer noise might drive city people into soundproof offices and secluded dwellings, damping the urge to communicate with neighbors. The range of threats that might trigger defensive closing is wide. Some of it may be sheer territoriality, as ethologists like Ardrey (1966) describe it — the kind of reaction a stickleback shows when defending his nest. No one has settled the question of what innate boundaries lie beneath cultural ones in humans. Conspicuous in the seventies was the "police dog and padlock" syndrome, a panicky response to crime on the streets as seen in the condominium boom. Sugar Creek, a town near Houston, Texas, was planned to hold 3,000 homes surrounded by an electronic "wall" automatically monitored by a guard force which could scrutinize people coming in. "Snob zoning" seemed to reflect a combination of economic interest in protecting property values and middle-class status-panic. Tariff walls dictated by economic interests are another kind of defensive closing. Community resistance to freeways, subdivisions, and new industries in the name of "balanced" or "zero" growth, as well as efforts to preserve historical sites from bulldozers, were also defensive closing to what might be loosely called modernization or progress. The "pure" and "organic" food movement and the antifluoridation movement were forms of closing against dietary impurities. Of course there were also the time-honored responses of censorship and expurgation as ways of closing out ideas that seem dangerous.

It would be all too easy to assume that closing is merely biologically defensive, like buffalo forming a circle against a predator, closing ranks to better defend themselves. But, among humans at least, we may presume that closing has much to do with gaining and preserving *higher symbolic orders* (so much redundancy we have and need), including identity — a sense of who we are personally or collectively — and the life-style supporting same. When an alien group or strange information invades a community, it should be no surprise to find that closing centers on sharpening collective identity and preserving it from the noise of conflicting styles.[4] This is perhaps a clue to the British immigration problem, described by Prime Minister Edward Heath as an "invisible danger" to the country: "something seems deeply wrong but nobody seems to know what it is . . . It is hard to pin down and put a value to. It concerns the kind of country we want to live in and the kind of people we want to be. It concerns our traditional British way of doing things." The trouble was expressed by a London woman as inability "to identify the enemy. We'd unite if we could unite against something" (Nelson, 1972). It seems reasonable that such a malaise of disunity, and the inability to focus on all its causes, should lead to proposals for immigration restriction like those of Enoch Powell. Was it an altogether different phenomenon that caused Israel to refuse admission to more black "Israelites" settling in the Negev desert town of Dimona? These people from the United States claimed to be "Hebrew Israelites" mentioned in the tenth chapter of the Book of Genesis. "We do not need entry visas," they said, claiming that about 2,000,000 blacks in the United States were waiting to join them. But those who arrived did not integrate themselves into the Jewish community in spite of the offered hospitality, but practiced a kind of isolationism, even taking their children out of school. After four years of this, exasperated Israeli officials refused to admit arrivals, explaining: "Color has never been a criterion in our immigration policy. Many thousands of our people are dark skinned. . . . But we exist for the ingathering of the Jewish people. The members of the Dimona community are not Jews." (Ofner, 1971). Way of life, life-style, collective identity, seems to be one of the important things protected by closing to immigration. Such concerns may easily underlie closing rationalized on other grounds, such as property protection or even fear of "lawlessness."

Stronger closing is found in cults, which shows more of what is sought than merely excluded in tightening ties with one's fellows. The Amish, for example, are well known for keeping apart, and for not permitting their children to attend public schools, because they wish to preserve something precious, a spiritual intensity and purity, which would not be possible if they opened to prevailing life-styles. This plainly goes beyond horse-drawn carriages, long beards, rough buttonless clothing, and flat-brimmed hats. Their farming is sanctified; they live entirely with each other in "full fellowship," which requires strict conformity. They believe themselves to be chosen, "God's peculiar people," who should not be "yoked together" with unbelievers, every act of their life being designed to keep their sacred way intact and unprofaned by contacts with people outside their boundaries. To not belong to their fellowship means damnation. As described by John Umble, excommunication of members is "an awful and solemn procedure": "The members to be expelled had been notified in advance and were absent. An air of tenseness filled the house. Sad-faced women wept quietly; stern men sat with faces drawn. The bishop arose; with trembling voice and with tears on his cheek he announced that the guilty parties had confessed their sin, that they were cast off from the fellowship of the church and committed to the devil and all his angels" (Loomis, 1960:235).

Looking at the positive side, what a cult achieves when closure is successful and members are in good standing is a higher spiritual and symbolic unity than that of the community at large, as in the peculiar grace enjoyed by the Shakers, who close not only themselves off from the community but even the sexes from each other in marriage (resulting in a kind of coeducational monastery, one might say). This sect, which reached its peak of some 6,000 members in the 1850s, apparently achieved a startling success in finding the perfect life, which we may judge not only by their creativity in beautiful and distinctive art and furniture, but by an unusual state of grace that is evident from their records. Their dances — shuffling dances, skipping dances, ring dances, and square order shuffles, which visitors often came to watch — showed their ecstasy in whirlings, quakings, jerks, falling into trances, speaking in unknown tongues, and spontaneous songs. The high point, however, comes in special exclusive ceremonies — love feasts and pilgrimages — in which there are hugging and kissing by groups of the same sex; drinking "spiritual wine" and then acting like "fools"; tub baths, giving each other good scrubbings; and spiritual feasts of imaginary pomegranates, wine, and honey, which remove hunger for real food even on lengthy pilgrimages. As their own poem tells us, they seem to do as well with their "spiritual cake" as moderns with psychedelics:

There's something in the Shaker Cake
That does make souls contented here . . .
'Tis called in Scripture "living bread,"
Because it quickens from the dead. . .
No earthly substance we employ,
But just our inward peace and joy,
Nor is it any natural yeast
That gives us this continual feast. . .
Those who do all sin forsake,
May freely feast on this good cake. . .
It fills our souls with great delight,
Though 'tis to nature out of sight. . .

When a modern cultist reaches such ecstasy, he might speak as a convert to the Crusade for Christ did: "Everything — even the flowers and the leaves on the trees — looked different. I was finding out for the first time the sweetness and joy of God, of being truly born again." Or as this convert to the Self Realization Fellowship of Southern California said:

Then came the . . . great moment which instantly changed my life: I came face to face with the Master himself. When he looked into my eyes all my antagonism, all my doubts fell away and vanished. I realized that Paramhansa represented what I had long craved . . . ultimate truth. I became . . . his follower . . . and came to the Golden World Colony to make my future home. I have found peace.

Though we need not suppose that all cultic closing reaches a Shaker level of ecstasy, nor that it is a constant feature even in very closed cults,[5] plainly it does give a stronger shared experience of such things as warm fellowship, familial bonds, faith, consonance ("good vibes," redundancy, resonance), and mystique — transcendental consciousness — through rituals and teachings of one kind or another. So cult members usually speak of harmony, peace, and joy within the group that they cannot find in the world outside, as did the member of a Zen Buddhist community quoted in Chapter 2.

If a cult so reduces entropy for its members, it is not surprising that closed sharing should be regarded as a holy of holies, to be shielded from the profane. All cults do not, of course, maintain barriers against interaction with outsiders; but, even when relatively open in an urban environment, they are found, when studied, to maintain a higher rate of close and very special interactions with their own members, as illustrated by the "Shalom" commune (W. Erickson, 1973).

Thus cults give perhaps the sharpest picture of the gains from closing — not just the redundancy that comes from any gathering with one's own kind, but a special synergy that might not be possible in other groups (though this does not rule out therapy, education, sports, and so on, these activities being cultlike). Such synergy is found in warmer love, commitment, centering, reborn identity, and transcendental meaning (mystique, grace, holiness, gift of tongues, and so on) — not to speak of serenity from bad vibes. Judging from great movements like Christianity and Buddhism, it is hard to say how much synergy can come from cultic closing.

This is a different picture from that of the defensive closing of snobbery, secrecy, and "keeping out" spasms. Such things do show the negative side of closing: selfish privilege, bigotry, prejudice, restriction of information. Conflict emphasizes such aspects of closing to keep enemies at a distance, screw up courage, or to gain cohesion by projecting bad feelings outside to images of villains (Chapter 6), or even by manufacturing scapegoats, as shown in sociological studies like those describing the New England Puritans (K. Erikson, 1966) or the Soviet purges between 1936 and 1938 (O'Connor, 1972; Leites and Bernaut, 1954).

Yet, having looked at various aspects of ingrouping — ethnic, nostalgic, separatistic, defensive, spasmodic, and cultic — we should balance the positive with the negative side. Cults, especially, more frequently close *for* than they close against. Before we say they pay too high a price in cutting off information, we should be sure we know what they are gaining. As with the Amish, it may be something of higher value than what is outside. At least they believe so.

More broadly, what I am arguing is that closing is as needed as opening, even — perhaps especially — in a pluralistic society that wishes to preserve differences in value and style. We see ingroups trying to do this at many levels: families, cliques, communes, colonies, companies, neighbors — to say nothing of cults and fraternal orders — all of which close ranks from time to time to accentuate their own cohesion and identities.

Gatekeepers help sort and control the flow, allowing time for decision, assimilation, and common will, of which avoiding information overload is no small part. So it seems that a pluralistic open society forms opinion through ingrouping — opinion that it cannot form through media held open by rules like "freedom of the press." In addition, closing generates valuable efforts through ingroups that feed into the broader effort of the whole society, as with the "ethnic" vote. Society mobilizes energy by enlisting ingroups, not by by-passing them. However open or closed the system may be, reduction of entropy sometimes requires ingrouping for gains of good redundancy and new synergy. As I have suggested, closing is typically triggered by overloads of banality and other noise.

Such rhythms of ingrouping seem part of a yet larger pattern. Let us see.

The communication pulse of nature

> To everything there is a season. . .
> a time to get and a time to lose;
> a time to keep and time to cast away. . .
> a time to keep silence, and a time to speak.
> (Ecclesiastes 3:1—7)

The eye opens and closes like a camera shutter. If we let our imagination go, there seems to be a sort of eye working as a gateway of information at various levels. I've already likened turning off to the mind pulling down a window shade to close out noise or anything boring. Many levels of life seem to have shutters whose opening and closing brings about a kind of communication "pulse," the flow varying from ebbs to surges.

Opening and closing seems to be even a basic property of protoplasm. Biologists say that coping with a changing environment requires a mechanism to control diffusion and interchange. To withstand drying, for example, pores must close or water be stored if more water cannot readily be found. Likewise for control of temperature, gas pressures, light, salt concentration, and so on. Jonas Salk (1973) says that the first enclosing in the evolution of life was formation of a cell membrane that allowed the creation and maintenance of an internal state different from the external environment, with the DNA molecule able to replicate such a system in genetic and somatic material. The semipermeable membrane of the cell has the job of remaining always closed to some things, and accepting others depending on need and relative concentration. This membrane is perhaps the first "shutter" of life. Of course life molecules such as DNA, enzymes, and antibodies select and reject one another. At any rate, closing seems a basic property of protoplasm: building and repeating its own structure for which the information is enclosed in a genetic code, rejecting what is not like itself, relying on a selective membrane if not more sophisticated defenses and gateways.

Going up the life scale, we see various kinds of organismic opening and closing: the seasonal greening of plants with the flow of sap then withering, a sea anemone in a tidepool extending and retracting its green tentacles (or the opening and closing of plants like the venus fly trap, morning glory, mimosa), and molluscs withdrawing into shells, the flow of impulses across nerve synapses, circulation and coagulation of blood, tensing and relaxing, and hibernation. There are passive and active styles of opening and closing illustrated by the sedentary clam, waiting with valves open for what comes along, shutting when it doesn't like it; the humming bird, seeking, darting in and out, quickly bored and moving on; and the anteater, a more aggressive opener, roving, thrusting his claws, ripping open ant hills, and devouring every scurrying insect. Such modes, active or passive, are gateways of an organismic opening and closing.

Similarly, at the level of an entire species there is opening and closing.[6] One kind is mating with one's own while failing to interbreed with other species — a way of protecting the gene pool from excessive variation or noise of combinations that might lack survival value. Another form of species closing is what Lorenz called flocking, and Ardrey the "social contract": an inherited need to be together in some kind of bunch, whether mating, or herd, or pack, or colony; and at other times a need to break from the group, to disperse for mating, food, or other reasons. Yet another form of species opening and closing is found in population "crashes," such as lemming migrations, in which, for obscure reasons, a species thins out its own numbers by suicidal behavior or surges that exhaust food supplies.

At the neural level also we experience the "ups" and "downs" of biorhythms, a whole procession of opening and closing moods: a shopping spree followed by saving austerity, euphoria and gloom, outgoingness and inwardness, friendliness and bad temper, drowsiness and alertness, interest and boredom, wakefulness and sleep, the child reaching out, then turning to its mother. Within our minds, thoughts move from thinking enclosed within logic to daydreaming, dreaming, and mysticism; brain waves from beta to alpha to theta. We note longer cycles of illness and health, menstrual periods, beginning and retiring from a career, and indeed the entire life as opening and closing, from the risks of youth to the stock-taking of age. Our senses are continually scanning for what is needed and avoiding what is detrimental — "turning off" ranging from momentary loss of interest to durable closing such as setting one's teeth against something (hardening the heart and will, being "through with" that), or alienated despair or anorexia, extreme forms of "closing the account" with life. In such ways, our inner rhythms are like a pulse.

At the level of society, as I said, it is a matter of communication pulse and social boundaries keeping a proper balance between inner and outer traffic.[7] People naturally try to maintain this balance by such devices as castes marrying according to rules, sects shunning and excommunicating, professions setting standards, nations forming immigration policies, or crusading movements (Klapp, 1969:257—311) trying to clean up corruption and purge villainy. So the societal "shutter" works to enforce boundaries against inimical messages, and to encourage internal communication such as fraternization, ceremony, and the sharing of we-reinforcing information to build up group memory, pride, identity, and will. Whether or not we agree with such aims, it seems to me wrong to characterize a closed group or "closed mind" as always bad. What is going on is an effort to find the best tradeoff between too much variety and too much banality, both of which are bad. A fixed policy, whether of opening or closing, cannot do this. The balance needed changes with circumstances. There are times when we need more reinforcement by good old redundancy, and times when exciting novelty and surprises are just the ticket.

The opening phase is illustrated by outgoing flows, such as mass tourism, more cultural exchanges, ecumenism, national expansion, a time of "letting go" as in the English Restoration after Cromwell, surges of student rebellion like the "Events of May" 1968 in France (Seeman, 1972), mass revivalism outside churches,[8] or the spiritual search for transcendence mentioned in Chapter 8.

So in saying that societies have a kind of shutter, I am only reiterating that at any level of life the natural pattern is alternation of opening and closing; the more alive a system is, the more alertly it does both. Closing is neither permanent, nor as some suppose merely a setback to progress, but evidence that the shutter of life is working selectively. A perpetually open society would suffer the fate of a perpetually open clam.

The English language gives a clue as to how important opening and closing are in daily life. As far as I can tell from exploring the dictionary and thesaurus, there are four broad categories of synonyms for opening and closing, two with good connotations and two with bad — thus favoring neither opening nor closing. To describe the process in a balanced way, one would have to use words from all the categories: (1) bad closing, (2) good closing, (3) bad opening, and (4) good opening, as already listed in Chapter 1. Plainly, wisdom has a place for all of these views: repression as bad closing, but self-control as good closing; folly and crime as bad opening, but self-expression as good opening; bigotry as bad closing, but a connoisseur's discrimination as good closing; indiscriminate taste as bad opening, but open-mindedness as good; secretiveness as bad closing; but discretion as good; tactlessness as bad opening, but honest outspokenness as good. Or in the manner of changing opinion: rigid as bad closing, but firm or incorruptible as good; licentious as bad opening, but libertarian as good. Or finally, at the biological level: degenerative inbreeding as bad closing, but selective breeding as good; or mongrelization as bad opening, but cross-fertilization good. There is little doubt that, should we find an individual with almost all the traits of bad closing, or bad opening, we should have an unpleasant man. On the other hand, if we found one with the judgment and self-control of an incorruptible saint or connoisseur, combined with open-mindedness, sympathy, and understanding, we should have someone close to the wisdom that philosophers have always sought. At the social level, a society full of bad closing would be boring and frustrating, like a prison; but if it were always opening badly, it would be a hodgepodge, eyesore, trash heap, or dump. If, on the other hand, it had qualities of good closing *and* good opening, it might be a treasury of fine things representing the best from everywhere, a selection of man's highest accomplishments, rather like the Louvre or the British Museum. Such seems the ideal of what civilization should be.

But, if one looks at the world today — its noise, bad vibes, and creeping banalities — one wonders if modern society does not seem to have been less than successful in getting on the good side of this balance sheet. Do not more words from both bad sectors of closing and opening apply than words from the good sectors? Society seems to have disturbed the natural rhythms of opening and closing by violating rules of good communication, by too often getting stuck in the bad sectors of opening (noise) and closing (banality).

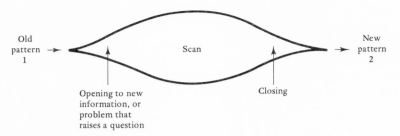

Figure 4. Discovery as closure

Steering a course requires closing to directions other than where one is going. Even discovery of what one does not yet know requires a certain amount of closure.

Discovery is closure

Writers, artists, scientists, and other creative people retire to secluded places to do their work. They know that discovery is not all scanning, and that it is possible to be swamped with information one cannot use. They realize what Gestalt psychologists have said about creativity: that it is closure to a *good* pattern from many possibilities, as one way of seeing things that necessarily excludes other ways at that moment. Or as John Dewey said and as Kenneth Burke (1936) reemphasized, "every insight is a blindness." Discovery is not an arrangement of all the information poured in, like a hand dealt in cards, but *closure* to what is needed for one's own jigsaw puzzle, and exclusion of the rest. Too many pieces might hide forever the finding of the fit. Once a pattern has been perceived, ninety percent of information becomes irrelevant (see Chapter 4). Discovery, in other words, is an outflow from within seeking what is needed to make a pattern, not an inflow from without.

Those who see only the *intake* side of learning are likely to overstress the *scanning* part of discovery — the enthusiastic collection of data and points of view without getting around to the output of pattern (design, theory), which by selecting information, makes discovery or creation possible. In other words, the diagram of discovery has *closure at both ends,* as is illustrated in Figure 4. For example, an artist finding interesting new material or discontented with what he has already done, sketches and models — and thereby scans the possibilities and draws on his inner resources, including redundancy, until he intuitively closes to a new design, then finishes to the degree of perfection required.[9] Likewise, a scientist, after using redundancy, which consists of the information available in his field, scans new data by observation and experiment, and looks for a solution to the problem to which he feels present answers are unsatisfactory. He closes but, instead of finishing to perfection, he reopens his new pattern to further verification and modification.

Intuitions, chance perceptions, even dreams, may help the scientist as well as the artist in both scanning and closure. Some psychologists hold that the function of sleep is to allow one to put the brain's computer "off line" (not available to input but still working) long enough for it to reprogram itself by dreams, which scan one's "interior landscape" (Evans, 1973). In short, the creative mind continually opens and closes; but, as I said, there is a tendency to overemphasize intake from outside, and to neglect the equally important fact that discovery requires closure — of course, *good* closing (as described by words like those in the category discussed above: wise, discriminating, expert, and so forth).

The creator, then, seeking good opening and good closing, and trying to avoid bad opening and bad closing, plays a sort of game. He will lose if he closes in the wrong ways; for example, in banality, stereotypy, rigidity, or bigotry, which function rather like a camera fastened in one position or with its shutter jammed. People become doctrinaire if their minds close for too long, as is seen in some Freudians and Marxists, or in an artist who settles down to one style for the rest of his career and does not continue to "grow." One kind of bad closing is to be so committed to a certain method that one applies it to every problem, even allowing it to select the problem. In the human sciences, one might see this among those who insist that all data must be "operationalized" or quantified. (As one devotee put it to me: "If you can't put it in a table, it's literature and to hell with it.")

Yet, to solve any problem, one must close on something. Opening is only a beginning, a search, not a solution. So error is possible both ways. *Romantic openers* are those who mistake the way (scanning) for the destination, those who hold that opening is inherently and always good, and closing always bad. Anarchists, for example, may propose discarding all enforced rules in society and relying on good will to provide consensus as needed. They would like to run the ball game, so to speak, without an umpire. Good luck to them! I fear they will need it.

Likewise modernists who embrace every change without reckoning side effects, and who throw away too much good redundancy (as explained in the last chapter), also need a lot of luck. On the other hand, *romantic closers* hanker too much for a golden age of morality and order, and call for more control, law, planning, logic, discipline, and consistency, and fail to appreciate the value of letting people try out things as they please. In short, the romantic opener has too much tolerance for variety: He wants to plunge into change, perhaps without even looking back. The romantic closer makes just the opposite error of not scanning for enough variety before turning back to good redundancy.

To a point, both closers and openers are right. That is, there is leeway in most environments for variety of styles (as with the clam and the hummingbird, or the goat who eats almost anything and the koala bear who eats only eucalyptus leaves). Among artists, one sees opening and closing styles. Picasso, for example, was hard to pin down to a particular style — at one time neoclassicist, at another Cubist or surrealist. His studio might almost have reminded one of a feverish monkey pulling open boxes, with its clutter of oddments — pieces of glass, a hollow elephant's foot, African drums, a bird cage, wooden crocodiles, bits of bicycles, old hats, bullfight posters, and so on — any of which he might use for serious or impish creations. He was a protean artist of many styles, whose whole life was an exploration. As he once said: "For me, a picture is neither an end nor an achievement but rather a lucky chance . . . I try to represent what I have found, not what I am seeking. I do not seek, — I find" (Whitman, 1973). When asked by a visitor, "What is art?" Picasso replied, "What is not?" and proved his point by joining a bicycle seat with handle bars to make a bull's head. In contrast with this eclectic genius, who improvised on impulse, lived in disorder, accepted clutter, and made use of everything, there are artists such as the classicist Degas[10] whose success seems due to almost the opposite strategy: every work planned, studios neat, and styles stable, however original the creations. The engraver Ingres and the painters Braque and Matisse developed a style and followed it fairly consistently. Matisse, a friend of Picasso, had almost an opposite temperament. Francoise Gilot describes Matisse's inner peace and self-contentment, which contrasted with Picasso's feverish energy: "Pablo had almost a reverence for Matisse because Matisse's manner reflected an inner balance, a calm that brought peace even to a man such as Pablo" (Gilot, 1964:32). Perhaps one might say that Picasso's disorder was an open game, whereas Matisse closed to perfection. In music, classical compositions show closed perfection whereas modernists such as Schoenberg or Cage seem to want to open scores to almost any kind or order of sound. Again, in literature, Proust was a great closer, writing, for example, from recollection of the flood of memories that came back from tasting a cookie. His creativity was in telling what *had* already happened instead of inventing what might happen. Zola constructed novels out of voluminous notebooks of observation, whereas Maupassant spun a story from the clue of a piece of string. So it would seem that opening and closing are both successful styles. Closed stylists evolve along a line, select what is to their own purpose, close out clutter, seek order in classic form, balance, poise, symmetry, perfect pattern. Open stylists take many directions, voraciously use ideas and media, accept clutter, often live in disorder, improvise impulsively, and achieve intensity — perhaps Dionysian, grotesque, or impish — rather than the calms of perfection.

I haven't meant to overdraw such a difference between artists, and still less to imply that an opener is always open and a closer always closed.[11] Most are somewhere between. The difference between open and closed styles is mostly in the *amount of scanning* felt necessary before solution. The opener stays open longer — perhaps one might say he more enjoys roaming, surveying, watching what others are doing, kibitzing, than does the closer. Staying open longer, he gains a better chance of finding everything, but also risks shallow eclecticism, even drowning in information. The closer, on the other hand, is more quickly satiated with variety, relies more on inner redundancy and intuition, emphasizes privacy, seeks perfection from selecting facts to fit an ideal, and makes fewer kinds of things out of fewer kinds of things. But, like the observer who leaves his post too soon, he may miss vital clues that the opener will catch. Yet the closer may have his design done before the opener even gets through scanning. You can't have it both ways.

Societies, too, can go to extremes of opening and closing. Perhaps the information overload described in Chapter 4 is such an extreme. If all citizens were Voltaires, a democracy might be late in experiencing information overload. But with a good proportion of Archie Bunkers, the limit of opening is reached sooner. However, it is not a question of level of education, as I have already implied. Let us put a democracy of Platos beside one of Voltaires. Then we should probably see a difference between closed and open styles of society, with both making the best of their chances. It is a question of the amount of order felt necessary to achieve good variety, and the amount of variety felt compatible with good order, with proportionate emphasis on boundaries. One can see such a contrast in the golden age of Greece, between Spartan collectivism and Athenian liberalism. Or today, some religions, for example the Amish, stress purity, sharp collective identity, high consensus, and stability by closing to variety from outside. The Quakers, on the other hand, keep open relations with the rest of society, scan more, change more, have less distinctive dogma and collective identity, and nevertheless reach consensus and high morale for what they wish to do — including resisting demands of the political system for military service. So the closure of an open group, when it comes, can be as firm as that of a closed group. Both styles are successful in their own way.

It is hard to deal with such a topic in an unbiased way, because we all come from societies and backgrounds with their own leanings toward closure or openness, and their own experience of extremes. Having sung the praises of redundancy in the last chapter, and deplored the ills of information overload, perhaps I have leaned toward closing at this time and place. But might there not also be a bias in social theorists who treat closure of mind or society as something always to be avoided, and who imply that opening is always better than closing? I think Karl Popper was rather unfair to Plato in labeling him a totalitarian for holding up his ideal of a closed society in which the wisdom of the few filtered justice to the many. Popper says Plato betrayed his teacher Socrates, who was "the champion of the open society and a friend of democracy," by his "grandiose efforts to construct the theory of the arrested society." (1952:191—4) So Plato:

spread doubt and confusion among equalitarians and individualists who, under the influence of his authority, began to ask themselves whether his idea of justice was not truer and better than theirs . . . equalitarianism was his archenemy, and he was out to destroy it . . . Plato recognizes only one ultimate standard, the interest of the state . . . this is the collectivist, the tribal, the totalitarian theory of morality. (Popper 1952:92—3, 107)

Yet, concedes Popper, Plato was a "sincere" totalitarian because his ideal was not exploitation of the people by the upper class but the "stability of the whole." (108) Plato's idea was that decision by the few people who have the most knowledge and virtue is better on the average than decision by many people. In fairness to Plato, one must ask, who has proven that rule by the wise would not work?

Is it not at least possible that some thinkers have been so enthralled by the ideal of a completely open society — especially by J. S. Mill's free market of ideas — that they lean too far toward opening and don't fully recognize needs for closure? I have in mind those already designated as romantic openers. But even social scientists are not immune to bias toward opening. The famous study, *The Authoritarian Personality* (Adorno, et al., 1950:976) cites a rather unpleasant list of characteristics associated with people of closed outlook, such as rigidity, bigotry, ethnocentrism, anxiety, repressiveness, power-orientation, aggressiveness, even potential fascism. Other studies find the advantage to be with openers, such as highly creative people who "show a preference for, an interest in, complexity and novelty," are less rigidly controlled, and have a better sense of humor (Berelson and Steiner, 1964:229—30). Psychologist Milton Rokeach (1960:23) finds the closed mind to be structurally (and, one presumes, more or less permanently) rigid, dogmatic, rejecting, and anxious: "The closed mind, through fear of the new, is a passive mind . . . There is a dynamic unwillingness to 'play along,' 'entertain' strange belief systems." Another psychologist, Charles Hampden-Turner (1971), finds the radical to be the good man, frank and open to others, tolerant, creative, synergic, and self-actualized; whereas the conservative is closed, avoids contact, does not reach out or use or give feedback to bridge the gap between himself and others, is cripplingly incompetent, and is therefore anomic. The open man goes up the helix of development, whereas the closed goes down to "failure of existence." (79)[12] Such a separation of openers and closers into categories of "saved" and "damned," respectively, does seem rather hard on the happy Amish and Shakers, as well as run against the view of those sociologists who, after Durkheim, see anomie as a predicament of some *openers* when they sacrifice too many group ties and try to go on their way alone. Why may not one say that both opening and closing can be creative, and that both opening and closing in some cases can be anomic, as with other extremes? To appreciate openness, is it necessary to have society rushing pell-mell into the limitless freedom and change of a "temporary society" (Bennis and Slater, 1968)?

Again, it is easy to understand the enthusiasm of an architect like Lawrence Halprin (1969:20) for "open scoring" as a way of developing a community plan or just about any complex enterprise — a public program, building, plaza, dance performance, or other communal art. But need one go so far as to deplore any system that is closed? — "a closed and defined body with a beginning and an end. A system has a goal and in order to achieve the goal establishes a specific way or technique of operation. A system is logical and sequential; it requires input, but not feedback. A system implies order . . . starts with a preordained mission" (195). So Halprin says that closed, goal-oriented systems "trap" us into failures, the "chaos of our cities and the confusion of our politics." The right approach is hope-oriented "open scoring," which − like open scores of dance, theater, and music − establishes "lines of action" to which performers contribute by improvising in constant interaction, changing as they go along, until they see what structure comes out, as in a "happening." (Halprin, 1969:4, 20, 195) Yet, for all the success of "open scoring" in arts such as modern jazz or dance, or ecological systems so vast that it is foolishness to imagine that one plans them, may one say that open is always better than closed planning for Beethoven as well as John Cage, for Frank Lloyd Wright as well as Halprin? Rather, a more tenable position seems to be that both closed plans and open scores are useful, depending on the occasion.

Romanticism, whether of openers or closers, goes too far in praising only one end of this spectrum. This analysis suggests that both opening and closing are right at proper times − and all solutions, even the most creative, sooner or later require closing. We should avoid seeing closing merely in terms of such concepts as rejection and narrowness, for this view fails to recognize that closing can be creative and wise − part of the strategy for living. Even an offensive spearhead gains stronger thrust from closing the defense perimeter or shortening lines of supply. As we have seen in Chapter 6, good closing has many advantages besides defensive ones: good redundancy − the strength of "old truths," "wisdom," renewed contact with one's own values and identity − which can help synergy, discovery, and meaning while reducing the information overload described in Chapter 4. In such light, one cannot say that openness (scanning for variety) is always good and closing always bad. Rather, they are both part of a natural oscillation in the game of life. If you bet always on one direction of a pendulum, you will be wrong half the time.

The game of life

In broadest terms I would define the game of life as the effort of living things, from the cell to the society, to win information from the environment and to build their own order − whether or not at the expense of others. So a biologist says: "All cells have built-in feedback controls that automatically tell them what to do to survive . . . indeed they are purposeful. Their purpose is to survive, and if they have an independent existence, their built-in purpose is to survive and multiply. Their adaptive stratagems to accomplish these ends are many and marvelous" (Potter, 1971:172). Living things maintain steady states by homeostasis, offsetting inputs that otherwise would change or destroy them. So life is dedicated to resist entropy, the tendency toward the disorder, randomness, "shuffledness," or "running down" described in the Second Law of Thermodynamics. The game against entropy is played by taking and using information, whether as organic molecules and genes on the one hand, or as codes, habits, memories, knowledge, and culture on the other hand. A biologist (Quastler, 1964:4) calculates that a bacterium contains one thousand bits of information — a particular pattern as unlikely as a coin toss turning up "heads" one thousand times in a row. Even in their molecules, living things are loaded with information drawn from environments and ancestors. So the famous dictum of the chemist Schrodinger, "Life feeds on negative entropy," says no more than that life hungers for information. Being organized to defeat entropy by encoding information and reading feedback from the environment is what makes life forms more alive than machines. So all organisms are committed to a mortal game of defeating entropy, a game in which the options are to win, in the sense of holding one's own or better, or to lose.

Such a game is played by scanning and sorting both food and information from the environment, opening and closing to get most of the best and least of the worst. There is a parallel between food[13] and information. For example, information can be scarce (as in the case of hunters tracking game) or plentiful but polluted (as in the case of misleading clues deliberately left by a criminal). Table 1 shows the parallel, from deprivation (pollution, scarcity) to overload. The organism responds to varying conditions of information, sometimes hungrily open and scanning, and sometimes closed or cautiously selective. For optimal intake, not just a certain amount but a *balance* of kinds of information (such as facts versus meanings, variety versus good redundancy, affection versus impersonality, honesty versus manipulation, ceremony versus matter-of-factness, we-reference versus thing-reference, nature versus artificiality) is needed. As I have said, the noise-filled environment of modern life gives a poor mix and is often inimical, requiring more closing than

Table 1. *Parallel between food and information*

	Food	Information
Overload	Gluttony and its illnesses	Information-overload, irrelevance (Chapter 3)
Optimum	Balanced nutrition	Problem-solving, adequate education
Scarcity	Starvation, malnutrition	Sensory deprivation, hunger for education, censorship, bafflement, banality, emotional flatlands
Pollution	Poisoning	Negative contagion, deception, manipulation betrayal, etc. (bad vibes)

opening even in the midst of hunger. As with food, we can become so used to pollution of information that we no longer notice how bad things taste.

If a camera shutter were to become stuck open, it could take in much that would spoil the film. If a ventilating system failed to either keep out or let in fresh air at appropriate times, it could not maintain the needed balance. So it is, I have suggested, with the shutters of the mind and of society. The game is played by alternately opening and closing to get more variety (fresh air) or more redundancy (warm air). When nothing of much worth is coming in, the mind has the capacity to internally generate either variety or redundancy, commonly called day-dreaming and creativity, or memories. So boredom from information poverty (banality) of the environment is lessened. A different situation may require all channels to open to what is coming in, to get the most of, for example, a work of art, an experience of grace, a friendship. The goal remains to get the most of the best and the least of the worst of what is out there. Whatever the items of such a balance may be, they can be summed up by putting them into the four categories[14] already identified: good opening, good closing, bad opening, bad closing. In this way we can reckon how well we are doing in the game of life.

Let us visualize this game occurring on a playing field with four sectors. The two northern sectors are good redundancy and good variety. The object of the game is to kick a ball as far as one can northwardly

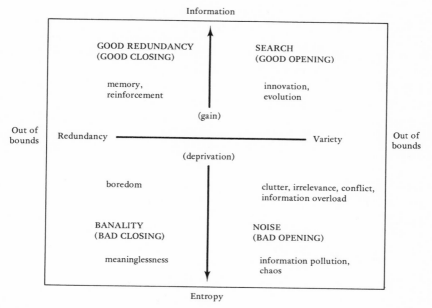

Figure 5. "Ballpark" of the game of life

toward the center line. But a strong, variable, southerly wind keeps blowing the ball back and to one side or the other. Landing in lower sectors means negative scores. One must play toward the center, for going off on either side requires starting at the bottom again. Figure 5 depicts this playing field. The winning movement of this game would be to go up the middle of the field, gaining information with every play and falling back as little as possible. Of course one can't keep the ball from veering to one side or the other. Sometimes one is kicking from a position of redundancy, sometimes from variety. The point is that one can't make a good play unless one knows in what sector he is. Being far out in variety requires a kick toward redundancy, rather than directly northward into discovery, as the wind might easily blow one out of bounds. On the other hand, to be deeply into redundancy calls for a kick toward search, even at risk of landing in noise. Opening and closing depend on where one is and how the wind is blowing. No constant policy (such as romantic opening or romantic closing) is right for all occasions. Getting the best score requires swinging from one side to the other.

I hope this metaphor makes plainer the plays of the game of life as swings between the adventure of opening to variety and closing to redundancy. Looking back at the words that English language speakers associate with opening and closing, one can see that they describe such kinds of success and mistakes. There are times when we should be open to criticism but closed to discouragement, open to suggestion but closed to bad advice, open to persuasion but closed to seduction, broadminded but not indiscriminate, critical but not intolerant, charitable but not an easy mark, frank but not tactless, discreet but not secretive, adventurous but not foolish. In more general terms, good variety is sought by scanning while bad variety is avoided by closing or filtering. Good redundancy is sought by closing, while bad is suffered as boring restriction from which one sooner or later tries to escape by opening to something new.

Information imbalance

Information imbalance, then, is being too long in a losing position in this game, that is, playing too much on one side or the other, especially in a lower sector of the field. In modern society most of us do play from lower sectors much of the time: we get too much banality and other kinds of noise, we are restricted mentally while we enjoy a mountain of consumer goods, we are enervated by pushbutton living that lacks the challenge of effort and the joy of creativity. Cut off from reality by blanding and cosmetics, we need good reinforcement while at the same time we suffer intrusions of physical and semantic noise in a general environment of information overload. Worse, "bad vibes" come in a flood of negative contagions, perceived manipulation, and threats to collective identity, which trigger backlashes and Archie Bunkerism. Meanwhile, others search from a fogged land for a transcending beacon. In such an information environment the ratio of noise to signals is too high; the stuck shutter lets in or closes out too many of the wrong things.

Such imbalance of information means a low-grade environment in which it is hard to get what one needs. Again, food supplies the parallel. Long before knowledge of vitamins, one could see that people were suffering from, for example, scurvy, which was in some mysterious way remedied by lime juice. Today people suffer from noise without realizing what is lacking. Balanced communication would be the right mix of messages frequently enough for people to feel well. In a polluted information environment, whatever is needed is not often enough available. And what is harmful is all too often available. For example, the person who needs friends may find nothing but manipulation. Even if a city does, in theory, offer rich enough diversity to find balance in communication, the opportunities may be so fragile, and the public domain of information so polluted by banality and other noise, that the very diversity is defeating, and triggers spasms of closing, as I have noted.

Strategies of coping

Whatever the situation, whether rich or poor in information, one must make a response involving: 1) scanning to see what is at hand; 2) awareness of gain or loss (interest awakened, gratification, bafflement, boredom, and so on) perhaps by comparison with a standard such as noise/signal ratio; 3) decision (closure) to some pattern as a goal; 4) opening and closing to get more of that goal and to avoid the rest. Sometimes scanning is the best policy; at other times it is turning off. For example, a person might climb a mountain looking for adventure, then after appraising his experience, either become a mountain climber or never climb again.

Coping requires continual maneuvering, depending on feedback (Singer, 1973), one's own state (fatigue, age, needs, satiation, and so forth), and one's position on the playing field. Inundated by noise and bad vibrations, one turns toward good closing. Stifled by the banality of a plastic world, one may seek good opening. In other words, there are two main lines of winning play, which range from bad opening to good closing, and from bad closing to good opening. And there are two losing directions: toward bad opening, and toward bad closing.

Bad opening to good closing

So the game of life gives us a picture in which we may place what has been said about lost past and identity (Chapter 6) and ingrouping: efforts to close out noise and bad vibes, and move toward resonance and synergy; or, one might put it, kicks toward the favorable sector of good redundancy.

Such a strategy is called for especially in conditions involving intrusive noise, information overload, insufficient reinforcement, and profanation. Intrusive noise should be distinguished from that which is merely fatiguing and boring (sometimes called "white" noise). People turn off easily from such lowgrade noise; but intrusive noise, because so stressful, demands prompt and vigorous closure — not just the yawn of boredom, but the slamming of a window or the soundproofing of walls. At such a point, noise and strangeness turn from interesting variety and adventure to threat. For example, when privacy is prized and habitual, bad opening will be soon felt as threat. The contrast between American openness and the British and French love of privacy has often been noted. Perhaps such a revealing television documentary as "An American Family" was possible only in a country with an ethic of openness and disclosure. But Americans, too, have their limit, at which telephones are unlisted and photographer's cameras are sometimes smashed.

Information overload (Chapter 3) also calls for good closing. When faced with the prospect of becoming scavengers or junk men if we take it all in, we dare not remain in the predicament of the open tape recorder, merely a conduit, but must select information according to our own needs: Scan, rank, pick from the top; take the best and ignore the rest. This may mean "skating on thin ice" as far as other information is concerned. Such trade-off is unavoidable, because, unless one scans and skates, he will be in deeper trouble from the irrelevance that will bog him down altogether. So the normal response to information overload is selective exposure (as when media audiences listen only to opinion leaders congenial to their own views), along with a certain amount of life-style insulation (as when a person tries to create for himself an island of taste), or "positive thinking," or specialization of work (in which other people or computers are perhaps used for scanning).

The third condition that often justifies good closing occurs when people don't get enough reinforcement by signals of redundancy, such as "that's okay" or "we are your kind." Because they don't hear the right accents or see familiar faces and gestures, they can't resonate and therefore easily feel alone. When there is no Royal Canadian Mounted Police to rush in, people feel on their own, defenseless, perhaps deserted. So they turn to smaller groups for the support on which they can count. High on the list of conditions inclining people to close is lack of reinforcement for identity, as pointed out in Chapter 6. Yet, mass society is precisely the kind that gives poor networks of support while overloading people with noise and banality, no small part of which is the multiplicity of models in the media which offer vicarious experience but which do not offer opportunity for validation by real reference groups. In such circumstances, people will close to some kind of redundancy, even the "pseudo-community" of suburbia (Sennett, 1970).

Oscar Newman's (1972) concept of "defensible space" describes the need for good closing to remedy the bad opening of cities — a need that could possibly be filled by architectural design. Anonymous cities have produced jungles of crime — public areas that are so open that anyone can come and go, but few notice or care what he does there. Such areas become "gauntlets" which citizens, even police, fear. The solution is to create "defensible space" by grouping dwelling units to encourage mutual activities, delineating paths, assigning areas near living quarters to particular users, and improving opportunities for visual surveillance so that residents can "easily perceive and control all activity taking place." By encouraging "territorial attitudes," people living in such an area, feeling it to be "their" place, become a group willing to defend it.

Profanation is a powerful closing trigger, a condition under which one feels called on to gird up one's loins, rally around the flag, or protect a holy symbol from degradation or impurity. Cults are especially sensitive because their sacred rituals and fragile higher states are so easily spoiled; even by "little things." So they often have special devices of boundary maintenance (Kanter, 1972) and keep closed to "the world" (Troeltsch, 1931).

Plainly, for such reasons, closing is a useful strategy, giving advantages that larger nets cannot. When it is too hard to get favorable signals from a noise-loaded society, falling back to the redundancy and synergy of smaller groups may seem the only way — so, at least, conclude many kinds of groups whose motto seems to be "take care of ourselves, let others go to hell." It is, one might say, a kind of purchase, a method of seeking a better rate of information exchange, whether through a cult, a fraternal organization, or by leaving the loneliness of an apartment for the involved community living of a mobile home park. What one gets, besides the practical advantages of closing ranks, is a richer mix of such things as congruent communication through better feedback, which enables one to become a more fulfilled person (Rogers, 1961). Indeed, there is no reason to suppose that closing into unions, reunions, happy hearths, communions, and so on cannot lead to "peak" experiences (Maslow, 1968). In other words, all peaks are not results of opening. The crusade is also a synergic closing movement, able to give stronger identity from its sense of striking a good blow to restore the right, as I have analyzed elsewhere (1969:257—311). For such benefits people seek good closing.

But of course there are serious mistakes of closing. It becomes a losing game when the tradeoff of variety for redundancy demands too high a price. The psychologist Hampden-Turner (1970) explains such costs in terms of anomie. Also, Karl Deutsch (1966:221—8) outlines six kinds of failure of political systems that become too closed for their own good: 1) loss of power over the environment; 2) loss of effectiveness of information channels from the outside world; 3) loss of steering capacity or coordination, that is, control over its own behavior; 4) loss of depth of memory — storage retrieval, recombination, and judgment of data; 5) rigidity in learning and rearranging inner patterns; 6) loss of capacity for deep changes such as reformation, rebirth, or conversion. Each of these failures comes from valuing some kind of data or memories over others that are neglected, so that systems become crippled, stagnant, imprisoned "in an invisible rut of their own making" (224). And so in Chapter 6 we have described the box of banality as bad closing.

W. Ross Ashby (1956)[15] has explained mathematically why a system must have a minimal amount of variety — more than the variety of that which it controls if it is to be dominant. A simple illustration comes from chess — a queen can defeat a bishop or castle because she has a greater variety of moves. This is another way of seeing the point at which closing ceases to be good strategy.

Perhaps the worst trade-offs come from *spasms*, which slam the door too hard, closing off much information for little, if any, gain. They are not the closure of discovery, of zeroing in on a target, but are motivated by negative feelings like anxiety, alienation, and hostility — as medieval people locked themselves in to escape plagues, at whatever cost in intercourse with the world outside. An obvious example is censorship, which deprives many of knowledge in order to protect a few from possible detriment or from their own weakness of judgment. A "busing backlash" (Rubin, 1972) deprives schoolchildren of interesting contacts with other races and classes for dubious gains beyond relief of parents' anxiety. Separatism for independence sometimes runs the risk of *self-ghettoization*, a danger encountered by the Welsh in relations with the English, or by Quebecers considering whether to follow the Parti Quebecois or to keep the economic benefits of Federalism in Canada. When wealthy city dwellers rush into guarded condominiums, they too run the risk of creating inverted ghettos, in which the law-abiding are locked in while criminals enjoy liberty outside. Another cost of spasmodic closing is that negativism takes the place of constructive policy. So sociologists (Horton and Thompson, 1962) found that alienated people, feeling powerless and resentful, turn out strongly to vote *against* things they don't like — an outlet for protest — but give little support to constructive measures that might do them more good. Such negative closing — censorship, self-ghettoization, and negativism — show that turning off can demand too high a price.

Scapegoating is in a class by itself as a kind of bad closing. Few words need be spent on its injustice and its part in prejudice and persecution (Allport, 1954:243—60). In the famous trial of Oscar Wilde, for example, we see that scapegoating was a closing of ranks by a more or less hypocritical society against someone who was blamed unfairly, and that people felt better for having driven him out (as the goat was driven out in the Book of Leviticus, 16:20—2). A scapegoat is cast as the villain in a social melodrama (Klapp, 1959, 1962, 1964b). Though people may have the satisfaction of seeing him properly punished, the costs are painfully apparent: chasing chimeras while real problems are neglected (and worse villains escape?). Yet even scapegoating is not without assets in the trade-off ledger. Since Durkheim, and Fauconnet (1920), it has been recognized that there are services to cohesion and the "collective conscience" from the fixing of responsibility and from a feeling of justice done. Even the notorious New England Puritan witch hunts, in spite of their paranoid unreality, did, according to the sociologist Kai Erikson (1966) help the Puritan colony to define its boundaries and defend its way of life against forces of secularization and dissident faiths. To them it seemed that the Devil himself was loose.[16] History, with its insights into suggestibility and the dangers of crowd hysteria, has a different verdict. Their spasm of closing gave the Puritans a momentary feeling of security, but we see it was a losing and costly rearguard defense.

But even without mistakes such as spasmodic closing, a social system can deteriorate into banality. However good something is, it can be made banal (Chapter 6). Every creative art, says Ehrenzweig (1970: 160), becomes closed and restrictive, so that artists have to break out again. Churches and other ritual institutions suffer from formalism (Cooley, 1927). After the Revolution, the Soviets thought they had a good thing going in the image of Lenin: They made an icon of him. Everywhere pictures, busts, banners, mottoes, songs, films, and televised documentaries proclaimed "Lenin Lives." Finally people became weary of "inundation of the land with Leniniana." A young Moscow engineer commented: "We are tired of the whole business. We don't need to be told to honor Lenin. We already do. Lenin was a simple, modest man. If he were here today, he would be appalled at this worship of his person" (Saikowski, 1970). The same might be true of Americans if inundated with images of Lincoln, or British with Churchill. Nothing is so good that repetition cannot make it less so.

About half the time, as I said, a given direction of opening and closing is wrong, especially toward the end of its swing. Good opening can extend too far toward bad opening, and good closing toward bad closing. Extremes may trigger spasms of closing or plunges into more change than people may be ready for.

Bad closing to good opening

The notion of a game on a playing field suggests that the other main direction of winning play is from bad closing to good opening. This gives us a picture in which to place the identity search, style rebellion, and consciousness-explosion of the sixties (Klapp, 1969), and the early stages of spiritual scanning (such as the flowering of gurus mentioned in Chapter 8) as kicks toward good opening, in hopes of transcending banality without falling into the other losing sector of noise.

As discontent with mental restriction deepens, people become ready to seek beyond for new things. Such a move begins with an awareness, such as boredom, that one has been deprived of needed variety. Rarely is this a jail predicament. It is often felt by small-town youth. It might be just a feeling of something missing, of no place to go, of resentment of rules, of being kept in the dark, or just a rut of what was once comfortable redundancy. We have mentioned how culture gets banalized in Chapter 6.

When bad closing is felt, a scanning sequence begins. A person may decide to take a trip to look for new people, places, dwellings, materials, groups, cultures — even a trip into outer space, or into the hidden sea of his own mind. He may drift toward settings where a variety of life styles and views can be encountered, such as Hyde Park Corner in London, or the campus and neighborhood of the University of California at

Berkeley. A sociological study (Love, 1973:161—209) describes two such parks in Portland, Oregon, whose fountains, designed by the architect Halprin, became "bazaars of people" that drew visitors from various walks of life. One fountain emphasized serenity and relaxation, the other a hubbub of interaction with people, including such diversions as wading in the fountain. Both offered lots of opportunities to watch the styles of other people. Visitors said of the exciting fountain: "You can watch . . . all kinds — not just hippies" . . . "a place for people to break down the communication-life style gap" . . . "All these people wouldn't be together in any other situation" (186—7, 194—5).

A person feeling a need for opening takes in and sends more messages, trying to spread information and spill what there is to spill. He favors such things as newsletters, gossip, inquiries, open hearings, exposés, and investigative reporting. He "shops" for experiences and communicational opportunities. Of course, he uses other people as scanners, by consultation, gossip, and so on.

Unfortunately, it is possible to be boxed into a kind of bad closing in which one does not know what one is missing and does not move toward opening. An example is professional secrecy. A study by a sociologist (Spector, 1973) found that lawyers were hunting jobs secretly. Even though working closely with others who were also hunting jobs, they were unable to work out a common solution such as a clearing house or simply a "grape vine," by which most might have found new positions more easily.

I find four main kinds of response that are ways out of the bad closing of banality: (1) *antics,* (2) *creativity,* (3) *mysticism,* and (4) *romanticism.* Most openers use such tactics. When boredom is the enemy, almost any lively antics are welcome as relief. Industrial workers try diversions like "banana time" (Roy, 1959) and "binging" (Homans, 1950). When people feel enclosed by banality, they try to extend their sensory horizons by "fun," horseplay, high jinks, pranks, revelry, "happenings," "freaking out," or "blowing one's mind," perhaps with the help of psychedelics. Such reactions were conspicuous in the counterculture, and are well described by writers such as Tom Wolfe (1968), Simmons and Winograde (1968), Harvey Cox (1969), and William Braden's (1970) portrayal of the "Age of Aquarius."

Banality can also be defied by creativity among those who have talent. The whole history of music, art, literature, and thought is a testimony to this. Less demanding of ability is the response of mysticism, a searching beyond rational thought through intuition or revelation for a reality beyond the surface of things, as we shall describe spiritual seeking in Chapter 8. A fourth banality-defying response is the opening kind of romanticism, which stresses fulfillment by letting oneself go, naturalness, wildness, questing, vagabondage, chivalric deeds, and bold strokes. Collective romantic surges find openings in rebellion, formation of utopian communities, hero worship, land and gold rushes, fads such as streaking, hits in popular music and shows (such as the songs of Bob Dylan, the rock musical "Hair," and the electrifying guitar virtuosity of Jimi Hendrix), and festivals such as Woodstock, 1969. By opening such doors, the bird of imagination escapes from the plastic cage.

However, there is no assurance that opening always cures bad closing. For example, the surge of middle class people toward "encountering" — sensitivity groups or T-groups — during the 1960s was by no means all gain. Therapy or spontaneity for one might mean family breakup or even mental breakdown for another. Opening oneself to a group was cathartic but also stressful when it involved criticism or attack. Critics concluded that encountering was "playing with fire," that twenty-five percent to forty percent of its participants gained nothing and very possibly lost much from it (Back, 1972:221). A Canadian psychologist, Lawrence LaFave, argued that people would be better off taking *in*sensitivity courses, as a protective buffer is needed for the noise, movement, and crowding of big cities; too much sensitivity can cause ulcers, high blood pressure, allergies, asthma, and failure in work (Klein, 1973). Some effects of encountering belong under the heading of information overload (Chapter 4): Overwhelming a person with variety he can't cope with is hardly an improvement over boring him with banality.

Such outcomes of the game of opening and closing tell us there are no guarantees against mistakes. Two ways of winning, good opening and good closing, are offset by two likely ways of losing, bad opening and bad closing. So modernization has proved an equivocal blessing to developing peoples. Like a blindfold game, it offers redemption to some but damnation to others (Berger, 1973:160) as in the "ethnocide" so often seen among tribal peoples.[17] To advanced societies, too, progress has come as a rude shock, sometimes a Pandora's box (Commoner, 1971; Ehrlich, 1968; Meadows, 1972). Only a romantic — whether opener or closer — would have the confidence to maintain, like the old country doctor who prescribed castor oil for everything, that one course is right all the time.

Nor are the proper doses of opening and closing the same for all kinds of societies. Some thrive on more redundancy, others on more variety. Different kinds of systems have different balance points and ranges of oscillation in opening and closing. Open pluralistic systems with high levels of learning and specialized work have an appetite for knowledge that requires a huge intake of variety in spite of the entropy that could threaten a more unified society. Often they are helped by "safety valves" — carnivals, games, escapes, drug-usage, and the like — which buffer tensions from varieties of information and conduct that could not be tolerated otherwise (Klapp, 1972:162–212). Even they have a point at which information turns to noise, as we have seen in Chapter 3. Tightly-knit societies, on the other hand, must close out variety sooner to avoid excessive entropy and dissonance. For example, tribal hunters who must band together for survival can permit only limited freedom; so with sects whose salvation hinges on purity of faith and the avoidance of sin. Such groups are "allergic" to the diversity that in liberal societies would be exhilarating. Yet all have a tipping point[18] at which a swing from opening to closing, or vice versa, is called for. The difference between closed and open pluralistic systems is in the location of the tipping point and the range of oscillation between variety and redundancy: What is good sailing wind for a clipper may be a hurricane for a canoe.

I hope that this chapter has given a picture of opening and closing as a natural process in which responses like turning off from social noise, and searches for variety and transcendence (as will be discussed in Chapter 8 in the section entitled, *Who is the guru?*), have their part. Even the most closed systems must open, and the most open systems close, at some point where overloads require a swing toward opposite directions and strategies. Pluralistic systems, for all their variety and openness, need to achieve closing by small groups coming together to screen out bad vibes and find the resonance of good redundancy — so preserving meaning and identity and often reaching higher levels of synergy.

A tipping point seems to be approaching now. Affluence has turned into a crisis in which bad opening and bad closing have generated noise, thus necessitating a new direction. Will this new direction be found? What will it be?

8. Movements and possibilities

This book attributes some of the sense of clutter and malaise in modern society to a high noise condition — noise taken in a social, not merely an acoustical, sense. The book has focused on three general conditions of social noise: information overload leading to consensus lags and meaning gaps; entropic communication of various sorts; and loss of reinforcement by good redundancy, accompanied by mounting banality. High social noise can be viewed as a price of indiscriminate modernism encouraged by a philosophy of unlimited openness. But other factors, such as commercialism, contagion, and the modeling noise of media have their own roots. However generated, social noise past a point leads to a sense of crisis, at which collectivities and movements aim at good opening for better information or at good closing for more redundancy. This chapter treats a few such responses that are prominent today.

Clutter consists of things out of place and scale that are somehow a threat to the human spirit. So, for example, seem automobiles roaring four abreast through the narrow streets of Athens and beneath the Parthenon, which crumbles from acidic fumes. This book has told a story of how clutter in the environment gives rise to noise in communication, which gives rise to confusion in the mind. When there is too much clutter in a scene, the mind becomes like a poorly organized photomontage. Some may thrive on clutter (keeping in mind Picasso's studio), but most are confused and fragmented by too much of it. A things-heaped, noise-filled, information-overloaded environment thwarts the human spirit in subtle ways. When information turns to noise, it puts us in the predicament of the open tape recorder, endless jigsaw puzzle, and Sysiphean striving. In the midst of such noise, with not enough reinforcement from good redundancy, people easily feel vulnerable, unplugged, and unnerved. This generates closing responses such as the joining of cults, ethnic ingrouping, hurrying into condominiums. So we saw that good closing is just as necessary as opening in the tides of life. I have

168

only scanned this problem, as one might an oil spill from a helicopter; but it does suggest that in noise production, as in energy production, something has gone wrong. This is a curious malaise of affluence.

This book assigns an important part to boredom, a form of alienation and no small motive for changes such as fashion, romantic rebellion, and other meaning-seeking movements. Mounting boredom suggests that a tipping point may be near, in which people will turn to something different.

On the physical environmental side, such turning has long since begun. Ecology gave early warning signals of destruction of the balances on which life depends. One painful instance is the tragedy of the commons. Will noise prove another tragedy of the commons? Will it go to a critical loss of social resonance? My supposition is that perceiving so much noise, people will not continue down the old road but seek a new direction. The problem for the next few decades will be how to get to clearer signals of it. Statements like the following suggest a coming turn in the tide: "Most Americans are overfed, overhoused, overdressed, and overheated. Consumption is a mania. External things have become masters. We enslave ourselves through self-indulgent greed and, in the process, push our nation to the brink of economic and ecological collapse." (Hubbard, 1975). To such disappointed people, what we have called affluence has turned out to be a kind of poverty.

Would it be a surprise, then, if the path before us were not straight but had a sharp turn? Many indications suggest a swing from the ideal of *productivity* to that of *fulfillment*.[1] In the old affluence, productivity meant the highest possible output with technology, saturation by input (ease, consumption, information), magnitude in quantity and scale, a flood of communication with poor feedback, and unlimited change and growth. Anything unlike this was regarded as poverty.

Perhaps just by turning all this around one can visualize what the new affluence might be like. If the old affluence was clutter and noise, the new would be simplicity and quiet. If the old affluence was pollution and waste, the new would be purity and conservation. Fulfillment would come from a higher level of personal output — seizing the privilege of doing things oneself. Fulfillment would come from human scale and balance between variety and redundancy. Fulfillment would come from a richer texture of communication and a broader horizon of sensibilities. When one likes such things, the old affluence looks like poverty.

Whichever of such moves occur, I don't suppose most will be by vast public decision but rather by countless choices which will reverse the assumptions of the old affluence, though many will not be recognized as noise-abating (just as, before air pollution was noticed, people sought the fresh air of the country).

Opening and closing always aims at better balance of information. Three movements are discernible today that reflect such oscillations. They are searches for: human scale, a mosaic rather than uniformity of life-styles, and transcendental meaning.

Human scale

It seems to me that in this world of megalopolis and megamachines producing piles of super-products, people are trying to recover a proportion lost somewhere along the path of progress. It is ironic that over two thousand years after Aristotle defined the limits of a good community (small enough that magistrates can know everyone and distinguish strangers from citizens), Athens should be bursting with motor traffic — for example, cars going three abreast around Kolonaki Square within a few feet of people sitting at outdoor tables — and that a conference should be held by the Greek Ministry of Culture and Sciences in 1977 to decide how to protect the Acropolis from air pollution — whether to remove the precious statues of six maidens known as Caryatids and replace them with plaster replicas. Nor are new towns all that much improved over the old. Reston, Virginia, for example, long known as a model modern community, a utopia of relaxed urban living at the head of a man-made lake, is reported by some to be boring to visit and sterile compared with a place like Georgetown; and to be afflicted by problems such as drug abuse, crime, and family conflicts. Few would claim to know yet what human scale is, but it is easy to see that much of the time we do not have it. The state of affairs in most cities is so bad that architect Paolo Soleri remarked grimly in 1970 that cities are evil; they work against man; outside the house is chaos.

Nevertheless, the search for human scale is on among planners, architects, environmentalists, scientists, and many others concerned about the human condition.[2] The Volvo factory in Sweden, for example, limits its plants to between 500 and 700 employees organized in teams that work at their own speed instead of in an assembly line, switch jobs, and participate in decisions about their work. Qualities of human scale can be glimpsed not only in the pages of utopia but in many places:

Henry Miller was gratefully surprised when, retiring to Big Sur after spending most of his life in cities, he found neighbors "popping up" out of the bushes: "For the first time in my life I found myself surrounded by kind souls who were not thinking exclusively of their own welfare. A strange new sense of security began to develop in me . . ." (Richard, 1973:238). Further illustrations are a country telephone switchboard operator who can identify all 150 callers on her exchange by voice alone; the existence of over 30,000 communes in North America; the "defensible space" of urban neighborhoods; or rural communities such as Appalachia, which are "cultures of poverty" from an economic standpoint but which sometimes turn out to be havens of "lost values" or oral tradition, human scale, and people-centered living.[3]

William Christian (1972) gives an intriguing glimpse of small villages in Spain's Nansa Valley. Here is a scale in which everyone counts; even little people become big in their scene. Say it is José (as we may imagine a farmer). Every day he is of some importance, and on some days of much importance: People call greetings and sallies to him wherever he passes; his name day is celebrated by all his friends; he enjoys the personal protection of the Virgin Mary as his village patron and carries a large candle in the procession on her feast day; he enjoys absolute equality in his share of village communal property and in the council a "right to his say" in all decisions; he is respected for his wealth of seventy cattle and everyone knows about his bull that took a prize in the fair at San Miguel. Furthermore, in the tavern he is appreciated as a storyteller and wit; people still remember his youthful bravado and pranks of ten years ago, one of which is celebrated in song. He has a nickname well known (as does everyone), which characterizes him in the "village drama," which consists of new episodes as well as long chains of stories told at the hearth, tavern church portal, barn, or wherever people gather for talk; even after death such public characters live on as stock figures in a sort of Comedia del Arte. He is rarely alone, as his family and the whole village turn out for funerals, festivals, work, worship, and play together; "everyone or no one does things." There is no need for such a man to feel left out; or to "keep up with the Joneses" in the nervous way of city dwellers; Miguel, Manuel, and the others know very well who he is, he needs no "front" to impress them. Here is a scale in which a man counts. If a community is to enjoy such a lively "village theater," says Christian, four things are necessary: It must be small enough for each person to be appreciated for distinctive traits; it must have the continuity provided by members who reside there long enough to become typified and familiar; it must have leisure time, and its concerns must be focused on a "stage" through activities such as fiestas, contests, gossip, and the like (1972:21—31). Would it not be a sure sign of human scale to find people so fascinated by the communal drama, which offers everyone a part in "our" show, that they were too busy to watch strangers perform in mass media? How does such a scale compare with that of the global village created by electric technology (McLuhan, 1964:298) in which media have "retribalized mankind" (265), bringing them closer and world events into sharper focus? Has it made people feel closer and given every man a part, or has it brought them into unnerving proximity without real relationship by gross distortion of human scale?[4]

Global theater has not made neighbors nor brought human affairs into better scale and focus for two main reasons: because instant closeups do not remedy disconnectedness; and because it lacks the fine texture of networks in which day-to-day relations — face-to-face or mouth-to-ear — give feedback to each person. On the contrary, such staggering shifts of scale have left people feeling vulnerable, intruded upon, confused — and time is more out of joint than ever. We have plenty of rhetoric and irrelevant exogenous information but not enough responsive feedback giving meaning to people. Of faraway events we hear more than we need, of those nearby less than we should. By such a high noise ratio, the global village shows how far short it falls of human scale. Nor can the mass media drama, which allow vast anonymous audiences to watch celebrities do interesting things, remedy this lack except as an aspirin the side effects of which awaken discontents.

Alongside mass media, others grow up that magnify what people are doing in their own worlds instead of focusing on celebrities and faraway affairs. For example, in the Los Angeles area over 300 community newspapers, such as the Valley News in Van Nuys or the South Bay Daily Breeze, pass up wire service material and what is covered by the Times and Herald-Examiner and hire their own reporters to dig in the local community, rub shoulders, and remain known and accountable to people for stories they write (unlike roving news crews). Meetings, weddings, potlucks, bowling leagues, lost dogs — nothing is too trifling to be reported; the ideal is to mention every person at least once a year. Such journalism functions as does gossip in the Nansa Valley: It helps people to feel important and it keeps community identification from being lost in urban sprawl. Its function is not merely a nostalgic hang-over, but needed more than ever today. As an editor put it: "The more a paper like the Times grows and prospers, the bigger the vacuum they leave, and the more a paper like ours can grow and succeed" (Shaw, 1975). In this case, the information market was able to generate com-pensatory institutions to balance the scale distortions of the mass media. Although we may not know exactly of what communication balance consists, we may be sure that it rests on networks[5] of sufficient texture and richness[6] to supply most people with enough feedback including good redundancy, to keep personal and collective identity alive.

Our glimpse of human scale and communication balance in this book comes not from studying them directly but from looking at the other end of the spectrum, at what they are not, such as too much informa-tion without meaning, or too little connectedness and good redundancy. Human scale is neither a heap of more facts than people can use, nor endlessly repeated, exactly duplicated units of anything. We must judge from such distortions what a balance would be, just as one would suppose that a diet too heavy in sweets would be better to have less of that and more of protein and minerals. I assume that in communica-tion, as in diet, there is an optimal "mix" that can be represented as a kind of profile of needed messages. Also, to conceive of communication balance one must assume that people are limited channels, so that an overload of anything, however useful, can become a deprivation of something else that is also needed. Whatever such balance may be, it is often missing from celebrity-filled but boring lives, and it is embarras-sing that the absence of boredom in some simpler societies suggests that they have balance and that we do not. The main point about imbalance is that sooner or later it moves people to do something about it, to swing in a different direction, as noted in the game of opening and closing.

Information overload gives us one glimpse of communication balance as a direction toward which people will turn. We have seen how the mind and society are limited channels that must cope with the battle of the inbasket and the endless jigsaw puzzle and which are in the predic-ament of the open tape recorder, which absorbs noise that is not only useless, but even harmful. The overload consists of facts without mean-ings, pseudodistinctions, and too many exogenous signals — coming from unknown sources, producing a sense of strangeness, often manipu-lated, and requiring cautious calculation — compared with the number of indigenous signals one can immediately understand and trust. This comes with a shortage of good redundancy, reinforcement, and meaning. Coping with such overload — trying to turn noise back into information, information into decisions, and facts into meanings — becomes the unending task of citizens as the flood of news, entertainment, education, claims, and "pitches" pours upon them. The price includes stress, decision lags, frustration from Sysiphean effort, a growing sense of absurdity, living in the front of one's mind while getting out of touch with oneself, and growing boredom with the mounting heap of information which, however accurate, does not add up to meaning. Such things are unlikely to change much — neither man's limits as a channel nor modern society's communication output.

It is not hard to guess that, suffering strains of overload, people will be trying to either process information more effectively or to avoid it. They will seek easy guides — capsules, digests, pundits — to facts and products, and better methods of scanning, processing, and selecting needed bits and patterns from a public domain of information conceived of as full of garbage. They will become "clean desk" and "clean kitchen" fanatics. Education will be expected to help, with courses in time-management, speed-reading, decision science, and computer programming. Yet, though data processing will improve, it is safe to say that it will not help much with the problem of meaning; that is, it does little to increase the rate of meaning formation for most people. The fact seems to be that, as one falls ever farther behind accumulating information, one feels like the man who couldn't catch a bus and therefore gave up, reconciled to going on foot or not at all. People recognize the facts, however correlated, do not of themselves create values; meanings are still constructed the old way, by reflection; and the best education is still a conversation with Socrates.

It is reasonable to suppose that, as a result of strains of information overload, people lacking enough Socrates will switch to pursuits of meaning that do not require sifting innumerable facts — direct routes such as intuition, meditation, astrology, prophesy, Oija boards, ESP, poetic imagination. From irritation with too many bits that do not add up, an antifactual intuitive holism will grow up (misnamed, I think as antiintellectualism). Values and meanings will be prized more than facts, and with or without facts. There will be more emphasis on religion, arts, and humanities, with the goal of getting one's head together and in better touch with oneself. The popularity of science will decline relatively,[7] except where it provides such things as biofeedback and confirmation for ESP and astrology. A new ethic of self-realization will generate hordes of seekers for transcendental wisdom, as will be noted later.

Lack of good redundancy (described in Chapter 6) gives another view of communication balance in terms of what it is not. I described it as lack of resonance, reinforcement, and connectedness, in the midst of information overload, with a resulting loss of the past and weakening of sentiments which, containing an irreducible amount of redundancy, must be replenished as must a battery. If redundancy is as important as I believe it is, people exposed to winds of noise will seek more good redundancy. They will slow down their rush into modernity. They will seek more connectedness in richer networks with human scale and better feedback. What is now called nostalgia will become deliberate efforts to slow mobility, to restore connections, to travel more to see old friends than to see new places, to ingroup with one's own kind, and to emphasize ceremonies and other experiences that give "that good feeling." Such communication will contain a stronger mixture of gossip and dialogue versus media output, subjectivity versus objectivity, nonverbal versus verbal feedback, sincerity versus manipulation, wisdom versus calculation, identity-building (news about me and we-relevant news about us) versus information about things. Indigenous networks, not exogenous sources, supply such good redundancy; it is not enough to print a card saying, "Need a friend? Call this number . . . talk to someone who cares." It is important to recognize that strengthening good redundancy in indigenous networks is not a matter of "going back" to anything, historically speaking, any more than getting well is "going back" to health. Going forward requires balance just as much as does standing still or going back. The new concept of progress and affluence will contain a better balance of redundancy.

Progress toward good redundancy will not be easy, however, for here we shall run a risk. Banalizing forces will be all too ready to rush in with their synthetic products to help those who yearn for "that good feeling." We must beware of their "help" and learn to distinguish it from good redundancy. (The secret of the distinction may prove to be this: Only indigenous networks, not exogenous sources, can generate good redundancy.)

I conjecture that in a world of increasing banality, people will be trying to *de*banalize life. Feeling boredom, they may try, for example, to dramatize and glamorize themselves through fashion, to freshen identities by novelties of style — with costumes, cosmetics, hairdos, wigs, dark glasses, sporty cars, faddish ideas, and so on. More people will enter the fashion race and it will speed up along with status anxiety.[8] Unfortunately, even if fashion temporarily relieves boredom, it sets in motion banalizing forces — multiplication of exactly repeated units — and adds to the burden of pseudo-distinctions that are so large a part of the information overload of modern times. Worse, as it becomes more extreme, fashion novelty fails to declare identity (when anybody can be anybody, nobody can be somebody), so the status rewards of being either distinctive or similar to everyone else fall off. A vicious circle of boredom to variation to boredom to variation may set in. We may expect boredom to stimulate wit, comedy, and general creativity.[9]

The monk's solution

It shouldn't be surprising that, invaded by noise, people are developing shells of avoidance, even capsules within which to achieve and protect life-styles, as a short term solution.[10] They will be building new kinds of screens, baffles, and filters between their own harmony and others' noise, searching for resonance with their own kind within clearer boundaries.

The monk's solution is the most familiar and time honored, and is especially useful to those with high moral or aesthetic standards. Recognizing danger in the world, he separates himself from it, whether by hermitage, monastery, or personal shield of austerity and guardedness while maintaining involvement in ordinary affairs. A sympathetic picture of such a way of life today among Trappists, Carthusians, Benedictines, Carmelites, Dominicans, Augustinians, and Jesuits is given by Moorhouse (1972). The monk concentrates on his work — prayer, worship, and contemplation — perhaps no more than the businessman does on his, except that the latter discriminates between profit and loss and the former between spiritual advancement and loss in the continual struggle to overcome the distractions, vanities, and temptations of a world most of which is viewed as inimical to higher life. The Cistercian Thomas Merton (1961:84, 86) advises: "Do everything you can to avoid the amusement and noise and the business of men . . . Do not read their newspapers if you can help it. Be glad if you can keep beyond reach of their radios . . . Keep your eyes clean and your ears quiet and your mind serene." So the monastery becomes an island, whose gatekeepers shield members from bad vibes, and whose channels supply an optimal mix of information for spiritual life. Within or outside, unceasing discrimination, mindfulness, is the key — control of the tongue and moods, inner serenity whatever the disturbance outside. Such voluntary isolation is a natural — perhaps the only — solution to the monk's problem, once one accepts his assumptions, that there is a higher good for man that is threatened by a world preponderantly evil unless boundaries are preserved. It is the same logic as that of a man, riding a felucca on the Nile, who was told that if he dipped his hand in the water he would run the danger of schistosomiasis; naturally he drew in his hand and stood aloof.

Compared with such guardedness, the ordinary modern man lives indiscriminately — one might almost say gulping the products of his society — living distractedly, rushing after this and that. Yet, for all such difference, the monk's solution may not be so irrelevant as it seems to modern life: Materialism is being reexamined; cultic movements like Vedanta, Buddhism, and the Children of God, are holding up spiritual — even monastic — ideals to many seekers (described later in "Who is the Guru?"). And even to modern secular men, the monk gives a model of perfected closing strategy, of making one's own life-style a support capsule. With mounting pressures of noise and congestion, it is likely that more people will be learning from the monk, seeking more skill at enclosure: screens, hedges, lattices, fences, walls, private gardens, arbors, nooks, niches, cubby holes, sound-baffles, headphones, ear stoppers; they will be trying to build capsules for themselves in penthouses, condominiums, yachts, artist's studios, where they can live with Walter Pater's gemlike flame of taste, according to their own style, away from noise and neighbors' eyes. Even the automobile, for all its noise, has offered a capsule in which alienated man can seek a world of his own — a bucket-seated fantasy of power, a place to talk or sing to himself, a shag-lined opulence of sound, or a rolling coach for escape.

Yet the purist's solution is not widely applicable, because austerities of commitment to a single goal will not do for most people; they want a more balanced pluralistic existence — to have all the styles they choose without giving up anything. Each wants his own cake while others enjoy theirs. Is there a collective solution that takes a leaf from the monk's notebook on the need for closing, yet goes beyond the cloister to the larger community, thus allowing freedom of choice while recognizing that no one gets fullest development of the style he chooses without some collective support and closure?

Mosaic of life-styles: a pattern for tomorrow?

In this era of clashing life-styles and distortions of scale, people are in-grouping, seeking roots and richer texture and balance of communication, as I have observed. They don't want a solitary cubicle, but a shared style with a safe boundary, yet with options of variety beyond. I conjecture that the solution that takes shape will be a mosaic of life-styles.[11]

Such a mosaic can be visualized by contrast with what we have now. Incompatible styles are practiced side by side, uneasily, often in conflict: smokers and nonsmokers, drinkers and nondrinkers, long hairs and straights, nudists and Sunday school picnics, swingers and Puritans, fundamentalists and atheists, ethnic varieties, and so on. What we call the freedom of a pluralistic society is often a conflict — a noise — of styles, in which each does as he chooses, more or less to the discomfort of others; for example, a family of Christian fundamentalists who dwell next to a house full of acid rock musicians who sit on the front porch smoking pot. The solutions for those who do not like a situation are to move or to ask the police to enforce the law, which restricts the freedom of the other party. Over this looms the fact of uniform legislation (often obtained by minority will of some pressure group), which regulates matters of personal choice, ranging from height of hedges[12] and buildings, walking of dogs, parking of vehicles, and style of structures, to moral matters such as burial practices and prohibition of alcohol, pornography, and private sex conduct. What such uniform legislation amounts to, if enforced, is a thinly-disguised tyranny of the majority, as Tocqueville (1840) described it — and an enormous enforcement problem for police and courts trying to impose the same standards on many who see no reason for obeying, who find arrangements to evade laws and avoid conflict, few explicit, some illicit. In short, under the aegis of equality and under uniform law (with some inspiration from the "melting pot" ideal), our society has strayed into a situation in which few get what they want, whether freedom to live as they please or comfortable conformity. Nor has suburbia, for all its banal uniformity, remedied this.

What arrangement would help solve such a problem? I conjecture that instead of a mishmash of disgruntled conformists and stifled libertarians, people will be trying a mosaic of life-styles, a form of structured pluralism that is neither separation nor homogenization. A pharmaceutical analogy will help define this. People will seek a stable emulsion, neither private capsules nor homogenized mixture. An emulsifying agent supplies boundaries to globules that may themselves be complex systems, which a mixer or detergent would destroy. The social emulsifying agent, I think, will be some kind of covenant: a voluntary agreement to make a life-style salient and to support it within a territory. This is what people are trying to do: to separáte into meaningful, harmonious communities that will have reasonable stability because people have chosen to support a common life-style. Within a covenant, freedom is like a ticket to an amusement park: valid for that kind of fun only within the grounds. Outside, other rules may prevail. A mosaic of life-styles is a natural development, covenants for which people are now groping, as in natural urban areas like Greenwich Village, smoking and nonsmoking compartments, nudist sections of public beaches, and the legalization of pot in some towns. *Non*uniform application of some laws is needed for a mosaic[13] of life-styles. Such an arrangement avoids the banality of one life-style for all, and gives a realistic choice provided one goes to the place where one may exercise it.

People will probably try out various kinds of covenants, aiming to make their community like a checkerboard of choices; but how they will work remains to be seen. In essence, a covenant is not a rule laid down from above but a collective agreement, supported or at least tolerated by external law. Under such, residents of a community can specify variations that do not violate the basic rights guaranteed by a constitution. One may suppose that once a covenant was established, people moving in would consent to it in writing and be required to leave if unwilling to comply with the life-style chosen for the area. If he wanted to do something different, he could go to another area where that was permitted: "Open" zones might designate where anything goes within minimum legal restrictions; experimental zones might allow trials of new life-styles to be supported by a future covenant. Buffer zones might separate highly incompatible sectors, such as a neighborhood for Mormons from a liberty area for sailors. "Incubator" zones for raising children would have different rules from those for "swinging singles" or senior citizens. Perhaps the rules of a zone would be posted at gateways to help mark the boundaries. By such devices, a life-style could be recognized and made salient, providing people with needed reinforcement instead of the conflict of pseudo-liberty. Changes in covenants might be made by democratic procedures, with provisions for buying out members outvoted and phasing changes slowly to allow for adjustments.

Such covenants may help remedy the confusion and self-defeating style conflicts that now exist in most cities. As it is, zoning specifies only general uses — residential, commercial, hospital, school, industrial, and so on — but not life-styles. Such patterns are not usually visible until one moves in and finds out the hard way what kinds of people live there. Without a covenant, commercial motives lead to renting or selling to anyone who will pay the price, with no consideration of what happens to the neighborhood — meaning costly readjustments, people moving, and moving again, looking for that "nice" place to live. Making life-style explicit in covenants would recognize what is being sought when "natural" areas of a city differentiate, and would slow down invasion and succession when a pattern appears valuable enough for dwellers to want to keep it. Among the advantages of posting a life-style would be that dwellers would gain a sense of defensible space (Newman, 1972) to which they could rally; also, raising children according to a chosen style would be far easier. Over it all, if the mosaic worked, would be more variety and choice for everyone, a true liberty.

One cannot anticipate the practical difficulties of programs that have not yet been really tried. Would there be, for example, more expense in law enforcement? (Some zones might require extra guard forces, while others minimal police and fire protection, with tax and insurance rates adjusted accordingly.) Yet, would there not be savings in law enforcement if, instead of trying to enforce a uniform life-style regarding such things as pets, hedge heights, setbacks, horses, liquor sales, and so on over an entire urban area, police activity were concentrated where it was really wanted? (For example, "nonvictim" offenses such as public intoxication, prostitution, gambling, and vagrancy constitute over forty percent of arrests.) It is yet to be seen whether specific codes in communities that care are harder to enforce than uniform codes over huge areas where few care.

Perhaps, when tried, a mosaic of life-styles will prove to be, along with communes and cooperatives, halfway houses on the road to tomorrow.

The surge of new religions: who is the Guru?

Last, I think that the surge of new religions so evident in the mid-seventies was partly a result of disappointment with the irrelevant and meaningless information, a closing to noise and clutter — bits that fail to fit into pattern and lead to meaning gap.

When conditions outside become too discouraging, one may seek the good life within one's own mind. Asia institutionalized this discovery millenia ago, whereas the West left spirituality to a few monks and mystics. At the same time, a flood of inward spiritual seeking in many new directions, especially in its earlier phases, is a vast collective groping for awareness — hence, in that sense, an opening.[14]

Seekers are persons conscious of lack of meaning in their lives who try to transcend the ordinary consciousness of institutions, which they feel as restriction, whether as noise or banality (bad closing). So they "shop" for more meaningful messages from view to view, fad to fad, cult to cult, guru to guru. They share the quest of the orange-robed, head-shaven disciple of the Hare Krishna movement, who says:

I . . . wanted a teacher to lead me into a world which I knew existed and which I felt was very near to me, yet somehow could not reach. (Dasa, n.d.)

Another seeker, an English convert to Buddhism, says:

The longing for Enlightenment . . . might manifest itself as a vague sort of longing. Being essentially a feeling of the heart, the intellect does not know what to do with it. There arises mistrust and fear about this feeling, though it is suppressed as much as possible. But it will pop up again and again, preparing the way to doubt — the great doubt. What am I? What is life all about? What am I here for? . . . And the search begins . . . It is exactly at this juncture that many of us came in contact with Buddhism. (*The Middle Way*, Journal of the Buddhist Society, London, May 1966:16)

A seeker is more eager to try extraordinary states of awareness because he knows he must transcend that of the society, which does not satisfy him. A recruit to Pentecostalism, for example, might wish to speak in tongues:

I had heard about the gift of tongues and my first reaction was that this was meaningless sound . . . The more I thought about it, the more real God became, the more a real possibility it seemed . . . When I was prayed over (for the Baptism), I asked for the gift of tongues. I didn't speak in tongues at that time . . . I had been advised that if I wanted tongues, I ought to try making sounds, so I did, thinking how stupid I would look later on; so I made a sound, and the gift was there, full-blown . . .

It was for me a specific proof that I had received the Holy Spirit. (Harrison, 1974: 405–6)

The restriction of ordinary consciousness is felt as a tangible obstruction to vision, as though a film of ice and mud were covering a windshield. Naturally, one would use a wiper if one could.

For such seekers, rarely before, at least in modern times, has the outlook been so interesting. Not only is science pouring forth its wonders, but the prophets, gurus, astrologers, necromancers, and alchemists are back in full force as though they had never been defeated in what that old rationalist Andrew D. Whyte (1896) called the warfare of science with religion. There is a mood of dissatisfaction with things as they ordinarily appear. People are peering by every means to see beyond, above, within, beneath surfaces — a surge of sensibility and awareness out of straightness and squareness. Slang shows the seeking state of mind with phrases such as "far out," "turn on," "stoned," "trip," "Jesus trip," "higher consciousness," and "bring me down" — a linguistic geography, one might say, of an inner or higher space now being explored by more and more people, no longer a preserve for a few "freaks," hippies, or cultists. Such words show that "far out" experience — whatever it was — had escaped from the institutional custody that certified certain ones (liturgy, grace, the holy) and disapproved of others (sin, sorcery, drug highs). Transcendental trips are offered in best sellers: Castaneda rides the broomstick with Don Juan; people turn out to greet the *Chariots of the Gods;* Jonathan Livingston Seagull trys to fly.

A bewildering variety of opportunities were tried. Drugstore paperback racks offered titles like *Sun Signs, Astrological Guide for 1974, The Psychic World of California* and *Mastering Witchcraft, a Practical Guide for Witches, Warlocks and Covens.* A *Catalogue of Ways People Grow* urges readers to look in Hasidism, shamanism, mysticism, astrology, tarot, hypnotism, analytic psychology, and bio-energetic analysis (Peterson, 1971). Witchcraft boutiques in major cities do a thriving business in talismans, tarot cards, candles, mystic jewelry, incense, and marvelous herbs. "Head shops" everywhere offer much the same. The educational offerings of experimental colleges and the Human Potentials Movement include such activities as witchcraft, Zen, Kung Fu, mind control, hypnotism, biofeedback, acupuncture, waking up with yoga, swimming pool feelies, and "what-its-like-to-be-me games." Jerry Rubin, the yippie star of the 1960s, announced:

I am totally into self-development now, almost completely working on my body, on my mind. I do yoga, go to massage school, run every day, am into bio-energetics (study of the natural rhythms of the body) . . . My energy was all external in the '60s; in the '70s I want to find out what's within . . . I want to lead a quiet life . . . I don't take drugs anymore. (Christian Science Monitor: February 16, 1973)

Advertisements in magazines invited people to see apparitions and "unravel the mystery of man": *Reader's Digest* offered "Meditation; Key to Peace of Mind, with an ancient discipline, that takes only minutes a day to practice" (September, 1973). Even the Stanford Research Institute, one of the most prestigious "think tanks," revealed it was delving into the world of psychic phenomena. A bumper sticker on a Volkswagen driven by a boy of about eighteen announced: "I have come to reveal the light — Guru Maharaj Ji."

With an estimated ten million people in the United States practicing astrology alone, there was reason to believe that transcendental seeking was reaching faddish if not hysterical epidemic proportions. A typical seeker might be "into" half a dozen things at once, having tried others before and ready to try more. A bewildering variety of "answer people" — from food pundits to what sociologist William Martin (1971) has called "God-hucksters" — were ready to meet the need. Who could say who had the answers? Who indeed was the guru, and which was the magic mantra?

Much of this ferment could be called truly religious by anyone's definition. Old faiths were revitalized by charismatic, pentecostal, or penitential experience: People were again seeking ecstasy in mainstream religion, speaking in tongues was popular, Hasidic Jews danced with beards flying. Various kinds of "Jesus-trippers" turned from worldliness to the simple ways of original Christianity, living by The Word in communal love, baptizing by immersion, giving up drugs, witnessing on the streets from house to house, and warning of Armageddon. Some, such as the Love Israel commune, used rather strenuous methods to "save" people, and were accused of "brainwashing" and "kidnapping" by alarmed parents. Their answer was: what are you worried about? Look at the life we are saving you from.

Exotic oriental cults of many kinds widened the spectrum of search. Yoga, based on the Indian Upanishads and distilled into the *Bhagavad-Gita*, was most popular. Introduced to North America by swamis such as Vivekenanda, Yogananda, Vishnu-Devanada (Sivananda Yoga Society), Prabahupada (Krishna Consciousness Society), Maharishi (Transcendental Meditation), Maharaj-Ji (Divine Light Mission), Aurobindo, Krishnamurti, and Chinmoy, to name but a few, yoga became an accepted part of human potentials training, university campuses, pastoral counselling, and ladies' weight-reducing programs. That was only the yogis. There were also the Buddhists — Tibetan, Mahayana, Hinayana, Zen — represented by teachers like D. T. Suzuki, Shunryu Suzuki Roshi (Zen Center San Francisco), and by Westerners such as Alan Watts and Christmas Humphreys. Most if not all such teachings made some use of meditation, aided by techniques — mantras, tantras, chants, breathing, postures, and so on — ranging from minutes to hours in length and from pleasantness to prolonged discomfort. The techniques, without exception, were aimed to suspend ordinary consciousness with its rational thinking and sensate focus.

On the fringes of mainstream religion were many forms of occultism, such as magic and fortune-telling. Psychics like Jeanne Dixon, Peter Hurkos, Carroll Wrighter, Maurice Woodroff, and Zolar made startling revelations. Theosophy advertisements offered to reveal the "hidden side of nature," the "thread of Ariadne given by the master to the disciple who ventures into the labyrinth of the mysterious being." Parapsychology and ESP investigations overlapped occultism, and encompassed everything from acupuncture to prayers for plant growth.

At the same time, attention was turning to outer space to see what new meaning could be found there. Astronomers explored possibilities of life on other planets, listened for celestial radio signals, and devised robot space probes. Reports of UFO sightings, landings, and encounters with strange creatures persisted in spite of the Air Force's discontinuance of its official observation project. Jackie Gleason reported he had seen UFOs twice. Groups, including police and air force personnel, reported collective sightings. The Children of God claimed in a leaflet distributed on the street: "These discs or circles of mysterious light which travel at speeds and changes of direction unknown to man or hover silently with a stability thus far unattained by any of man's space vehicles are nothing more or less than angelic creatures or spirit beings commonly known as angels and often represented by halos in early Christian art." Sociologists (Buckner, 1968) studied the flying saucer cult. Astronauts reported an odd spiritual change: the "astro-effect" as a result of trips into space. One moon veteran, James B. Irwin, described as a "nuts and bolts" type of technician before his Apollo 13 trip, came back calling himself a "moon missionary," and made preaching trips about the country to tell audiences of his new way of looking at the earth as if "with the eyes of God." An Apollo 14 veteran, Rusty Schweickart, took up transcendental meditation, saying, "I'm not the same man. None of us are."

Sports and amusements also had mind-blowing dimensions. Rock music, of course, transcended all limits. Strenuous sports, especially those involving danger to self or others such as Kung Fu, car racing, and parachute jumping had mystiques that were hard to explain. A psychiatrist (Noyes, 1972) reported that in experiences of sudden death or of near death there were mystical states of consciousness not unlike those brought on by LSD. Less dangerous sports offered their moments of transcendence: Surfers talked of being "reborn in the green womb of Mother Ocean."

Then there were drugs, of course. Since the beginning of the psychedelic movement, signaled by Huxley's *Doors of Perception* (1954) and the celebrated experiments of pioneers like Alan Watts, Timothy Leary, and Richard Alpert,[15] an increasing number of psychotropic (mind-altering) drugs were pouring into the market. Over 900 were listed by the National Institute of Mental Health in 1971, including an opiatelike substance 10,000 times as potent as morphine. Clearly everything from rose leaves and catnip to the most advanced pharmaceuticals was being tried for mind-altering effects. The average teenager knew about drugs his parents had never heard of and inquired about cautiously to avoid showing ignorance. After alcohol, marijuana was the favorite. It was estimated in 1974 to have nine to ten million occasional users in the United States. A study of working-class pot users (Schwartz, 1973) showed that escape from boredom was the common reason for getting stoned; these users would then listen to rock and so remove themselves from the "hassles" of nine-to-five jobs. Although getting stoned to listen to rock is not the same as "shooting the tube" or greeting UFOs or speaking in tongues or meditating in the lotus posture, they do have in common transcendence of ordinary ways of experiencing life.

In terms of communication, such searches are forms of scanning. In scanning we do just as we would with a radio receiver if we were to get too much noise or if we became aware that a band were limited: Twirl the dial and seek bands where the signals are better. Turning from conventional religion to occultism, comet-watching to drugs, and so on, people were turning the dial and trying to tune in on new signals and escape from the old band with its static and tiresome signals. In this way they were shopping for extraordinary states of consciousness: peering inward and outward to extend the spectrum of sensibilities. Today there is plenty of scientific scanning as outward search. But if anything describes the new temper of the times, to my view it would be the term *spiritual* scanning.

Spirit is a name for special kinds of information that neither physical instruments nor words catch. Such signals are so subtle that they are called leadings, graces, auras, omens, and so on. Mystics are typically speechless about their higher states of consciousness; the only words they offer are exceedingly uninformative and do not produce a corresponding state in the listener. Physics cannot describe what, for example, a fortune-teller reads in tea leaves; nor can alpha and delta brain waves registered by biofeedback devices register the *content* of intuitions.

As I have implied, the restriction from which shoppers are trying to escape by inward and outward scanning is *banal, ordinary* consciousness, which might happen to include the ugliness of a "rat race" glazed over by folksy or wisecracking humor, pious clichés, admen's puffery, and Disneyland wonders. The restriction of banal consciousness, like the glaze on an apple, is invisible to ordinary consciousness; but people can become aware of it. The claims of the gurus and teachings of the mystics[16] help us to become aware of this glaze of banality, if not to see things without it.

Just what is the transcendental experience beyond the restriction of banal consciousness? Though there can be little doubt that people are reaching extraordinary states by various routes, there is no way to tell from objective evidence whether they are all the same or different, or how many there are, or who really has them and who not. For example, when a psychic goes into a trance, he claims to be entering a higher state of consciousness where he is able to see into the future and past and make contact with the spirits of dead people. A Zen Buddhist, on the other hand, aims to go into a state that he describes as "the great mind," which he describes as follows:

We stop thinking; we stop emotional activity; we just sit . . . When you sit maybe many things will happen. You may hear the sound from the stream, or you may think of something, but your mind does not care. Your great mind is there, just sitting. Even though you don't see things or you don't hear, or you don't think . . . still maybe something is going on in the big mind. (Shunryu Suzuki-Roshi, 1973:3)

Again, a yogi goes into his trance in front of us: His eyes turn upward, eyelids close, his face assumes a beatific expression; he remains for minutes or hours hardly breathing. He reports that he has been experiencing "samadhi"; whereas the Buddhist may speak of "satori," "illumination," "nirvana"; and the spiritualist of auras and higher planes. To reach a higher state, one uses a mantra, another a tantra (mystic sound), a third a chant, a fourth a breathing exercise, and a fifth simply sits counting his breaths. Guru Maharaj Ji is said to use a manipulative technique, involving a certain way of pressing on the eyeballs, to show his disciples the Divine Light. The result is described as a sunburst of light in the center of the forehead. At least we may be sure there are many ways to transcendental states (after all, three yogas — Karma, Bhakti, and Jnana — are recommended by the *Bhagavad-Gita;* and there are many variants of Buddha's eight-fold path — Tibetan, Hinayana, Mahayana, and Zen). But no one seems to be able to speak with authority about whether they are all similar, or different, and which are authentic. The reason is simply that very few people have had more than one kind of transcending experience, and no one of whom I have ever heard has had them all. Is an LSD trip like a mystical one, Castaneda's journey like that of a Tibetan monk, Samadhi like pentecostal grace, speaking in tongues like Satori? Are they all "peak" experiences as described by Maslow (1962), or abreactions (Sargent, 1973)?[17] All we seem to know for sure is that there are quite a few ways of bypassing what Huxley (1954:23) called the "reducing valve" of ordinary consciousness, by which the brain avoids information overload and forms concepts. According to this, our ordinary view is a slit compared with the full spectrum of reality. Huxley concluded that the best way to transcendence was yoga (Vedanta). At any rate, transcendence seems to be more than the "uplift" that people ordinarily get listening to a Sunday sermon, yet one should not depreciate even such feelings, for they are a sign that ordinariness is transcended, if only for a moment.

A psychiatrist, Andrew Weil (1972), has put forth the startling suggestion that "stoned" thinking is not drug-created, but a natural state that most of us would be better off in more of the time. His controlled (double-blind) experiments with marijuana users showed that biochemical effects were slight, but placebo effects large. Marijuana, he holds, is "quieter pharmacologically" than alcohol — so how could remarkable mental effects attributed to it really be due to it? On the contrary, he asserts, "stoned" is a *natural* state of higher consciousness reached in various ways by mystics, celebrants, artists, and other creative people.

"Stoned" thinking is characterized by feelings of unity, selflessness, joy, and reality. By contrast, straight thinking is "straight in the way an interstate highway is straight. Unlike a winding country road it does not follow the natural contours of reality" (135). So why not cultivate "stoned" thinking instead of regarding it as an abnormal state?

Surely we are justified in concluding from the variety of searches by sincere and reputable people that there are natural ways of knowing that are transcendental rather than ordinary, unitive rather than separative in that they stress wholeness, and that these ways are intuitive, not derived from reasoning about facts or sense data, not ordinarily subject to voluntary control, and drawn from unconscious sources. Not only are people aware that such intuitive knowledge has been neglected, but a *new consensus* seems to be emerging: that it is *all right* to have extraordinary nonrational consciousness. Even Timothy Leary's (1966:93) heresy: "I think that anyone who wants to have a psychedelic experience and is willing to prepare for it . . . should be allowed to have a crack at it" is closer to being accepted. What was once the "counterculture" is becoming part of common culture. Gurus are not so queer as they once seemed. Nor do fads seem so silly.[18]

Indeed, faddism, as in shopping from one guru or placebo to another, should not be put down as a waste of time — especially when compared with banal activities. Of course, some of the things tried are silly and some people are fooled. But, since there is no way to find out possibilities without trying them, the flowering of gurus at this time might be a useful thing. At any rate, science, for all the reliability of its methods, has taught that errors are part of the price that must be paid for truth. From the variety of searches now going on, at least one can tell that many people are dissatisfied with the restriction — I have called it banality — of the ordinary fact-filled view of things, so are hopefully scanning horizons for something better. The best way seems yet to be found. Of those who know, who tells? Of those who tell, who listens? Of those who try, which succeed? We don't quite know how to tune our minds to new bands of reception, but a lot of people are trying and saying they are getting something interesting. It might be well, for now, to leave it at that.

Conclusion

The main hypothesis of this book is that opening and closing reflect a sort of game to get the best information, a game that is played in a field with four quarters: good opening, good closing, bad opening, and bad closing.

So social noise, when it defeats meaning and resonance, triggers responses of closing that aim to get good redundancy and, hopefully, synergy for opening and growth. Those who suffer the heaviest loads of social noise swell the river of seekers for solutions such as I have described: human scale and balanced communication, denser networks, the monk's solution, a mosaic of life-styles, or the answer given by a cult or guru.

Other sorts of responses to social noise have been noted, for example, in Chapter 4, selective perception and exposure, insulation, apathy, avoidance, specialization, chunking, queuing, magic formulas, lags of decision and consensus, resistance to modernization; in Chapter 5, hostile responses, fears, loss of trust, alienation; in Chapter 6, ingrouping, rising ethnicity, emphasizing boundaries, nostalgia; in Chapter 7, romanticism, separatism, backlashes, defensive closing, scapegoating, and cultism.

After closing, what trips the lever toward opening, I think, is boredom and a sense of information restriction (bad redundancy — with possible resentment of the extremes to which heroes or villains of closing have gone. Such feelings are signs that the swing has gone too far; what was felt as good redundancy comes to be too much of a good thing — bad redundancy (monotony, mechanicalness, formalism, rigidity, banality). I suggest that the hero has a vanguard role, as does the villain (Chapter 5) in pushing things too far, whether toward opening or closing.

Such descriptions of things already happening are hardly predictions of a sort to test hypotheses. Still less are speculations about a mosaic of life-styles or the role of heroes and villains in bringing about swings of opening and closing. Rather, they are an effort to visualize a few of the responses people might make to a world filled with noise.

To get to testing hypotheses, an analytical typology of possible responses to social noise needs to be spelled out, bearing in mind that opening and closing responses are *strategies* that depend on particular circumstances. There is need to be more specific about type of group, sector, and level of organization. Opening at one level might mean closing at another. For example, an expanding firm takes on new ventures, but its growth puts a strain on departments such as assembly, accounting, or research and development, which tend to slow down, specialize, or otherwise restrict their stress from growth of the organization. When a typology of opening and closing at specific levels is made, a paradigm can be set up as a probability matrix predicting types of response to various conditions of social noise, as hypothesized in Chapter 4.

Because social noise is doubtless translatable into anomie (both being forms of entropy), the well-known scheme of Robert K. Merton (1968:194) — conformity, innovation, ritualism, retreatism, rebellion — is suggestive. Retreatism includes some responses I have called closing. Innovation and rebellion apply to opening. Yet I would be reluctant to use it because, for one thing, it is based on the success or failure of achievement in a structure, not on a communication failure of noise. Second, it fails to account for the anomie of affluence (Mizruchi, 1964; Simon and Gagnon, 1976) as well as, in my opinion, does social noise. That is, Merton's scheme does not take enough account of anomie among those who *attain* culturally prescribed goals, yet experience social noise that may drive them toward cults or other sorts of closing. Nor, it seems to me, do retreatism and ritualism quite describe cultic searches.

Testing hypotheses about social noise requires better indicators of its various forms: semantic, stylistic, informational, and contagious. Noise has here been defined in subjective terms of relevance to receivers' needs — and perhaps must be. Also, the distinction between good and bad redundancy remains partly subjective: namely, in terms of how good or bored people feel about it; nor have I been able to avoid this. To sociologists raised on theories of the subjective meaningfulness of social relations, like those of Charles H. Cooley, George H. Mead, Bronislaw Malinowski, and Max Weber, this subjectivity is hardly surprising, though no less knotty a problem.

Leaving such theoretical and empirical tasks for the future, I have here drawn together the threads of a theory of opening and closing and speculated about specific implications and hypotheses in the hope of stimulating research.

Notes

Chapter 1. Social noise

1 R. Murray Schafer writes (1973:33) that increasing noise more than offsets advances in high fidelity; our "soundscape" is becoming "low-fi." See also: Robert Baron (1970); Theodore Berland (1970); David C. Glass and Jerome E. Singer (1972), experimental studies of noise and other stressors such as electric shock on task performance and physiology; Lucy Kavaler (1975); Karl D. Kryter (1970); John Gabriel Navarra (1969); Henry Still (1970); Rupert Taylor (1970).

2 Unrest is the starting point for collective behavior, according to the theory of Herbert Blumer (1939). See also O. Klapp (1972).

3 This conception plainly goes beyond the usual definition of noise in information theory, as disturbances leading to uncertainties (stated as entropy in bits) of senders and receivers about messages; or the cause of information loss, wrong reception or interpretation of signals; such as equivocation, "uncertainty as to which symbol was transmitted when a given signal is received" (Pierce, 1961:154); and "bogus information" produced by the noise source (Cherry, 1966:205). My concept goes beyond uncertainties about messages to such things as ugliness, stylistic conflict, and information that is damaging (entropic) to the receiver, however true and new. It also includes perfectly good information that is irrelevant, or in the wrong time, place, amount, subject matter, order, chunks, and so forth, according to receivers' needs; as well as bad redundancy, which, instead of helping transmission, interferes with new and needed information one might have gotten from a channel during that time. By extending noise beyond the somewhat restricted technical meaning, I have tried to gain the benefits of using it as a sensitizing concept (Blumer, 1954; Glaser and Strauss, 1967:241) — which does not preclude the possibility of treating such things mathematically.

4 In thermodynamics, in which the concept of entropy was first developed, a change in entropy is defined by a ratio of the reversible heat energy added to or absorbed by a system to the absolute temperature. Momentous steps were taken when Shannon and Weaver (1949) applied the term entropy to the uncertainty reduced by a signal; and theorists such as Erwin Schrödinger, L. Brillouin, and Richard C. Raymond conceived the information on which life is built, such as that of DNA, as the negative reciprocal of entropy (negentropy). (For their views, see Walter Buckley, ed., 1968:143–65.) Anatol Rapoport (1976:233) says, "In thermodynamics entropy is defined in terms of the relation between energy and temperature. In communication theory entropy refers to the uncertainty associated with messages. A more far-fetched connection is difficult to imagine, but it has been conclusively demonstrated by the mathematical isomorphism between the two."

5 Such meaninglessness is referred to in contemporary literature by terms such as existentialist despair, alienation, anomie, legitimation crisis (Habermas, 1975), and inauthenticity of institutions (Etzioni, 1968:635).

6 The distribution of noise, depending as it does on communication, is probably unlike that of physical pollution, which does strike the poor harder. A study of air pollution by the

191

Energy Policy Project of the Ford Foundation (*Environment*, March, 1976) found that of families living in Washington, D.C., less than one percent making over $7,000 a year were exposed to carbon monoxide levels above the federal standard in 1969; but thirteen percent of the families below this level were so afflicted.

There is probably a relationship among city size, literacy, income per capita, and information load (so, presumably, noise). R. Meier (1962:132) estimated that an inhabitant of a city like New York receives 100 times the information flow received by an inhabitant of a city like Addis Ababa with low literacy and income per capita.

7   Having more education than one's work calls for is a principal cause of job dissatisfaction when advancement chances are slim. A study by the Survey Research Center at the University òf Michigan found that twenty-seven percent of America's workers are "overqualified" for their jobs.

8   An instance of social closing triggered by acoustical noise is given in an experiment by psychologists Kenneth Matthews, Jr. and Lance Canon (1975) which showed that a high level of noise made people less kind and willing to help one another. When a field worker dropped books on the street during normal noise (about 50 decibels), 20 percent of random passers-by stopped to help. With noise at 87 decibels, only 10 percent played the good Samaritan. Laboratory experiments showed that failure to help was not due simply to the wish to get away from noise sooner, as the time in the noisy room could not be shortened. My interpretation would be that noise, past a point, triggers a generalized closing, which discourages giving or receiving information, helping, or any exchange likely to increase stress already felt to be too high.

Holloway and Hornstein (1976) found what I would call closing to social noise. Their experiments showed that bad news, such as of an assassination, made people less cooperative and socially responsible, damaged social bonds with strangers, and produced rank prejudice.

Chapter 2. Opening and closing in open societies

1   Picasso said, "I was filled with green so I painted green" (Florsheim).

2   By denying necessity of synchronicity, I merely wish to avoid the implication of society marching in step according to opening and closing rhythms. Such a picture would be simplistic even for a small society, let alone a complex pluralistic one with groups in varying relationships with one another. Three reasons for not expecting much synchronicity may here be mentioned. The first is varying contingencies. Living systems vary in their needs and states and so do opportunites offered by environments. Not only does a complex society offer many different sorts of environment, but the same environment could offer opposite stimuli to open or close to different sorts of persons or collectivities; for example, travel to an ethnocentric tourist versus a cosmopolitan, or the high noise of a city to a religious sect versus a university research team. And in any case one may invoke the old standby of multiple causation theory: that whatever tendency there may be to open or close is only one factor in whatever is happening. Many forces, ranging from sudden disasters to steady trends like bureaucratization, are not very responsive to vital rhythms. Such contingencies may obscure the pattern of opening and closing.

A second reason for not expecting much synchronicity is varying time periods, so that, even where cycles are plainly occurring, peaks and troughs do not coincide. One source of such variation is plainly difference in natural length of cycles at different system levels — if we use J. G. Miller's (1965) classification: cell, organ, organism, group, organization, society, supranational system. At one end (cellular and organismic), opening and closing consist of such things as nerve-firing and synchronization, orienting reflex and attention span, measured in from fractions of seconds to at most hours; whereas at the other end (societal, supranational) the individual may be involved in cycles such as ecumenical-mindedness or internationalism, or fashions (Richardson and Kroeber, 1940), which take decades or even longer.

Another source of variation of time periods is that all responses are subject to lags of one sort or another. It takes time to get people going — communicate, promote, educate, legislate, and so on. They may also persevere in policies not in tune with the current mood. So one might find a law restricting immigration or opening a school system to minorities passed after the mood that initiated it had shifted. Lags help cycles to vary and put indicators out of step.

A third reason for not expecting much synchronicity of opening and closing is that any policy acted on is likely to produce eddies of opposite reaction. So in Egypt in 1976 an upsurge of Islamic orthodoxy appeared to be a direct result of President Anwar Sadat's liberalization policies, permitting public consumption of alcohol, liberalizing divorce laws, and improving the status of women. In the United States, backlashes responded to movements like civil rights, women's lib, and school busing. The more vigorously a policy is effected, the more likely seem reactions of opposition. At such times it is hard to tell whether the overall situation is opening or closing.

Nevertheless, such difficulties should not discourage search for synchronicity among indicators of opening and closing. Indeed, it seems to me that with so many things working against it, to find even a little synchronicity has more evidential weight than not finding it; a small amount among, say, institutions at the same level, supports the hypothesis whereas lack of synchronicity does not necessarily challenge it.

3 For example, some indicators of mass media content suggest that there was a closing from the mid-sixties to the mid-seventies. Preliminary comparison of American television programming in February, 1966, and February, 1976, indicated a decrease in variety, both overall and in given time slots — certain viewing hours becoming more standardized in terms of what one could expect to see. Another change in content that may indicate closing was the virtual disappearance of Westerns (from 11 percent to 0 percent of total broadcasting time) along with a rise in crime and law enforcement dramas (from 6 percent to 20 percent of total broadcasting time). If it is fair to assume that Westerns portray lawless violence in the open spaces and freedom of the frontier, whereas crime dramas show violence in a regulated urban setting followed by law enforcement, then such a shift in content might be in step with general loss of variety, both indicating closing.

In another sector of media, comparison of titles of magazine stories and articles for 1965 and 1975 in the *Readers' Guide to Periodical Literature* showed an increase in topics classified as closing (such as nostalgia and moral reinforcement) and a decline in those classified as opening (such as speculations about outer space).

Villain images in media are also an indicator of closing to entropy, if the theorizing presented in Chapter 5 is correct. An increase in frequency of such characterizations should be expected at the same times as other signs of closing.

Such tentative observations are offered not as fact but merely as illustration of the sort of agreement among indicators that it would be reasonable to look for if there were, indeed, a closing in popular mood from the mid-sixties to the mid-seventies.

4 Adapted from Klapp (1975) with permission.

Chapter 3. The feast of the media

1 Art historian Anne Hollander (1974:20—1) notes that during the late eighteenth and nineteenth centuries, public reaction to art seems to have been keener than it now is in our

media-saturated society: " . . . paintings often had an exciting public existence quite different from the one they experience today. Long before movies, people loved to see fantasies brought to life and popular attitudes dramatically depicted. In Paris and London, eager crowds would stand in line and pay to see a single huge canvas by Benjamin Haydon or Jacques Louis David, and they would often respond to it with strong emotions, participating actively in the event by strewing flowers or shaking their fists or fainting."

2 Marshall McLuhan (1964) claimed that electronic media are restoring the sensory balance lost in a print culture. But our consideration of oral systems suggests that one would not be really "retribalized" by plunging into media systems deprived of dialogical communication. Extension of media *at the expense* of the oral system would mean trouble because many believe (Matson and Montagu, 1967) that health, wisdom, happiness, and freedom depend on oral networks.

3 According to a small business subcommittee of the Senate, the government was using 5,298 different kinds of forms in 1973; ten billion sheets of paper are shuffled by government employees every year. *Congressional Quarterly (Christian Science Monitor,* October 15, 1975).

4 This happens to be the same number of hours per day that workers in Chinese communes are bombarded by radio propaganda (Printz, 1974).

5 Eric Sevareid commented, "Now, you can bring every ill in the world into everybody's ken, violence or whatever . . . It . . . [makes] a difference in the whole nervous system of society. Another idea I have . . . [is] news every other day . . . We could do a better job and let everybody's nerves rest a little while. There is a kind of news pollution" (Quoted by Arthur Unger, *Christian Science Monitor,* August 19, 1976).

6 See *Control of the Direct Broadcast Satellite* (1974).

7 Laser transmission by optical fibers, developed by the International Telephone and Telegraph Corporation, was by 1975 able to handle simultaneously 1,400 voice conversations – ultimately perhaps 10,000 conversations, 20 channels of color TV, or one billion bits of information per second (equivalent to the entire Bible in one-tenth of a second), according to Dr. Albert E. Cookson, senior vice president and technical director of ITT in New York.

Chapter 4. When information turns to noise

1 Richard Meier (1962:132—6) also early recognized the threat of information overload in modern society, estimating that by 1992 the practical limits of human communication would be reached, and that growth in variety and quantity of cultural interaction in the urban environment "is coming to an end."

2 MacKay and McCulloch (1952). A bit is a binary unit of information; for example, whether "heads" or "tails." Technically, a bit is the logarithm of two (choices) to the base 2 (Rapoport, 1953). Hence, if a signal tells you which of four suits a card belongs to, it contains two bits of information.

3 Lerner's (1958) hypothesis that media use leads to rising frustrations has been questioned by Hornik (1977), whose findings from a study of Salvadorean seventh to ninth grade students were that aspirations and dissatisfaction of students with television did not increase faster than of those without television, and that television somewhat lessened desire to live and work in the city. Hornik's hypothesis is that impact of media is not simple and direct, but depends on selective perception and especially how the environment is perceived: media raise expectations and aspirations only when the environment also rewards such increase, otherwise their effect is minimal. "People choose aspirations for themselves consistent with their perception of their environment" (411). The matter remains inconclusive, needing further research on other populations.

4 The selective exposure hypothesis is favored over mere avoidance as a response to dissonance, according to research by Carter et al. (1969).

5 It is the difference — irrelevance of subjects to one another and perhaps to the student's career — more than the sheer amount of information that makes the load so heavy. Were courses scheduled to reinforce one another (rather than the "cafeteria-style" curriculum) some of this difficulty could be eliminated.

6 Noted to be a function of rumors by Festinger et al. (1948).

7 Henry Ford announced on February 19, 1975: "In my 30 years as a businessman, I have never before felt so uncertain and so troubled about the future of both my country and my company . . . Day by day the problems mount and nothing is decided. People are rapidly coming to the conclusion that nobody knows what to do, nobody is steering, the problems are running away with us and the country is headed straight for disaster" (Free Press Wire Service).

Almost in dismal confirmation of Ford's misgiving came the report of Stewart L. Udall, former Secretary of the Interior (1978), that: "Four tedious years after the Arab oil embargo convincingly demonstrated just how precarious the United States' energy position is, the only verdict we can pronounce is that the democratic process has broken down. Indeed, for the first time in the postwar period the American government has failed completely to come to grips with a critical domestic problem. Three successive Presidents have attempted to implement energy plans, and three different Congresses — after endless arguments — have refused to pass the laws needed to deal with the shortages which threaten the future of our economic system. . . A failure of leadership . . . encompasses both political parties, and all levels of government. As a result, there is still no national will with which to attack the energy crisis because there is still no consensus about the nature and dimension of the energy problem itself."

James G. Miller (1975:501) holds that large societies as wholes are spared many stresses of information overload because they "have many channels to process inputs and many adjustment processes for diminishing information flows over their numerous input channels." Nevertheless, decider components are vulnerable to overloads such as meeting short-term goals and coping with immediate emergencies, leaving no time for long-term planning. "Warnings of obvious impending shortages of energy in many parts of the world . . . did not receive sufficient attention from deciders of these societies until a crisis occurred. Development of alternative energy sources has generally lagged behind what would have been possible. Deciders dealt with more urgent emergency situations or more compelling political issues. For years little money was allocated or effort devoted to research and development on solutions to the energy shortage."

8 Kenneth Boulding (1971) visualizes an "entropy trap," perhaps in one hundred years, "in which the stock of knowledge will be so large that the whole effort of the knowledge industry will have to be devoted to transmitting it from one generation to the next" (Quoted in Roszak, 1972:211).

9 The failure of social science to solve social problems has many more roots than information overload. I do not mean to imply that it is the chief, let alone sole, cause of problems that are growing faster than solutions.

10 James R. Taylor (1972) recommends that the simple channel model applied to individuals be replaced by more complex models of networks with feedback loops, and of programs with varying goals and subroutines. In terms of James G. Miller's study (1971), group response (assuming it is part of a channel) includes all processes of transduction, encoding, decoding, association, memory, deciding, and feedback that go into group response to an information input.

11 Hypotheses about information overload are inferred to extend to other sorts of social noise. For the sake of brevity, I assume that every hypothesis about social noise is divisible

into subhypotheses about informational, semantic, stylistic, and contagious forms.

12 For instance, very young children tolerate more confusion and are less bored by repetition than are older children and adults, because they have not yet formed mental models and expectations that information should be relevant, make sense, and not be silly (Glassman, 1976); therefore, they are less bothered by high variety or redundancy of information.

13 The uncommitted are expected to be distractible and variable as contrasted with the ritualism of the bureaucratic virtuoso, who likes closure in rules (Merton, 1968:253).

14 Social network density is defined as interconnectedness, measured by the ratio of the number of actual to possible relationships among people who know one another (Mitchell, 1969:18). It is also described as relationships that are close-knit (E. Bott, 1971), or interlocking (Laumann, 1973).

15 Network uniformity is here defined as similarity among members in such things as occupation, faith, ethnicity, status, and background. Combined with network density, it resembles what Durkheim called mechanical solidarity. Low density and high diversity make people more masslike, as Kornhauser (1959) describes the availability for mass movements, which result from looseness of communal ties. High density and uniformity make people less masslike, whether bound in communally, or available for mobilization — as Pinard (1971) portrays joining a new movement because of communal or religious obligations, ties, and pressures.

Chapter 5. Entropic communication

1 The physicist Clerk Maxwell proposed to reverse heat degradation — essentially to achieve perpetual motion — by conceiving of gas in a container with two compartments, with a tiny hole in the wall separating them. There a demon would preside, opening and closing a door, allowing fast-moving molecules to pass and stopping the slow. So the temperature of one side would rise while that of the other fell — defeating the thermodynamic law that heat never flows from less to more without work. The trouble was, as critics pointed out, that the demon *would* have to work, and even to see the particles would use light energy.

2 Norbert Wiener (1950) noted that the law of entropy implies an Augustinian view of progress: The world is a dangerous place, peace and order are temporary, man lacks ability to save himself, a happy outcome is not guaranteed in the earthly city.

3 An offshoot was the food panic of 1974 (*Forbes*, February 1, 1975) — a rush to buy canned and dehydrated foods for long-term storage, which had "blossomed" in eighteen months into a thirty million dollar business supporting twenty to thirty companies.

4 D. Phillips (1974) found that suicides increase immediately after a suicide story has been publicized in newspapers in Britain and the United States, and that the more publicity the greater the increase in suicide. Such influence of suggestion on suicide he calls the "Werther effect."

5 An interesting conception has emerged in parapsychological research. Dr. Karagulla (1967:158—70) describes "energy fields around human beings," perceived by "sensitives" though not yet verified by instrumentation. Some people can "brighten," others muddy and drain one's psychic energy; a "sapper," says Karagulla, exerts a pull on others, dragging them into exhaustion, irritability, even illness. Sensitives report seeing "streamers" or "tentacles" shooting out and hooking into the field of a person close by. "Sappers" are usually self-centered, unaware of their energy pull.

6 Eva Le Gallienne (1955), who played the part and translated the play, describes Hedda as a tormented creature who made up for her barrenness of spirit through romanticism. Ibsen described her as "cold — ice cold."

7 Klapp (1949, 1954, 1956, 1958, 1959, 1962, 1964a, 1964b).

8 Suicide may be predictable from the decline of violent villains (while other kinds rise?).

This is inferred from the inverse relationship of rates of aggression and suicide (Binstock, 1974).

9   McClelland (1975) used content-analysis of children's texts, best-selling novels, and hymns to predict war from a drop in the need for affiliation and a growing aggressive spirit represented by high need for power, which led to a self-righteousness favoring war. Plausibly, the treatment of villains could reflect such things.

10 The National Commission on the Causes and Prevention of Violence directed its Media Task Force to investigate the relationship of mass media programming and violence. This led to a contract with Dean George Gerbner and his staff at the Annenberg School of Communications to analyze the violence content of TV entertainment programming. See David L. Lange, Robert K. Baker, and Sandra J. Ball (1969:311—39). A television Violence Index was developed from percentage of violent programs, rate of violent episodes, and number of roles calling for characterization as violent or victim (George Gerbner and Larry Gross, 1976:173—99). The National Citizens Committee for Broadcasting issued a violence index which showed that of the ten most violent television shows in the summer of 1976, four were on ABC, four on NBC, and two on CBS; and that viewers watching ABC could count on an average of 4.4 gunfights, fistfights, and other mayhem per hour of "action" programming (*Newsweek*, September 6, 1976:46).

11 Imitation is also variously called modeling, identification, role-playing, emulation, vicarious learning, contagion, and suggestion. Unlike most communication, a special feature of imitation is that even in close interaction it is usually one-way: Both parties don't do it equally; and except in coaching and tutoring, the model is unaware of the copier and his own impact on him, gets little feedback, and feels no responsibility. An extreme case is hero worship: intense, prolonged idolization by unknown fans. The paradox is that a relationship so lopsided in terms of feedback should be so powerful: Many cases can be found of people who have modeled their careers on one hero. Hysterias and crazes also show the power of imitation. Both these kinds of imitation have effects approaching the hypnotic, though neither gives the model much inkling of the impact he has on others. Psychologists (especially Bandura and Walters, 1963; Bandura, 1969, 1971) have studied experimentally conditions (such as direct and vicarious reinforcement, emotional arousal, dependency, status-envy, uniformity of cultural models) that encourage imitation.

12 Historians (Carlyle, 1841; Wecter, 1941; Johnson, 1943; Hook, 1943; Fishwick, 1954) have shown the influence of "great men," whereas sociologists (Czarnowski, 1919; Riddle, 1931; Mecklin, 1941; Duncan, 1962; Klapp, 1962, 1964) have studied the social functions of heroes in ritual, control, and cohesion.

13 A survey of three television networks, CBS, NBC, and ABC, by the *Christian Science Monitor* in 1975, found that alcoholic beverages were being seen or mentioned on an average of once every seventeen minutes of prime time (8:00 to 11:00 P.M.). Liquor was most frequently used for a prop to give an actor something to do, humor, an impression of sophistication, or relief of tension. A tally of NBC showed that over twice as many scenes involved alcoholic as any kind of nonalcoholic drink. All this emphasis persisted in spite of a quiet campaign by federal officials to get liquor off the tube.

14 B. Greene (1974:296—7) tells the story of the Alice Cooper Band's use of theatrical sadism for mass hysteria. Cooper's comment was: "America loves stars. It's part of the American way. That's one of the reasons our group could make it. Billy the Kid was a rotten guy, you know . . . he always walked up behind the guy and shot him in the head. Look at Dillinger . . . He was thought of as a Robin Hood . . . America certainly does consider gangsters heroes, Al Capone, people like that . . . Look at us."

15 One author, Brian Garfield, was so appalled that his story of an urban vigilante hero who took up a career killing muggers (*Death Wish*), might possibly glorify and legitimize violence that he asked CBS to ban its presentation on television, even offering to forego his

own royalty. Their response was to schedule it at a late hour with a warning about its content.

16 Such as baseball and football players crediting their performance to energy from a candy bar or certain brand of sugar. Domino Sugar was required to use the following corrective for one-fourth of its advertising over a one-year period: "Do you recall some of our past messages saying that Domino Sugar gives you strength, energy, and stamina? Actually, Domino is not a special or unique source of strength, energy and stamina. No sugar is, because what you need is a balanced diet and plenty of rest and exercise."

17 Plea bargaining was a main way that Watergate offenders escaped punishment. High-ranking officials received lighter sentences than pawns in the original burglary. Deploring the suspended sentence on a minor charge given former Attorney General Kleindienst in lieu of prosecution for the felony of perjury, the *Christian Science Monitor* (June 12, 1974) said: "A judge goes too far when, in imposing a suspended minimum sentence, he lavishly praises America's first former attorney general to have been convicted of a crime. As the ordeal goes on, Americans need to be assured . . . that the forces of law are giving proper weight to wrongdoing and striving for . . . equal application of . . . justice."

18 Another survey using a scale of political alienation, reported, even among more successful people, a seeping sense of isolation from political leaders and concern that the "whole American way of life is a fraud" (Robert S. Gilmore and Robert S. Lamb, 1976). A survey of children aged five to twelve years by T. G. Bever, M. L. Smith, Barbara Bengen, and T. G. Johnson, published in the *Harvard Business Review*, found that misleading television advertising is turning preadolescent children into cynics, who already believe that, like advertising, business and other institutions are riddled with hypocrisy (Francis, 1976).

19 Christie and Geis (1970) found in experimental games what Pareto's famous theory of circulation of elites took for granted.

20 "A young man who had fairly well recovered from an acute schizophrenic episode was visited in the hospital by his mother. He was glad to see her and impulsively put his arm around her shoulders, whereupon she stiffened. He withdrew his arm and she asked, 'Don't you love me anymore?' He then blushed, and she said, 'Dear, you must not be so easily embarrassed and afraid of your feelings.' The patient was able to stay with her only a few minutes more and following her departure he assaulted an aide and was put in the tubs" Bateson (1972:217). Ray Birdwhistell (1970) shows such a "double bind" even in the handling of a baby while changing his diaper.

21 Analyzed by Buckley, Burns, and Meeker (1974).

22 The commercialism of television is so strong that President Ford was interrupted to make way for a commercial during his appearance on NBC's "Meet the Press," on November 9, 1975.

   Despite all that had been said about not exploiting the minds of children, a study by Action for Children's Television (ACT), reported in December, 1975, found that commercials interrupt programs directed to the under-twelve viewing audience "on average of once every 2.9 minutes." Peggy Charren, president of ACT, said that the practice of selling multiple items in the same commercial is becoming increasingly common and fosters a "want" mentality in young children.

Chapter 6. Good redundancy: identity as playback

1 *Redundancy:* That which is redundant or in excess; anything superfluous or superabundant . . . Syn. − tautology, pleonasm, verbosity, verbiage, prolixity, diffuseness, circumlocution, periphrasis" (*Webster's New International Dictionary*).

2 Some sociologists hold that people on the political right wing have a "greater symbolic in-

vestment in the past than the present" — the "quondam complex," in the United States at least (Lipset and Raab, 1970:504). If this is true, the converse would not follow: that is, that most people attached to the past or feeling loss of a personal past are right-wingers. It would be surprising to find such a fundamental need as redundancy distributed according to a political spectrum.

3 Resonance is seen in the phenomenon of two separate things vibrating together according to the same frequency. In physics it is conceived as a vibration of large amplitude resulting from an application of a forced vibration to a system, when the period of the force equals that of a natural vibration of the system. The notion is sometimes used to distinguish warm social relationships from those that are impersonal, plastic, alienating; being signified by colloquial expressions such as: "good vibes," "warmed up to," "sympathize with," "turned on," "heart-to-heart," "swinging," "engrossed," *"en rapport,"* "we-feeling." I would define social resonance as mutual responsiveness of a warm sort among two or more persons, induced by signals, whether from an outside source or as feedback from the relationship, which actuates recall of valued parts of the memory and identity of each that can be shared — that is, good redundancy. For example, two persons might resonate from listening to a tune or from their own responses to one another. The main idea is that the goal of human communication is not merely transfer of information but responsiveness — resonance — reached through attunement and kept by good redundancy in feedback loops.

4 "Counterculture arises in those sectors of a society in which day-to-day experience substantially contradicts or insufficiently reinforces the society's ideology . . . Analytically, there are two ways their commitment to the ideology can be weakened, first by lack of contact with plausibility structures that uphold the ideology, and second by experiences that the ideology cannot explain" (Westhues, 1972:28).

5 Webster's Dictionary defines banality as "commonplace, trite; used until so common as to have lost novelty and interest; hackneyed, stale; stereotyped; vapid."

6 Usually described as the "girl next door," cute, wholesome, the "kind of girl you'd like to marry;" but bland rather than exciting or glamorous (questionnaire data).

7 Psychologists say boredom is a deprivation. D. E. Berlyne (1960:187) says it is a tension, a state of arousal of a drive which occurs when "external stimuli are excessively scarce or are excessively monotonous." Both of these conditions ". . . mean a meager influx of information — in the one case because signals are lacking and in the other case because signals are highly predictable. The drive in question we usually call boredom." Unlike drowsiness, boredom "works through a rise in arousal" first expressed in restlessness (like doodling) and a tendency to escape physically or by daydreaming or artistic activity; it can lead to mounting struggles for variety, even agonizing agitation and emotional upset. Even when it comes with satiation, say with food or entertainment, boredom is a deprivation as real as hunger, with severe effects as shown by Donald O. Hebb and other psychologists at McGill University in studies of sensory deprivation begun in the early fifties. For example, men were paid to lie on a comfortable bed around the clock in a lighted cubicle, wearing eye covers admitting diffuse light, gloves and cardboard muffs to limit touch perception, and soundproofing masking noise. About the only interesting experiences these men had were eating and trips to the bathroom. Though the pay was good, and there seemed to be hardly any stress, most could stand no more than two to three days. Even after four or five hours, they could not follow a connected train of thought and found their ability to concentrate disturbed for twenty—four hours or more after coming out of isolation. Monkeys, too, raised in a box with just a dim light under conditions of sensory deprivation become debilitated or aggressive (Prescott, 1974; Harlow, 1962). Woodburn Heron, one of the McGill psychologists, concluded that a changing sensory environment seems essential for normal mental functioning of humans. Variety is not only the spice of life but the very

stuff of it. A review of sensory deprivation studies is given by Suedfeld (1975). Earlier studies dramatized adverse effects, whereas later ones showed that sensory deprivation can also help perceptual and intellectual functioning, and even be therapeutic. Most important for our purposes: It is motivational, arousing subjects to be more open, aware, and ready to react and change.

8   J. R. Pierce (1961) says all completely random (Gaussian) noise sounds alike, hence monotonous, even if it is most various and unpredictable. This is because to recognize a thing as new, one must be able to distinguish it from what is old. But, to be distinguishable, some of the sounds and other things we perceive must be similar enough as classes or patterns for us to compare what is new with them; this means that some kind of similarity is necessary to appreciate anything, new or old. So totally unfamiliar languages or music — perhaps jazz, rock, or flamenco — sound alike to the uninitiated. "To be appreciated art must be in a language familiar to the audience; otherwise no matter how great the variety may be, the audience will have an impression of monotony, of sameness. We can be surprised repeatedly only by contrast with that which is familiar, not by chaos" (267). We might compare receiving over a teletype machine either of the following series of signals: "XDROTVLPZNE . . ." — or "DDDDDDDDDD . . ." Both the jumble and the repetitious series would be a "blah" of boring sameness. Again, suppose one is watching a baseball game. It goes on for nine innings, no hits, no runs, no errors — or *all* home runs! It would not take many games like this before the audience stopped coming out. Or suppose the opposite extreme of random variety: Everything is changing and surprising, runners go either way, fouls are played, some balls are pitched from the grandstands. Soon it all becomes boring nonsense and the audience goes home. Bad redundancy can result from either too much sameness or too much variety.

9   As with noise defined in terms of receivers' intentions (Chapter 1), there is an undeniable element of subjectivity in the distinction of good from bad redundancy: namely, how people feel about it, whether boredom or "that good feeling" of warmth of heart and reinforcement of identity. As an example, the sameness of Howard Johnson's restaurants may be boring to some, but welcome to others who are looking for an oasis of familiarity and reliable standards while traveling strange highways. Again, an American at home might be bored by hamburgers but get "that good feeling" encountering one in another country; and yet another American seeking authentic travel experience might be disappointed to see hamburgers displacing fish and chips in Britain and tacos in Mexico. Do we, then, in the distinction of good from bad redundancy have a research difficulty of the sort faced by students of "happiness" (such as Bradburn and Caplovitz, 1965) who feel they must identify it solely by subjective report or give it up as a scientific category?

It may be that there is no entirely objective distinction of good from bad redundancy, or of good variety from noise. Nevertheless, I should not wish at this point to conclude that objective properties of messages and social forms cannot help such distinction. For one thing, information is measured statistically (however incompletely) in "bits." If it is poorer in bad redundancy this should be registered. Also D. Berlyne and colleagues (1973, 1974) found that objective properties of figures, such as complexity, produce differences in subjective responses such as interest, liking, and boredom. Besides, I have mentioned at least two distinctions between good and bad redundancy that can be objective. One is exact and mechanical, versus artistic, lively repetition. The other is the historical fact of whether information of a redundant message is related to one's background and identity, matching important memories, as does one's mother tongue distinguished from languages learned later. Such characteristics may not replace subjective criteria but should help the research distinction.

10   I have emphasized how much a person or society needs the resonance from repeated, familiar signals. The main thrust is that there are minimal and optimal levels of good redun-

dancy for all systems that have, or claim to have, an identity. Yet there are a number of unanswered questions about kinds and levels of good and bad redundancy. I assume that the amount of redundancy can be determined in part from properties or a message or signal, for example, how much repetition or pattern can be found in it (see A. C. Staniland, 1966:193—8). But I also assume that redundancy is relative to the kind and state of the system, that is, its need for information, channel capacities, functions of the moment. In general, a closed (static or traditional) society needs redundancy more than does an open one. But questions such as how much redundancy a given system needs, or what generates banality leading to boredom and alienation, need considerable empirical sociological study.

Chapter 7. Theory of opening and closing

1 See Vidmar and Rokeach (1974).

2 According to *The New York Times* of December 17, 1970, there were then over 2,000 communes in the United States, not including several thousand urban co-ops (Fairfield, 1971:3).

3 Some results of supposedly successful busing were also discouraging. A ten-year study of school desegregation in Riverside, California, where one-way busing had distributed black and Chicano children among eleven schools, found neither better education nor less segregation for minority children. "We found, instead, that the children in each ethnic group became more and more cliquish over the years and less accepting of those outside their own group" (Miller and Gerard, 1976:66—70, 100).

4 Sociologist Bernard J. Siegal (1970) finds closing with cultivation of identity symbols as a defensive adaptation when groups cannot respond aggressively, among, for example, Pueblo Indians, Hutterites, Amish, Mormons, and Jews in *shtetls*. See also Comeau and Driedger, 1978.

5 J. Whitworth (1975:216) found "alternating periods of relative openness to the world and purificatory withdrawal" in the history of three sects: Shakers, the Oneida community, and Bruderhof.

6 Mayr (1975) finds both open and closed behavior programs among species' evolutionary strategies. Natural selection sometimes favors a genetically "closed" program, sometimes an "open" one. For example, intraspecific communication tends to be closed, as when courtship displays serve as isolating mechanisms; whereas open programs for food and habitat selection have more survival value. Imprinting of young is an interesting example of openness in learning the object of a fixed behavior program.

7 More technical terms are input and internal transduction of information, as distinguished by J. G. Miller (1971:290).

8 The "Great Awakening" of intense revivalism in New England between 1730 and 1745 seems to have been a surge of opening similar to a mass movement. Though it triggered hysterical spasms like witch hunts, persecution of Quakers, and jeremiads from the Puritan theocracy, it prepared the way for a new form of social order: individualism, voluntarism, and democracy of a heterogeneous nationalism, relieving strains between Puritan orthodoxy and the individualism of commercial development (Rossel, 1970).

9 A prize-winning photographer describes the closure of artistic decision in this way: "Sometimes I have the feeling that here are all the makings of a perfect picture but one element is missing . . . that third something . . . I know not what. Then suddenly things begin to change. I wait, move in, the shutter clicks. I have that knowing feeling that I've captured something very, very special" (Converse, 1973).

10 Degas, according to Sir Kenneth Clark, was a severe classicist who did not like profusion of color; he could be so disturbed by a bouquet of flowers that he would ask that it be removed. He reached the peak of classical discipline, the "chiseling of reality until it reaches the idea.

11 Matisse is described as a purist "in search of the absolute." His goal was a calm that he considered all artists should strive to attain: "I want a balanced and pure art, neither disturbing nor distressing." The ideal that haunted his development was the blue harmony of Cezanne's *Trois Baigneuses,* which he kept in his studio. Nevertheless, in attaining his ideal, it could not be said that he was always closed. In early life he associated with the Fauves, tried all kinds of experiments, and sedulously copied masters in a search for a pure act of painting. Yet he put faith in the inner "revelations" of his unconscious and felt that the mind should "keep a sort of virginity towards the chosen elements and reject all that is offered by reasoning." He regarded contact with others not as something to be avoided but as a test of his own integrity: "I have never avoided the influence of others . . . I should have thought it a form of cowardice and a lack of sincerity towards myself. I believe the artist's personality owes its development and its strength to the struggles it undergoes . . . if he is overpowered, he deserves no better fate" (Escolier, 1960:41, 43, 158).

12 Another theorist whom I class as an opener is George T. L. Land (1973), a vigorous advocate of growth. He sees equilibrium as unnatural, the goal of life being not to preserve or adapt to but to transform the environment. Technology is not artificial and against man but a natural extension of biological functions such as locomotion. Land regards disruption of the environment — including the cries of environmentalists — as crises useful to challenge better technology. Closure of a system is treated in unfavorable terms compared with mutualistic growth.

13 Food is here taken as a synecdoche for matter and energy intake. The distinction from information is clearly stated by J. G. Miller (1971:279—81).

14 Such dichotomization into "good" and "bad" redundancy and variety implied by the chart of the "playing field" is for simplicity of initial theorizing. It does not rule out a middle ground, neither good nor bad, on a continuum between extremes.

15 The Law of Requisite Variety. "Let us . . . suppose we are watching two players, R., D. who are engaged in a game . . . if the variety in the outcomes is to be reduced . . . R's variety *must* be increased to at least the appropriate minimum. Only variety in R's moves can force down the variety in the outcomes . . . only variety in R can force down the variety due to D; only variety can destroy variety" W. R. Ashby (1956:202—18).

16 James Inverarity (1976) applied Kai Erikson's (1966) theory (following Durkheim, that boundary crises caused Puritan persecution and Antinomians, Quakers, and witches in New England) to outbreaks of lynching in Louisiana between 1889 and 1896, which peaked during disruption of the Solid South by the populist rebellion against class inequities. He concluded that "boundary crises produce repressive justice," but this depends on the degree of mechanical solidarity in the community (208). Such boundary crisis I would call bad opening in the terminology of this book.

17 A case being American Samoans, described as 28,000 people, including 4,000 bureaucrats, totally dependent on the United States, "wandering in their chrome wilderness alongside its polluted bay" (*Manchester Guardian,* November 9, 1974). See John H. Bodley (1974).

18 Sociologist Peter Blau (1974) generalizes about the point at which people in pluralistic societies will turn from ingroups to contacts with outsiders as an alternative to no associates: Increasing heterogeneity reaches a point at which people are forced to choose between having no ingroup for the time being and going to outsiders for interaction. On the assumption that people prefer outgroup associates to no associates, "proliferation of boundaries implicit in great heterogeneity lessens these barriers and encourages intergroup relations" (622). The concept of supersaturation is also useful in analyzing where tipping points may be. Boulding (1965:vii) says: "Societies, like solutions, get supersaturated or supercooled; that is, they reach a situation in which their present state is intrinsically unstable, but does not change because of the absence of some kind of nucleus around which

change can grow. Under these conditions, protest is like the seed crystal or the silver iodide in the cloud.'' Boulding mentions hypocrisy as a condition of supersaturation, where there is a strong hope of change waiting to be realized. In such terms accumulating social noise — of which people finally become aware — is a supersaturation that approaches a tipping point. Widespread "turning off" would indicate that the tipping was collective, not merely individual.

Chapter 8. Movements and possibilities

1 Auguries of such a turn in the tide can be seen in writings such as E. Fromm (1968); T. Roszak (1969); Klapp (1969); H. Cox (1969); C. Reich (1970); W. Braden (1970); and D. Yankelovich's (1974) survey of changes in attitudes of people between the ages of sixteen and twenty-four.

2 On the economic side an appealing picture of human scale is given by E. F. Schumacher (1973). Another example is the pioneering effort of a group led by Dr. Peter Goldmark, (inventor of color TV and the long-playing record), funded by the U.S. Department of Housing and Urban Development, to achieve the New Rural Society, reversing the rural-to-urban migration, revitalizing small towns by new ways of communication making possible dispersal of jobs and industry, face-to-face conference over a distance, and cultural enrichment in communication centers (Salisbury, 1975). All this seems to meet the wish, already expressed in polls, of fifty-five percent of Americans to live in the country.

A back-to-the-land movement was revealed by U.S. Census figures for 1970—1974, published in 1975. Population gains in rural and nonmetropolitan areas outpaced growth in metropolitan areas, especially in four regions: the Upper Great Lakes, Rocky Mountains, southern Appalachia, and the Ozark-Ouachita. Overall, metropolitan areas grew 2.9 percent while nonmetropolitan advanced 4.0 partly a spillover from suburbs. So a revival of small town and rural living seemed to be reversing a long trend. (*Christian Science Monitor*, July 3, 1975).

In a historic decision, Santa Barbara, California, regulated its own size. The City Council voted on April 22, 1975, on recommendation of the planning commission, despite opposition from growth advocates, to set a population limit of about 85,000 as all that could be accommodated without smog, traffic, sewage, and water problems significantly diminishing the quality of life. (The General Plan had previously allowed about 120,000 people.) It was to be done by "down-zoning" multiple-family residential areas from forty-three to twelve units per acre, a method already tested in courts.

In another historic decision, on August 13, 1975, the Ninth U.S. Circuit Court of Appeals in San Francisco backed the right of cities to curb growth, upholding an ordinance enacted by the city of Petaluma in 1972 restricting new housing to 500 units a year and establishing a green belt. That year Petaluma had reached a population of 30,500 after twenty-five percent increase in two years. The court held that such zoning restrictions were a valid use of police power, that a village had a right to use the zoning power delegated to it by the state for family values, youth values, quiet seclusion, and clean air; nor did such restriction wall out any particular income class nor any racial minority group.

3 So one writer describes the mountain folk with whom he lived for fourteen years: "They want to enjoy you as you are. Uniquely, mountain folk concentrate on 'reading' other people . . . They're people centered.'' This is the key to their inquisitiveness, not a desire to gossip maliciously. "They build fellowship and community . . . These folk, historically, have not yearned to grasp material things for themselves. Things are not prized above independence and self-reliance. When a Harlan, Kentucky, miner sang, "I don't want your millions mister,' he expressed the Appalachian spirit. Beyond plain food, humble shelter, and

open space their wants are minimal. No one ever accused them of being materialistic. They have not stolen our nation's natural resources. In fact, they sold their birthright titles to enterprises from the outside for a pittance. If America at the edge of its third century is searching for lost values which satisfy the human soul, it would do well to listen to the mountain voice placing people above things" (Grieser, 1976).

4 "At instant speeds . . . the public begins to participate directly in actions it had previously heard about at a distance in space and time." But "electric speed may . . . have violated human scale, tending as it does to transport man instantly everywhere" Marshall McLuhan (1974:56).

5 By network I mean a structure of channels, formal or informal, direct or mediated, which a substantial number of the same people share continually. It might take forms such as talk and gossip (Mitchell, 1969), visiting patterns (Loomis and McKinney, 1956), effective feedback of a town (Singer, 1973), or matrices of reinforcement of communal coopera-tion (Kunkel, 1970). The point is that the readership of large metropolitan newspapers or a typical suburban neighborhood or even sometimes the place where one works is *not* such a network.

6 The sociological term for such texture that overcomes disconnectedness is network densi-ty (J. C. Mitchell, 1969), also described as relationships that are close-knit (E. Bott, 1971) or interlocking (E. Laumann, 1973).

7 Many have charged positivistic science with treating information at the expense of mean-ing, such as Joad (1950), Matson (1964), or Roszak (1972) who blames science for having imposed on man "single vision" (417, 420) and dehumanizing objectivity (175, 222).

8 The status anxiety at the root of fashion was long ago noted by sociologists such as Sim-mel (1950) and C. W. Mills (1951). Recent studies such as C. Booker (1970) and John Weitz (1974) stress its nervous and frantic character.

9 I part here from Huizinga's (1950:199, 206) gloomy view that the play-spirit of civiliza-tion is threatened with extinction by technical organization and scientific thoroughness (Max Weber's matter-of-factness). Huizinga admits that there is an "agonistic principle" in communication that carries the world "back in the direction of play."

10 Kobo Abe (1974) gives a whimsical view of a life-style capsule made by a homeless man out of a corrugated paper box, worn over his head and shoulders and carried about like a snail's shell — a sort of mobile survival shelter.

11 This is a proposal to recognize and formalize some of what sociologists call natural urban areas when they serve a legitimate collective style or identity. Such collectively-defined places are distinct form personal space (Hall, 1966; Sommer, 1969) and privacy (B. Schwartz, 1968) on the one hand, and public territory on the other. Lyman and Scott (1967) call them home territories, which arise when groups informally take over parts of public territories and make them their own — makeshift clubhouses of children, hobo jun-gles, gangs' turf, ethnic enclaves, colonies, and so on. Home territories have boundaries, culture, and rules understood though not officially promulgated. Defense against invasion comes in part from concern to protect such identity and culture — which I here call good redundancy and elsewhere (1969) place as a basis of identity. A device such as a covenant is one way of formalizing what groups are trying to do anyway. Norman Mailer in his semi-serious campaign for the mayoralty of New York had such an idea when he proposed that the city be divided into districts, each of which could choose its own way of life, free love and marijuana legal in one, divorce and drugs outlawed in another, and so on. In 1976, some American cities were trying to create such areas by zoning; for example, Boston's "combat zones," Detroit's restriction of pornography, and Berkeley's licensing of massage parlors.

Another expression of the same tendency is the growth of mobile home communities across America. A U.S. Census in 1974 found almost four million people living in mobile homes; and the figure was fast climbing toward five million in 1977, according to the Manufactured Housing Institute (formerly the Mobile Home Manufacturers Association). Such communities are not merely an economical sort of housing but fill a void left by the decline of small towns and the decay of formerly closely knit, familistic, ethnic neighborhoods in cities. Many mobile home parks supply remarkably warm cameraderie and collective identity, a neighborhood of like-minded people who can boast that they know everyone else by first names. Social and recreational centers offer organized activities from which no one is left out, and residents participate in setting the goals of the community (Reuters, 1977).

Of course, in these days of easy communication and mobility, it is not necessary to suppose that network density high enough to support life-styles comes only from *spatial* proximity and boundaries, but they help.

12 Many cities regulate hedge and fence heights and require building setbacks that deny privacy, forcing homeowners into maintaining grounds as a show to others but as no comfort to themselves.

13 Other words for life-style territories are pejorative in one way or another; for example, ghetto, segregation, snob zone, parochialism. Separatism, though neutral, implies disconnection. Accommodation, also neutral, stresses conflict reduced rather than the positive side. Symbiosis is more favorable, stressing advantages of cooperation among different parties. Mosaic, in my judgment, has the right connotations, for it implies elements valuable in themselves, in a union or pattern superior to parts. One may note that Canada officially accepted the concept of an ethnic mosaic, announced as multicultural policy in October, 1971, to encourage groups to develop their own cultures; differentiation, not uniformity, was the goal.

14 Arnold Toynbee (1947:217, 220) recognized the opening and closing movement, with respect to mysticism, as "withdrawal and return." Turning to inner life for enrichment, the mystic withdraws from communication. "The withdrawal makes it possible for the personality to realize powers within himself which might have remained dormant if he had not been released for the time being from his social toils and trammels . . . This movement of Withdrawal-and-Return is not a peculiarity of human life which is only to be observed in the relations of human beings with their fellows. It is something that is characteristic of life in general."

15 I have described the psychedelic movement in *Collective Search for Identity* (1969: 170–6).

16 See the excellent collections of teachings of the mystics by Stace (1960) and Huxley (1944).

17 "Clairvoyant reality" is described in a symposium on paranormal communication in the *Journal of Communication* as a Psi-conducive state in which it is easier to get and send telepathic messages and such. It is different from ordinary sensory reality in that a person is aware of (1) the unity of all things (with less ego concern and more caring for others), (2) the illusoriness of time, (3) nonsensory ways of communicating and knowing, and (4) the illusoriness of "good" and "evil" (Braud, 1975).

A national survey of Americans by Greeley and McCready (N = 1467) found that 35 percent of Americans said they had at least once or twice felt "close to a powerful, spiritual force that seemed to lift you out of yourself." "Descriptors" of such mystical experience were: feeling of deep peace (55 percent); certainty things will work out for good (48 percent); need to contribute to others (43 percent); love at center of everything (43 percent); joy and laughter (43 percent); great emotional intensity (38 percent); increased understanding and knowledge (32 percent); unity of everything (29 percent); new life or new world (27 percent); confidence in personal survival (27 percent); cannot describe what is happening (26 percent); universe feels alive (25 percent); sense of being taken over by something more powerful (24 percent); personal expansion (22 percent); warmth or fire (22 percent); feeling alone (19 percent); loss of worldly concern (19 percent); bathed in light (14 percent); desolation (8 percent); something else (4 percent). [The above descriptors have been paraphrased slightly.] (Greeley, 1974: 140−1).

L. LeShan (1974) finds that clairvoyant and mystical reality are alike in transcending: sensory perception, separateness (asserting unity of all things), time (past, present, and future coexisting), and good and evil; and that advanced physicists share such a perspective.

I. M. Lewis (1971) asserts the universality of trance states and states of possession, though cultural interpretations vary. It seems to me precarious to conclude yet that all such states − clairvoyant, mystical, trance, and possession − are subjectively identical, if only for the reason that no observer has experienced all kinds.

18 "This is the news. It's not easy to report in the newspaper this kind of news, but this is the news" (Buckminster Fuller as quoted in Forem, 1973: 108). A Christian clergyman, William V. Rauscher (1975), reproaches the church for neglecting psychic experiences and paranormal events such as telepathy, healing, clairvoyance, and prophecy.

References

Abe, Kobo, 1974. *The Box Man*. New York: Knopf.

"Action for Children's Television (ACT)," study reported in *Christian Science Monitor* (December 28, 1975).

Adorno, T.W. et al., 1950. *The Authoritarian Personality*. New York: Harper & Row.

Allen, Frederick Lewis, 1931. *Only Yesterday, the Fabulous Twenties*. New York: Harper & Row.

Allport, Gordon, 1954. *The Nature of Prejudice*. Cambridge, Mass.: Addison-Wesley Publishing Co.

Alpert, Hollis, 1974. "The Devil, you say!" *Saturday Review/World* (February 9):56—7.

Amory, Cleveland, 1960. *Who Killed Society?* New York: Harper & Row.

Ardrey, Robert, 1966. *The Territorial Imperative*. New York: Atheneum.

Armer, Paul, 1966. "What will the computer do next?" *New York Times* (April 24):16—17.

Asch, S. E., 1952. *Social Psychology*. New York: Prentice-Hall, Ch. 16.

Ashby, W. Ross, 1956. *Introduction to Cybernetics*. New York: Wiley.

Astrachan, Anthony, 1973. "The cultural revolution on our doorstep." *Saturday Review World* (September 25):4—19.

Attneave, Fred, 1959. *Applications of Information Theory to Psychology: A Summary of Basic Concepts, Methods, and Results*. New York: Holt, Rinehart and Winston.

Back, Kurt W., 1972. *Beyond Words, The Story of Sensitivity Training and the Encounter Movement*. New York: Russell Sage Foundation.

Bagdikian, Ben H., 1971. *The Information Machines, Their Impact on Men and Media*. New York: Harper & Row.

Bandura, Albert, 1963. "What TV violence can do to your child." *Look* (October 22):46—52.
    1969. *Principles of Behavior Modification*. New York: Holt, Rinehart and Winston.
    1971. *Psychological Modeling, Conflicting Theories*. Chicago: Aldine-Atherton.

Bandura, Albert, and Richard H. Walters, 1963. *Social Learning and Personality Development*. New York: Holt, Rinehart and Winston.

Baron, Robert Alex, 1970. *The Tyranny of Noise*. New York: St. Martin's Press.

Barzun, Jacques, 1964. *Science: The Glorious Entertainment*. New York: Harper & Row.

Bateson, Gregory, 1972. *Steps to an Ecology of Mind*. New York: Ballantine Books.

Bavelas, A., 1946—1948. "A Mathematical Model for Group Structures," *Applied Anthropology*:5—7, 7(3), 16—30.

Beckett, Samuel, 1967. *Stories and Texts for Nothing*. New York: Grove Press.

Beer, Stafford, 1972. *Brain of the Firm, the Managerial Cybernetics of Organization*. London: Penguin.

Bennett, John W., Herbert Passin, and Robert K. McKnight, 1958. *In Search of Identity, The Japanese Overseas Scholar in America and Japan*. Minneapolis: University of Minnesota Press.

Bennis, Warren G., and Philip E. Slater, 1968. *The Temporary Society*. New York: Harper & Row.

Berelson, Bernard, and Gary A. Steiner, 1964. *Human Behavior, an Inventory of Scientific Findings.* New York: Harcourt Brace Jovanovich.

Berger, Peter, Brigitte Berger, and Hansfried Kellner, 1973. *The Homeless Mind, Modernization and Consciousness.* New York: Random House.

Berland, Theodore, 1970. *The Fight for Quiet.* Englewood Cliffs, N.J.: Prentice-Hall.

Berlyne, D. E., 1960. *Conflict, Arousal and Curiosity.* New York: McGraw-Hill.

Berlyne, D. E., ed., 1974. *Studies in the New Experimental Aesthetics: Steps Toward an Objective Psychology of Appreciation.* Washington, D.C.: Hemisphere Publishing Corp.

Berlyne, D. E., and K. B. Madsen, eds., 1973. *Pleasure, Reward, Preference.* New York: Academic Press.

Bernstein, Basil, 1964. "Elaborated and Restricted Codes: Their Social Origins and Some Consequences," in Alfred G. Smith, ed., *Communication and Culture.* New York: Holt, Rinehart and Winston.

Bethel, May, 1969. *How to Live in Our Polluted World.* New York: Pyramid Publishers.

Biderman, Albert D., 1963. *March to Calumny, the Story of American POWs in the Korean War.* New York: Macmillan.

Binstock, Jeanne, 1974. "Choosing to die, the decline of aggression and the rise of suicide." *The Futurist* (April):68–71.

Birdwhistell, Ray L., 1970. *Kinesics and Context, Essays on Body Motion Communication.* New York: Ballantine Books.

Blatty, William Peter, 1971. *The Exorcist.* New York: Harper and Row.

Blau, Peter M., 1974. "Parameters of social structure." *American Sociological Review,* 39 (October):615–35.

Blumenthal, Albert, 1932. *Small Town Stuff.* Chicago: University of Chicago Press.

Blumer, Herbert, 1939. "Collective Behavior," in Park (ed.), *An Outline of the Principles of Sociology.* New York: Barnes & Noble Books.

1954. "What is Wrong with Social Theory?" *American Sociological Review* 19 (February): 3–10.

Bode, Carl, 1959. *The Anatomy of American Popular Culture, 1840–1861.* Berkeley and Los Angeles: University of California Press.

Bodley, John H., 1974. *Victims of Progress.* New York: Addison-Wesley.

Booker, Christopher, 1970. *The Neophiliacs.* London: Gambit.

Boorstin, Daniel J., 1962. *The Image, or What Happened to the American Dream?* New York: Atheneum.

Bott, Elizabeth, 1971. *Family and Social Network.* 2d ed. New York: Free Press.

Boulding, Kenneth, 1965. "Towards a theory of protest." *Bulletin of the Atomic Scientists* (October). Reprinted in Walt Anderson, ed., 1969. *The Age of Protest,* vi–viii. Pacific Palisades, California: Goodyear Publishing Co..

1971. "The Diminishing Returns of Science," *New Scientist* (London) (March 25). Quoted in Roszak, 1972:211.

Bradburn, Norman M., 1969. *Structure of Psychological Well-Being.* Chicago: Aldine.

Bradburn, Norman M., and David Caplovitz, 1965. *Reports on Happiness, a Pilot Study of Behavior Related to Mental Health.* Chicago: Aldine.

Braden, William, 1970. *The Age of Aquarius, Technology and the Cultural Revolution.* Chicago: Quadrangle.

Braud, William G., 1975. "Paranormal communication: Psi-conducive states." *J. of Communication,* 25 (Winter):142–61.

Buckley, Walter, ed., 1968. *Modern Systems Research for the Behavioral Scientist.* Chicago: Aldine.

Buckley, Walter, T. Burns, and L. D. Meeker, 1974. "Structural resolutions of collective action problems." *Behavioral Science,* 15 (September):277–97.

Buckner, H. Taylor. "The Flying Saucerians, an open door cult." In Marcello Truzzi, ed., 1968. *Sociology and Everyday Life*, 223–30. Englewood Cliffs, N.J.: Prentice-Hall.

Burke, Kenneth, 1936. *Permanence and Change: An Anatomy of Purpose*. New York: New Republic, Inc.

Campbell, Angus, P. E. Converse, W. E. Miller, and D. E. Stokes, 1964. *The American Voter, an Abridgement*. New York: Wiley.

Cannon, Walter B., 1939. *The Wisdom of the Body*. New York: Norton.

Carlyle, Thomas, 1841. *On Heroes, Hero Worship and the Heroic in History*. London: Oxford University Press; Humphrey Milford.

Carter, Richard F., Ronald H. Pyszka, and Jose L. Guerraro, 1969. "Dissonance and exposure to aversive information." *Journalism Quarterly* (Spring):37–42.

Chapin, F. Stuart, 1924. "A theory of synchronous culture cycles." *Journal of Social Forces* (May).

Charbonnier, G., 1969. *Conversations with Claude Levi-Strauss*. London: Jonathan Cape.

Cherry, Colin, 1966. *On Human Communication; a Review, a Survey, and a Criticism*, 2nd edition. Cambridge, Mass.: M.I.T. Press.

Christian, William A., Jr., 1972. *Person and God in a Spanish Village*. New York: Seminar Press.

Christie, L. S., R. D. Luce, and J. Macy, Jr., 1952. "Communication and Learning in Task-oriented Groups." Cambridge, Mass.: Research Laboratory of Electronics, M.I.T. Technical Report Number 231, May 13.

Christie, Richard, and Florence Geis, 1970. *Studies in Machiavellianism*. New York: Academic Press.

Church, Richard, 1969. "Days of routine." *Christian Science Monitor* (September 12).

Clark, Sir Kenneth. "Romanticism in Art," televised documentary film.

Clear, Warren J., 1943. "Glory through hara-kiri." *Reader's Digest* (August):103–4.

Colby, Benjamin N., 1958. "Behavioral redundancy." *Behavioral Science*, 3:317–22.

Comeau, Larry, and Leo Driedger, 1978. "Ethnic Opening and Closing in an Open System: a Canadian Example," *Social Forces*, December (forthcoming).

Commoner, Barry, 1971. *The Closing Circle: Nature, Man and Technology*. New York: Knopf.

Control of the Direct Broadcast Satellite. An Occasional Paper of the Aspen Institute Program on Communications and Society, 770 Welch Road, Palo Alto, California 94304. In association with the Office of External Research, U.S. Department of State, 1974.

Converse, Gordon N., 1973. Comment of Chief Photographer, Christian Science Monitor.

Cooley, Charles Horton, 1909. *Social Organization: A Study of the Larger Mind*. New York: Scribner.

Cooper, Eunice, and Marie Jahoda, 1947. "The evasion of propaganda: how prejudicial people respond to antiprejudice propaganda." *J. Psychol.* 23:15–25.

Cottle, Thomas. *The Abandoners: Portraits of Loss, Separation and Neglect*. Boston: Little, Brown.

Cox, Harvey, 1969a. *The Feast of Fools*. Cambridge: Harvard University Press.

Crain, Robert L., Elihu Katz, and Donald B. Rosenthal, 1969. *The Politics of Community Conflict: The Foundation Decision*. Indianapolis: Bobbs-Merrill.

Czarnowski, Stefan, 1919. *Le culte des heros et les conditiones sociales*. Paris: Alcan.

Dance, Frank E. X., ed., 1967. *Human Communication Theory, Original Essays*. New York: Holt, Rinehart and Winston.

Dasa, Hayagriva, n.d. *Back to Godhead*, pamphlet number 46. Street handout of Hare Krishna movement.

Davies, Hunter, 1968. "The Beatles." *Life* (September 20):82.

Davies, James C., 1969. "The J-curve of rising and declining satisfactions as a cause of some great revolutions and a contained rebellion." In Graham and Gurr, eds., *Violence in America, Historical and Comparative Perspectives*. New York: New American Library.

Deutsch, Karl W., 1961. "On social communication and the metropolis." *Daedalus* (90):99—110.
1966. *The Nerves of Government, Models of Political Communication and Control.* New York: Free Press.

Dewey, John, 1916. *Democracy and Education, an Introduction to the Philosophy of Education.* New York: Macmillan.

Dixon, Norman F., 1971. *Subliminal Perception: The Nature of a Controversy.* London: McGraw-Hill.

Dobyns, Henry F., Paul S. Doughty, and Allan R. Holmberg, 1968. *Peace Corps Program Impact in the Andes.* Ithaca, N.Y.: Cornell University Department of Anthropology.

Dohrenwend, Bruce P., and Barbara S. Dohrenwend, 1969. *Social Status and Psychological Disorder, a Causal Inquiry.* New York: Wiley-Interscience.

Dorfles, Gillo, 1969. *Kitsch, the World of Bad Taste.* New York: Universe Books.

Douglas, Mary, 1966. *Purity and Danger, an Analysis of Concepts of Pollution and Taboo.* London: Routledge and Kegan Paul.

Dube, S. C., 1967. "Communication, innovation, and planned change in India." In Daniel Lerner and Wilbur Schramm, eds., *Communication and Change in the Developing Countries,* 139—46. Honolulu: East-West Center Press.

Duncan, Hugh Dalziel, 1962. *Communication and Social Order.* New York: The Bedminster Press.

Eddy, Roger, 1966. "On Staying Put," *Mademoiselle,* (May):108, 110.

Efron, Edith, 1971. *The News Twisters.* New York: Nash Publications.

Ehrenzweig, Anton, 1970. *The Hidden Order in Art.* London: Palladin.

Ehrlich, Paul, 1968. *The Population Bomb.* New York: Ballantine Books.

Eisenstadt, S. N., 1952. "Communication processes among immigrants in Israel." *Public Opinion Quarterly* (16):42—58.

Eliade, Mircea, 1954. *The Myth of the Eternal Return.* New York: Pantheon Books.
1958. *Birth and Rebirth, the Religious Meanings of Initiation in Human Culture.* New York: Harper & Row.

Erickson, William, 1973. "The social organization of an urban commune." *Urban Life and Culture* 2, No. 2 (July):231—56.

Erikson, Erik H., 1963. *Childhood and Society.* 2d ed. New York: Norton.

Erikson, Kai T., 1966. *Wayward Puritans; a Study in the Sociology of Deviance.* New York: Wiley.

Escolier, Raymond, 1960. *Matisse from the Life.* London: Faber & Faber, Ltd.

Essien-Udom, E. U., 1963. *Black Nationalism, a Search for Identity in America.* Chicago: University of Chicago Press. Reprinted by Dell 1964.

"Ethnicity is In," *Time.*Essay (September 3, 1973).

Etzioni, Amitai, 1968. *The Active Society: A Theory of Societal and Political Processes.* New York: Free Press.

Evans, Christopher, 1973. "Evans Dream Theory, an interview by Barbara Boynton." *Intellectual Digest* (October).

Eysenck, H. J., 1967. *The Biological Basis of Personality.* Springfield, Illinois: C. C. Thomas.
1972. *Psychology is About People.* London: Allen Lane.

Fairfield, Richard, 1971. *Communes USA, a Personal Tour.* Baltimore: Penguin Books.

Fauconnet, Paul, 1920. *La Responsabilité.* Paris: Alcan.

Feierabend, Ivo K., Rosalind L. Feierabend, and Betty A. Nesvold, 1969. "Social change and political violence: cross-national patterns." In Graham and Gurr, eds., *Violence in America, Historical and Comparative Perspectives.* New York: New American Library.

Festinger, Leon, 1957. *A Theory of Cognitive Dissonance.* Evanston, Ill.: Row, Peterson.

Festinger, Leon, et al., 1948. "A study of rumor: its origin and spread." *Human Relations* 1: 464—86.

Festinger, Leon, H. W. Riecken, and Stanley Schachter, 1956. *When Prophecy Fails.* Minneapolis: University of Minnesota Press.

Filler, Louis, 1961. *Crusaders for American Liberalism.* 2d ed. Yellow Springs, Ohio: The Antioch Press.

Firth, Raymond, 1956. "Rumor in a primitive society." *J. Abn. & Soc. Psychol* 53:122–32.

Fischer, C. S., 1973. "On urban alienations and anomie: powerlessness and social isolation." *Amer. Sociological Review* 38 (June):311–26.

Fishwick, Marshall W., 1954. *American Heroes: Myth and Reality.* Washington: Public Affairs Press.

Fiske, Edward B., 1972. "The selling of the deity, 1973." *Saturday Review* (December 9):17–18.

Florsheim, Richard A., (artist), n. d. Personal communication.

Fogel, Lawrence J., 1963. *Biotechnology: Concepts and Applications.* Englewood Cliffs, N.J.: Prentice-Hall.

Forem, Jack, 1973. *Transcendental Meditation, Maharishi Mahesh Yogi and the Science of Creative Intelligence.* New York: Dutton.

Francis, David R., 1976. "TV ad hypocrisy . . ." *Christian Science Monitor* (March 22).

Freedman, Jonathan L., 1975. *Crowding and Behavior.* San Francisco: Freeman.

Fromm, Erich, 1968. *The Revolution of Hope.* New York: Harper & Row.

Garland, Hamlin, 1899. *Boys Life on the Prairie.* New York: Washington Square Press, reprinted 1965.

Gentry, C., 1969. *Last Days of the Late, Great State of California.* New York: Ballantine Books.

Gerbner, George, and Larry Gross, 1976. "Living With Television: The Violence Profile," *J. of Communication* 26 (Spring):173–99.

Gilchrist, J., M. Shaw, and L. Walker, 1955. "Some effects of unequal distribution of information in a wheel group structure." *J. Abn. & Soc. Psy.* 51:119–22.

Gilmore, Robert S., and Robert S. Lamb, 1976. *Political Alienation in Contemporary America.* New York: St. Martin's Press.

Gilot, Francoise, 1964. "Pablo had almost a reverence for Matisse." *Observer Magazine:*32.

Glaser, Barney G., and Anselm L. Strauss, 1967. *The Discovery of Grounded Theory, Strategies for Qualitative Research.* Chicago: Aldine.

Glass, David C., and Jerome E. Singer, 1972. *Urban Stress, Experiments on Noise and Social Stressors.* New York: Academic Press.

Glassman, Robert B., 1976. "A Neural Systems Theory of Schizophrenia and Tardive Dyskenesia," *Behavioral Science* 21:274–88.

Glassman, Ronald, 1974. Review of *Picture Tube Imperialism* by Alan Wells. *Contemporary Sociology* 1 (January):75–7.

Gottlieb, Allan E., and Richard J. Gwynn, 1972. "Social planning of communication." In B. Singer, ed., *Communications in Canadian Society.* Toronto: Copp Clark Publishing Co.

Graham, Billy, 1974. "Billy Graham Tells Why He's Afraid to See 'The Exorcist,' an Exclusive Interview," *National Enquirer* (March 3).

Graham, Hugh D., and Ted R. Gurr, eds., 1969. *Violence in America, Historical and Comparative Perspectives.* New York: New American Library.

Greeley, Andrew M., 1974. *Ecstasy, a Way of Knowing.* Englewood Cliffs, N.J.: Prentice-Hall.

Greene, Bob, 1974. *Billion Dollar Baby.* New York: New American Library.

Greiff, Constance M., ed., 1972. *Lost America.* 2 vols. Princeton, N.J.: Pyne Press.

Grieser, Ralph, 1976. "In search of America." *Christian Science Monitor* (June 9).

Gross, Bertram M., 1964. "Operation BASIC: the retrieval of wasted knowledge." In Dexter, Lewis A., and David M. White, eds., *People, Society, and Mass Communications.* New York: Free Press.

Grosser, George M., Henry Wechsler, and Milton Greenblatt, eds., 1964. *The Threat of Impending Disaster.* Cambridge, Mass.: M.I.T. Press.

Habermas, Jurgen, 1975. *Legitimation Crisis,* trans. Thomas McCarthy. Boston: Beacon Press.

Hajda, Jan, 1961. "Alienation and integration of student intellectuals." *Am. Soc. Review* 26:

758—77.

Hall, E. T., 1959. *The Silent Language.* New York: Doubleday.

1966. *The Hidden Dimension.* New York: Doubleday.

Halprin, Lawrence, 1969. *The RSVP Cycles, Creative Processes in the Human Environment.* New York: Braziller.

Hampden-Turner, Charles, 1970. *Radical Man, the Process of Psycho-Social Development.* Cambridge, Mass.: Schenkman.

Hardin, Garrett James, 1972. *Exploring New Ethics for Survival; the Voyage of the Spaceship Beagle.* New York: Viking Press.

Harlow, Harry F., 1962. "The heterosexual affectional system in monkeys." *American Psychologist* (January).

Harris, Thomas A., 1967. *I'm OK — You're OK.* New York: Harper & Row.

Harrison, Michael I., 1974. "Preparation for life in the spirit: the process of initial commitment to a religious organization." *Urban Life and Culture* 2 (January):387—414.

Hart, Hornell, 1945. "Logistic social trends." *Amer. J. of Sociology* (March):337—52.

Hauser, Philip M., 1969. "The chaotic society — product of the morphological revolution." *ASR* 34 (February):1—19.

Hecker, Justus F.C., 1837. *The Dancing Mania of the Middle Ages,* trans. by B. G. Babington. New York: Cassell, 1888. Reprinted by Burt Franklin, New York, 1970.

Henry, Jules., 1964. *Culture Against Man.* New York: Random House.

Herzog, Arthur, 1973. *The B.S. Factor: The Theory and Technique of Faking It.* New York: Simon & Schuster.

Hoffman, Arthur S., ed., 1968. *International Communication and the New Diplomacy.* Bloomington: Indiana University Press.

Hofstadter, Richard, 1955. *The Age of Reform.* New York: Random House.

Hollander, Anne, 1974. "The first picture show." Review of *The Romantic Rebellion: Romantic vs. Classic Art* by Kenneth Clark. *Saturday Review/World* (May 18):20—1.

Holloway, Stephen M., and Harvey A. Hornstein, 1976. "How Good News Makes Us Good," *Psychology Today* (December):76—8, 106, 108.

Holmberg, Allan R., 1968. *See* Dobyns.

Homans, George C., 1950. *The Human Group.* New York: Harcourt Brace Jovanovich.

Hook, Sidney, 1943. *The Hero in History.* New York: John Day Co.

Hornik, Robert C., 1977. "Mass Media Use and the 'Revolution of Rising Frustrations': a Reconsideration of the Theory," *Communication Research,* IV, 4 (October):387—412.

Horton, John E., and Wayne E. Thompson, 1962. "Powerlessness and political negativism: a study of defeated local referendums." *Amer. J. Sociology* LXVII (March):485—93.

Hubbard, Helen F., 1975. "How much is enough?" *Christian Science Monitor* (March 10).

Huizinga, Johan, 1950. *Homo Ludens, A Study of the Play Element in Culture.* Boston: Beacon Press.

Huxley, Aldous, 1944. *The Perennial Philosophy.* New York: Harper & Row.

1954. *Doors of Perception.* New York: Harpers.

Immerwahr, Raymond, 1974. "Romanticism: past and present." *Carleton Germanic Papers* No. 2:31—48. Ottawa: Carleton University, Department of German.

Inverarity, James, 1976. "Populism and lynching in Louisiana, 1889—1896: a test of Erikson's theory of the relationship between boundary crises and repressive justice." *ASR* 41 (April):262—80.

Janis, Irving L., *Victims of Groupthink, a Psychological Study of Foreign Policy Decisions and Fiascoes.* Boston: Houghton Mifflin.

Jaspan, Norman, 1974. *Mind Your Own Business.* Englewood Cliffs, N.J.: Prentice-Hall.

Joad, C. E. M., 1950. *A Critique of Logical Positivism.* Chicago: University of Chicago Press.

Johnson, Gerald W., 1943. *American Heroes and Hero Worship.* New York: Harper & Row.

Kahl, Joseph A., 1968. *The Measurement of Modernism, a study of Values in Brazil and Mexico.* Austin: University of Texas Press.

Kanter, Rosabeth Moss, 1972. *Commitment and Community, Communes and Utopias in Sociological Perspective.* Cambridge, Mass.: Harvard University Press.

Karagulla, Shafica, M.D., 1967. *Breakthrough to Creativity, Your Higher Sense Perception.* Los Angeles: De Vorss & Co.

Katz, Elihu, 1961. "The Social Itinerary of Technical Change," *Human Organization* 20:70—82.

Katz, Elihu, and Paul Lazarsfeld, 1955. *Personal Influence, the Part Played by People in the Flow of Mass Communications.* Glenco, Ill.: Free Press.

Kavaler, Lucy, 1974. *Noise: The New Menace.* New York: John Day.

Keesing, Felix M., and Marie M. Keesing, 1956. *Elite Communication in Samoa, a Study of Leadership.* Stanford, Calif.: Stanford University Press.

Kerckhoff, Alan C., and Kurt W. Back, 1968. *The June Bug: A Study of Hysterical Contagion.* New York: Prentice-Hall.

Key, Wilson Bryan, 1973. *Subliminal Seduction: Ad Media's Manipulation of a Not So Innocent America.* Englewood Cliffs, N.J.: Prentice-Hall.

Klapp, Orrin E., 1949. "The folk hero." *Amer. J. of Folklore* 62:17—25.

1954. "The clever hero." *J. Amer. Folklore* 67:21—34.

1956. "American villain types." *Amer. Sociol. Review* 21:337—40.

1958. "Tragedy and the American climate of opinion." *Centennial Review* (Michigan State University) 2:396—413. Reprinted in John D. Hurrell, ed., 1961. *Two Modern American Tragedies.* New York: Scribner.

1959. "Vilification as a social process." *Pacific Sociological Review* 2:71—6.

1962. *Heroes, Villains and Fools; The Changing American Character.* Englewood Cliffs, N.J.: Prentice-Hall.

1964a. "Mexican Social Types," *American J. of Sociology,* LXIX:404—14.

1964b. *Symbolic Leaders, Public Dramas and Public Men.* Chicago, Ill.: Aldine.

1969. *Collective Search for Identity.* New York: Holt, Rinehart and Winston.

1972. *Currents of Unrest, an Introduction to Collective Behavior.* New York: Holt, Rinehart and Winston.

1975. "Opening and closing." *Behavioral Science* 20 (July):251—7.

Klein, David, 1973. "Encounter groups make people too sensitive." *National Enquirer* (January 7).

Kornhauser, William, 1959. *The Politics of Mass Society.* Glencoe, Illinois: The Free Press.

Kostelanetz, Richard, ed., 1972. *Seeing Through Shuck.* New York: Ballantine Books.

Kriesberg, Martin, 1949. "Cross-pressures and attitudes: a study of the influence of conflicting propaganda on opinions regarding American-Soviet relations." *P.O. Quar.* 13 (Spring): 5—16.

Krutch, Joseph Wood, 1929. *The Modern Temper.* New York: Harcourt, Brace Jovanovich.

1965. "Can we survive the fun explosion?" *Saturday Review* (January 16):14—16.

Kryter, Karl D., 1970. *The Effects of Noise on Man.* New York: Academic Press.

Kunkel, John H., 1970. *Society and Economic Growth, a Behavioral Perspective of Social Change.* New York: Oxford University Press.

La Barre, Weston, 1967. "Paralinguistics, kinesics, and cultural anthropology." In F.W. Matson and Ashley Montagu, eds., *The Human Dialogue, Perspectives on Communication,* 456—90. New York: Free Press.

Laing, R. D., 1967. *The Politics of Experience.* New York: Ballantine Books.

Land, George T. Lock, 1973. *Grow or Die: The Unifying Principle of Transformation.* New York: Random House.

Lange, David L., Robert K. Baker, and Sandra J. Ball, 1969. *Mass Media and Violence* XI. "A Staff Report to the National Commission on the Causes and Prevention of Violence."

Washington: Government Printing Office:311—39.

Laski, Marghanita, 1961. *Ecstasy, A Study of Some Secular and Religious Experiences.* London: Cresset Press.

Laumann, Edward O., 1973. *Bonds of Pluralism: The Form and Substance of Urban Social Networks.* New York: Wiley.

Laurence, Margaret, 1973. Interviewed by Graeme Gibson, *Eleven Canadian Novelists.* Toronto, Canada: House of Anansi Press, Ltd.

La Vey, Anton S., 1969. *The Satanic Bible.* New York: Avon Press.

Lazarsfeld, Paul, 1944. "The election is over." *P.O. Quar.* 8 (Fall):317—30.

Lazarsfeld, Paul, and Robert K. Merton, 1954. "Friendship as a social process." In M. Berger, T. Abel, and C. Page, *Freedom and Control in Modern Society.* New York: Van Nostrand.

Lazarsfeld, Paul, and Wagner Thielens, Jr., 1958. *The Academic Mind.* Glencoe, Ill.: The Free Press.

Le Gallienne, Eva, trans., 1955. Preface to Henrik Ibsen, *Hedda Gabler.* Washington Square, N.Y.: New York University Press.

Leary, Timothy, 1966. "Interview with Timothy Leary," *Playboy,* (Sept.):93.

Leites, Nathan, and Elsa Bernaut, 1954. *Ritual of Liquidation, the Case of the Moscow Trials.* Glencoe, Ill.: The Free Press.

Lerner, Daniel, 1958. *The Passing of Traditional Society.* New York: Free Press.

Le Shan, Lawrence, 1974. *The Medium, the Mystic, and the Physicist.* New York: Viking Press.

Lessing, Erich, 1966. *The Voyages of Ulysses, a Photographic Interpretation of Homer's Classic.* London: Macmillan.

Levi-Strauss, C., 1969. *See* Charbonnier, G.

Levy, Mark R., and Michael S. Kramer, 1972. *The Ethnic Factor, How America's Minorities Decide Elections.* New York: Simon & Schuster.

Lewis, I. M., 1971. *Ecstatic Religion, an Anthropological Study of Spirit Possession and Shamanism.* Harmondsworth, Middlesex, England: Penguin Books, Ltd.

Lewis, Oscar, 1961. *The Children of Sanchez, Autobiography of a Mexican Family.* New York: Random House.

Lifton, R. J., 1956. "Thought reform of Western civilians in Chinese Communist prisons." *Psychiatry* 19:173—95.

Lincoln, C. Eric, 1961. *The Black Muslims of America.* Boston: Beacon Press.

Linder, Staffan Burenstam, 1970. *The Harried Leisure Class.* New York: Columbia University Press.

Lipset, Seymour M., and Earl Raab, 1970. *The Politics of Unreason; Right-Wing Extremism in America, 1790—1970.* New York: Harper & Row.

Loomis, Charles P., 1960. *Social Systems.* New York: Van Nostrand.

Loomis, Charles P., and John C. McKinney, 1956. "Systemic differences between Latin-American communities of family farms and large estates." *Amer. J. Sociology* LXI:404—12.

Love, Ruth Leeds, 1973. "The fountains of urban life." *Urban Life and Culture* 2, No. 2 (July): 161—209.

Lowenthal, Leo, and Norbert Guterman, 1949. *Prophets of Deceit, a Study of the Techniques of the American Agitator.* New York: Harper & Row.

Lyman, Stanford M., and Marvin B. Scott, 1967. "Territoriality: a Neglected Dimension," *Social Problems,* 15 (Fall):236—45.

Lynn, R., 1971. *Personality and National Character.* Oxford, New York, and Toronto: Pergamon Press.

MacCannell, Dean, 1973. "Staged authenticity: arrangement of social space in tourist settings." *Amer. J. Sociology* 79 (November):589—603.

    1976. *The Tourist, a New Theory of the Leisure Class.* New York: Schocken Books.

MacKay, Charles, 1932. *Extraordinary Popular Delusions and the Madness of Crowds.* Boston:

L. C. Page. Originally published 1841.

MacKay, D. M., and W. S. McCulloch, 1952. "The limiting information capacity of a neural link." *Bull Math. Biophys.* 14:127—35.

Maltz, Maxwell, 1960. *Psycho-Cybernetics.* Englewood Cliffs, N.J.: Prentice-Hall.

Mandel. Loring, 1970. "Television pollutes us all." *New York Times* (March 25). Reprinted in Alan Wells, ed., 1972. *Mass Media and Society.* Palo Alto, Calif.: National Press Books.

Manning, Robert, 1968. "International news media." In Arthur S. Hoffman, ed., *International Communication and the New Diplomacy.* Bloomington: Indiana University Press.

Marcuse, Herbert, 1964. *One-Dimensional Man.* London: Routledge & Kegan Paul Ltd.

Marquis, D. G., and T. J. Allen, 1966. "Communication Patterns in Applied Technology," *American Psychologist* 21:1052—60.

Martin, William C., 1971. "This Man Says He's the Divine Sweetheart of the Universe," *Esquire* (June):76—8ff.

Maruyama, Magoroh, 1968. "The second cybernetics: deviance-amplifying mutual causal processes." In Walter Buckley, ed., *Modern Systems Research for the Behavioral Scientist,* 304—13. Chicago: Aldine.

Maslow, Abraham H., 1968. *Toward a Psychology of Being.* New York: Van Nostrand Reinhold.

Matthews, Kenneth E., Jr., and Lance K. Canon, 1975. "Environmental noise level as a determinant of helping behavior." *J. of Personality and Social Psychology* 32, No. 4:571—77.

Matson, Floyd W., 1964. *The Broken Image.* Garden City, N.Y.: Doubleday.

Matson, Floyd W., and Ashley Montagu, eds., 1967. *The Human Dialogue, Perspectives on Communication.* New York: Free Press (Macmillan).

Mayr, Ernst, 1974. "Behavior programs and evolutionary strategies." *American Scientist* 62 (November—December):650—9.

McClelland, David C., 1975. "Love and power: the psychological signals of war." *Psychology Today* (January):44—8.

McLuhan, Marshall, 1964. *Understanding the Media: The Extensions of Man.* New York: McGraw-Hill.

1968. Preface to Robert Wallis, *Time: Fourth Dimension of the Mind,* vii. New York: Harcourt, Brace Jovanovich.

1974. "Global theatre." *J. of Communication* 24 (Winter):48—58.

Mead, Margaret, 1969. "Generation Gap." Symposium, oral presentation, San Diego, California (June 2).

Meadows, Donella H., et al., 1972. *The Limits to Growth. A Report for the Club of Rome's Project on the Predicament of Mankind.* New American Library Edition. New York: Universe Books.

Mecklin, John M., 1941. *The Passing of the Saint, a Study of a Cultural Type.* Chicago: University of Chicago Press.

Meerloo, Joost A. M., 1967. *See* Dance, 133.

Meier, Richard L., 1962. *A Communications Theory of Urban Growth.* Cambridge, Mass.: M.I.T. Press.

1965. "Information Input Overload: Features of Growth in Communications-oriented Institutions," in F. Massarik and P. Ratoosh, eds., *Mathematical Explorations in Behavioral Science.* Homewood, Illinois: Richard D. Irwin and Dorsey Press.

1971. *Organized Responses to Communications Stress in the Future Urban Environment.* Working Paper 149. Berkeley, Calif.: Institute of Urban and Regional Development, University of California (April).

1972. "Communication stress." *Annual Review of Ecology and Systematics* 3:289—314.

Melville, Keith, 1972. *Communes in the Counterculture: Origins, Theories, Styles of Life.* New York: Morrow.

Menninger, Karl, 1973. *Whatever Became of Sin?* New York: Hawthorn Books.

Merton, Robert K., 1968. *Social Theory and Social Structure.* New York: Free Press.

Merton, Thomas, 1961. *New Seeds of Contemplation.* New York: New Directions Books.

The Middle Way, Journal of the Buddhist Society, 52 Eccleston Square, London, England, May, 1966.

Milgram, Stanley, 1963. "Behavioral study of obedience." *J. Abn. & Soc. Psy.* 67:371–8.

——— 1970. "The experience of living in cities." *Science* 167:1461–8.

Miller, George A., 1967. *Psychology of Communication, Seven Essays.* New York: Basic Books.

Miller, James Grier, 1960. "Information input overload and psychopathology." *Am. J. Psychiatry* 116 (February):695–704.

——— 1965. "Living systems." *Behavioral Science* 10:193–237, 337–411.

——— 1971. "Living systems: the group." *Behavioral Science* 16:277–398.

——— 1972. "Living systems: the organization." *Behavioral Science* 17:1–182.

——— 1975. "Living systems: the society." *Behavioral Science* 20 (November):366–535.

Miller, Norman, and Harold B. Gerard, 1976. "How Busing Failed in Riverside," *Psychology Today* (June):66–70, 100.

Mills, C. Wright, 1951. *Whitecollar, the American Middle Classes.* New York: Oxford University Press.

Mitchell, J. Clyde, ed., 1969. "The concept and use of social networks." *Social Networks in Urban Situations, Analyses of Personal Relationships in Central African Towns.* Manchester: University of Manchester Press.

The Modern Romans, The Decline of Western Civilization. Pasadena, Calif.: Ambassador College Press, 1971.

Moore, Shirley, 1967. *Biological Clocks and Patterns.* New York: Criterion Books.

Moorhouse, Geoffrey, 1972. *Against All Reason: The Religious Life in the Modern World.* Harmondsworth, Middlesex, England: Penguin Books Ltd.

Mulder, M., 1959. "Group Structure and Group Performance," *Acta psychol. Amst.* 16: 356–402.

Navarra, John Gabriel, 1969. *Our Noisy World.* Garden City, New York: Doubleday.

Nelson, Robert, 1972. "Britons trace malaise to disunity." *Christian Science Monitor* (March 1).

Nevin, David, 1969. "Autocrat in the action arena." *Life:* 51–2.

Nevins, Allan, 1968. "The tradition of the future." *Saturday Review:* 32–3ff.

Newman, Oscar, 1972. *Defensible Space.* New York: Macmillan.

Novak, Michael, 1971. *The Rise of the Unmeltable Ethnics, Politics and Culture in the Seventies.* New York: Macmillan.

Noyes, Russell, Jr., 1972. Paper in *Psychiatry,* reported in "The Pleasures of Dying," *Time* (December 4).

O'Connor, Walter D., 1972. "The manufacture of deviance: the case of the Soviet purge, 1936–38." *Amer. Sociol. Review* 37 (August):403–13.

O'Connor, William Van, 1943. *Climates of Tragedy.* Baton Rouge: Louisiana State University Press.

Ofner, Francis, 1971. "Israel halts flow of U.S. black immigrants." *Christian Science Monitor* (October 14).

Ogburn, William Fielding, 1922. *Social Change.* New York: B. W. Huebsch.

Opie, Iona, and Peter Opie, 1959. *The Lore and Language of School Children.* Oxford: Clarendon Press.

Packard, Vance, 1957. *The Hidden Persuaders.* New York: McKay.

Patterson, Thomas E., and Robert D. McClure, 1974. *Political Advertising: Voter Reaction to Televised Political Commercials.* Study by Citizens Research Foundation, Princeton, New Jersey.

Penfield, Wilder, 1952. "Memory mechanisms." A.M.A. *Archives of Neurology and Psychiatry* 67:178–98.

Peterson, Severin, ed., 1971. *A Catalog of the Ways People Grow*. New York: Ballantine Books.

Phillips, David P., 1974. "The influence of suggestion on suicide: substantive and theoretical implications of the Werther Effect." *Amer. Sociol. Review* 39 (June):340–54.

Pierce, John R., 1961. *Symbols, Signals and Noise*. New York: Harper & Row.

Pinard, Maurice, 1971. *The Rise of a Third Party, a Case Study in Crisis Politics*. Englewood Cliffs, N.J.: Prentice-Hall.

"Pleasures and Pains of the Simple Life," *Time*, (September 15, 1967):37.

Pool, Ithiel de Sola, ed., 1973. *Citizen Feedback and Cable Technology*. Cambridge, Mass.: M.I.T. Press.

Popper, K. R., 1952. *The Open Society and Its Enemies*. rev. 2d ed., 2 vols. London: Routledge and Kegan Paul Ltd.

Potter, Van Rensselaer, 1971. *Bioethics, Bridge to the Future*. Englewood Cliffs, N.J.: Prentice-Hall.

Prescott, James, 1974. "Touching. An interview by Barbara Boynton." *Intellectual Digest* (March):6–10.

Preston, Robert L., 1971. *How to Prepare for the Coming Crash*. New York: Hawkes Publishing, Inc.

Printz, N., 1974. "Chinese Commune," *Christian Science Monitor* (March 29):F-1.

Pye, Lucian W., ed., 1963. *Communications and Political Development*. Princeton, N.J.: Princeton University Press.

Quastler, Henry, 1964. *The Emergence of Biological Organization*. New Haven: Yale University Press.

Quastler, Henry, and V. J. Wulff, "Human performance in information transmission." *Control System Laboratory Report R-62*, University of Illinois.

Rapoport, Anatol, 1953. "What is information?" *Etc.* 10:247–60. Reprinted in Alfred G. Smith, 1966. *Communication and Culture, Readings in the Codes of Human Interaction*, 41–55.

———— 1976. "General Systems Theory: a Bridge Between Two Cultures." *Behavioral Science* 21: 228–39.

Rauscher, William V., 1975. *The Spiritual Frontier*. Garden City, New York: Doubleday.

Raymond, R. C., 1962. "Betting on the new technologies." In J. R. Bright, *Technological Planning at the Corporate Level*. Boston: Division of Research, Harvard School of Business.

Reich, Charles A., 1970. *The Greening of America*. New York: Random House.

Reuters, 1977. "Mobile-home communities filling void across U.S.," *Christian Science Monitor*, (December 7):36.

Richard, Jerry, ed., 1973. *The Good Earth, Utopian Communities and Communes in America*. New York: New American Library.

Richardson, Jane, and Alfred L. Kroeber, 1940. *Three Centuries of Women's Dress Fashions: A Quantitative Analysis*. University of California, Anthropological Records V: No. 2.

Richardson, Lewis F., 1960. *Arms and Insecurity*, ed. N. Rashevsky and N. Trucco. Pittsburgh, Pa.: Boxwood Press.

Riddle, David, 1931. *The Martyrs, a Study in Social Control*. Chicago: University of Chicago Press.

Rogers, Carl R., 1961. *On Becoming a Person*. Boston: Houghton Mifflin.

Rogers, Everett M., 1962. *Diffusion of Innovations*. New York: Free Press.

Rogers, Everett M., in association with Lynne Svenning, 1969. *Modernization Among Peasants: The Impact of Communication*. New York: Holt, Rinehart and Winston.

Rogers, Everett M., and F. Floyd Shoemaker, 1971. *Communication of Innovations, a Cross-Cultural Approach*. New York: Free Press.

Rokeach, Milton, 1960. *The Open and Closed Mind*. New York: Basic Books.

Rossel, Robert D., 1970. "The great awakening: an historical analysis." *A.J.S.* 75:907–25.

Roszak, Theodore, 1969. *The Making of a Counter Culture; Reflections on the Technocratic*

Society and Its Youthful Opposition. New York: Doubleday.

1972. *Where the Wasteland Ends, Politics and Transcendence in Postindustrial Society.* Garden City, N.Y.: Doubleday.

Roy, Donald F., 1959. "Banana time." *Human Organization* 18, No. 4 (Winter):158–68.

Royce, Joseph R., 1964. *The Encapsulated man, An Interdisciplinary Essay on the Search for Meaning.* Princeton, N.J.: Van Nostrand.

Rubin, Lillian B., 1972. *Busing and Backlash: White Against White in a California School District.* Berkeley: University of California Press.

Rubinstein, Eli A., 1974. "The TV violence report: what's next?" *J. Comm.* 24 (Winter):80–8.

Rudwin, Maximilian, 1931. *The Devil in Legend and Literature.* Chicago: Open Court Publishing House.

Russell, Bertrand, 1951. *The Impact of Science on Society.* New York: Columbia University Press.

Saikowski, Charlotte, 1970. "But where has all the fervor gone?" *Christian Science Monitor* (January 23).

1970. "What do Russians really think about?" *Christian Science Monitor* (January 30).

Salisbury, David F., 1975. "Inventor of LP records works to revitalize small towns." *Christian Science Monitor* (April 9).

Salk, Jonas, 1973. *Survival of the Wise.* New York: Harper & Row.

Sapir, Edward, 1949. *Culture, Language and Personality.* Berkeley: University of California Press.

Sargeant, William, 1973. *The Mind Possessed, a Physiology of Possession, Mysticism and Faith Healing.* New York: Penguin Books.

Schafer, R. Murray, 1970. *The Book of Noise.* Burnaby, B. C.: Communications Centre, Simon Fraser University.

1971. *The New Soundscape.* London and Vienna: Universal Edition.

1973. *The Music of the Environment.* Burnaby, B. C.: World Soundscape Project, Department of Communication Studies, Simon Fraser University.

Schein, Edgar, 1961. *Coercive Persuasion.* New York: Norton.

Schiller, Herbert L., 1973. *The Mind Managers.* Boston: Beacon Press.

Schramm, Wilbur Lang, 1964. *Mass Media and National Development, the Role of Information in the Developing Countries.* Stanford, Calif.: Stanford University Press.

Schumacher, E. F., 1973. *Small Is Beautiful: Economics as if People Mattered.* New York: Harper & Row.

Schwartz, Barry, 1968. "The social psychology of privacy." *Amer. J. Soc.* 73:741–52.

ed., 1973. *Human Connection and the New Media.* Englewood Cliffs, N.J.: Prentice-Hall.

Schwartz, Gary; Paul Turner, and Emil Peluso, 1973. "Neither heads nor freaks: working class drug culture." *Urban Life and Culture* 2 (October):288–313.

Scitovsky, Tebor, 1976. *The Joyless Economy.* New York: Oxford University Press.

Seeman, Melvin, 1958. "The intellectual and the language of minorities." *Amer. J. Soc.* 64: 25–35.

1972. "Alienation in pre-crisis France." *ASR* 37 (August):385–402.

Self-Realization Fellowship of Southern California, undated pamphlet.

Selye, Hans, 1974. *Stress Without Distress.* Boston: Lippincott.

Sennett, Richard, 1970. *The Uses of Disorder: Personal Identity and City Life.* New York: Knopf.

Seymour, John, and Sally Seymour, 1976. *Farming for Self-Sufficiency Independence on a Five Acre Farm.* New York: Schocken Books.

Shannon, Claude E. and Warren Weaver, 1949. *The Mathematical Theory of Communication.* Urbana: University of Illinois Press.

Shaw, David, 1975. "Suburban papers: many thrive in hard times." Los Angeles *Times* (June 22).

Sheed, F. J., ed., 1973. *Soundings in Satanism*. New York: Sheed and Ward, Inc.

Sherif, Muzafer, 1936. *The Psychology of Social Norms*. New York: Harper & Row.

Shibutani, Tamotsu, 1966. *Improvised News, a Sociological Study of Rumor*. Indianapolis: Bobbs-Merrill.

Shostrom, Everett L., 1967. *Man, the Manipulator, the Inner Journey from Manipulation to Actualization*. New York: Abingdon. Reprinted by Bantam, 1968.

Siegal, Bernard J., 1970. "Defensive structuring and environmental stress." *AJS* 76 (July):11–32.

Simmel, Georg, 1950. *The Sociology of Georg Simmel*, ed. and trans. Kurt H. Wolff. Glencoe, Ill.: The Free Press.

Simmons, J. L., and Barry Winograd, 1968. *It's Happening*. New York: Marc-Laird Publications.

Singer, Benjamin D., 1968. "The report's critique of television." *Columbia Journalism Review* (Fall):54–8.

   1973. *Feedback and Society, A Study of the Uses of Mass Channels for Coping*. Lexington, Mass.: Heath.

Sommer, Robert, 1969. *Personal Space: The Behavioral Basis of Design*. Englewood Cliffs, N.J.: Prentice-Hall.

Sorokin, Pitirim, 1941. *The Crisis of Our Age*. New York: E. P. Dutton.

   1950. *Altruistic Love, a Study of American "Good Neighbors" and Christian Saints*. Boston: Beacon Press.

Spector, Malcolm, 1973. "Secrecy in job seeking among government attorneys: two contingencies in the theory of subcultures." *Urban Life and Culture* 2, No. 2 (July):211–29.

Stace, Walter T., 1960. *The Teachings of the Mystics*. New York: New American Library.

Stanford, Neal, 1971. "Flood of scientific data rises." *Christian Science Monitor* (January 23).

Staniland, A. C., 1966. *Patterns of Redundancy, a Psychological Study*. Cambridge: Cambridge University Press.

Stewart, J. Q., 1950. "The development of social physics." *Amer. J. Physics*, 18:239–53.

Still, Henry, 1970. *In Quest of Quiet; Meeting the Menace of Noise Pollution: Call to Citizen Action*. Harrisburg, Pa.: Stackpole Books.

Suedfeld, Peter, 1975. "The benefits of boredom: sensory deprivation reconsidered." *American Scientist* 63 (January-February):60–9.

Sumner, W. G., 1906. *Folkways*. New York: Ginn & Co.

Suzuki-roshi, Shunryu, 1973. "First Sandokai lecture." *Wind Bell* (Publication of Zen Center, San Francisco) Vol. XII.

Tawney, Richard Henry, 1920. *The Acquisitive Society*. New York: Harcourt Brace Jovanovich.

Taylor, G. R., 1970. *The Doomsday Book, Can the World Survive?* New York: World Publishing Co.

Taylor, James R., 1972. *The Overload of Communication Systems*. Report to Canadian Department of Communications, Ottawa. Montreal, Quebec: Section de Communication, Université de Montréal.

Taylor, Rupert, 1970. *Noise*. Harmondsworth: Penguin Books.

Terkel, Studs, 1974. *Working: People Talk About What they Do All Day and How They Feel About What They Do*. New York: Pantheon Books.

Tocqueville, Alexis de, 1840. *Democracy in America*, trans. by George Lawrence. New York: Harper & Row.

Toffler, Alvin, 1970. *Future Shock*. New York: Random House.

Toynbee, Arnold J., 1947. *A Study of History*. New York: Oxford University Press.

Troeltsch, Ernst, 1931. *The Social Teaching of the Christian Churches*. New York: Macmillan.

Turner, Victor, 1967. *The Forest of Symbols, Aspects of Ndembu Ritual*. Ithaca, N.Y.: Cornell University Press.

Udall, Stewart L., 1978. "Inaction has turned the energy issue into America's worst postwar crisis," *Los Angeles Times,* January 1.

University of Michigan Center for Political Studies, August, 1973. Opinion Survey, Ann Arbor.

Van Gigh, John P., 1976. "The Physical and Mental Load Components of Objective Complexity in Production Systems," *Behavioral Science* 21:490—7.

Vassiliou, George, and Vasso Vassiliou, 1967. "Poll of Greeks." Athens: Institute of Research in Communication.

Vidmar, Neil, and Milton Rokeach, 1974. "Archie Bunker's bigotry: a study in selective perception and exposure." *J. of Communication* 24 (Winter):36—47.

Wecter, Dixon, 1941. *The Hero in America, a Chronicle of Hero Worship.* New York: Scribner.

Weil, Andrew, 1972. *The Natural Mind: A New Way of Looking at Drugs and the Higher Consciousness.* Boston: Houghton Mifflin.

Weitz, John, 1974. *Man in Charge.* New York: Macmillan.

Wells, Alan, 1972. *Picture Tube Imperialism.* Mary Knoll, N.Y.: Orbis Books.

Wendling, Aubrey, and Kenneth Polk, 1958. "Suicide and social areas." *Pacific Sociological Review* 1 (Fall):50—3.

Westhues, Kenneth, 1972. *Society's Shadow — Studies in the Sociology of Counter-Cultures.* Toronto: McGraw-Hill, Ryerson.

White, David M., 1964. "The gatekeeper, a case study in the diffusion of news." In L. A. Dexter and D. M. White, eds., *People, Society, and Mass Communication.* New York: The Free Press.

White, W. L., 1957. *The Captives of Korea, an Unofficial White Paper.* New York: Scribner.

Whitman, Alden, 1973. "Arch wizard of modern art." *The Glove and Mail* (April 9).

Whitworth, John McKelvie, 1975. *God's Blueprints, a Sociological Study of Three Utopian Sects.* London and Boston: Routledge & Kegan Paul.

Whorf, Benjamin L. 1956. *Language, Thought and Reality.* New York: Wiley.

Whyte, Andrew D., 1896. *History of the Warfare of Science With Theology.* Out of print.

Wiener, Norbert, 1948. *Cybernetics; or Control and Communication in the Animal and the Machine.* New York: M.I.T. Press.

1950. *The Human Use of Human Beings, Cybernetics and Society.* Boston: Houghton Mifflin.

Windbell, 1970—71. Publication of Zen Center, San Francisco, California (Fall-Winter).

Wolfe, Tom, 1968. *The Electric Kool-Aid Acid Test.* New York: Farrar, Straus & Giroux.

Wrighter, Carl P., 1972. *I Can Sell You Anything.* New York: Ballantine Books.

Yankelovich, Daniel, 1974. *The New Morality: A Profile of American Youth in the '70s.* New York: McGraw-Hill.

Yevtushenko, Yevgeni, 1967. *Bratsk Station and Other New Poems.* Tr. Tina Tupikina-Glaessner et al. New York: Praeger (copyright 1966). Pp. 165—6.

Yoors, Jan, 1967. *The Gypsies.* New York: Simon & Schuster.

Zajonc, Robert B., 1960. "The concepts of balance, congruity and dissonance." *P.O. Quar.* 24:280—96.

Zurcher, Louis A., 1972. "The mutable self." *The Futurist* (October):181—6.

Index